M000166125

THE
HEAVENS
DECLARE

Books by the author

LARA'S FIRST CHRISTMAS

THE BEEJUM BOOK

THE WEB IN THE SEA:
Jung, Sophia, and the Geometry of the Soul

HOW LIKE AN ANGEL CAME I DOWN:
A. Bronson Alcott's Conversations with
Children on the Gospels

THE DOVE IN THE STONE:
Finding the Sacred in the Commonplace

JUNGIAN SYMBOLISM IN ASTROLOGY

*

THE
HEAVENS
DECLARE

Astrological Ages *and*
the Evolution *of* Consciousness

ALICE O. HOWELL

Theosophical Publishing House

Wheaton, Illinois ◆ Chennai (Madras), India

Copyright © 1990, 2006 by Alice O. Howell
Second edition 2006

All rights reserved. No part of this book may be reproduced
in any manner without written permission except for quota-
tions embodied in critical articles or reviews. For additional
information write to

Quest Books
The Theosophical Publishing House
PO Box 270
Wheaton, IL 60189-0270

www.questbooks.net

Photo credits:
Page 224: Cartoon by Jack Ziegler reproduced by permission of
Advance Magazine Group
Cover image: Harnett/Hanzon, courtesy Getty Images

Cover design, book design, and typesetting by Dan Doolin

Library of Congress Cataloging-in-Publication Data
Howell, Alice O. 1922 –
The heavens declare: astrological ages and the evolution of
consciousness / Alice O. Howell.—2nd ed.
      p. cm.
Rev. ed. of: Jungian synchronicity in astrological signs and ages.
1st ed. 1990.
Includes bibliographical references and index.
ISBN-13: 978-0-8356-0835-0
ISBN-10: 0-8356-0835-2
1. Astrology.   2. Coincidence.   3. Jung, C. G. (Carl Gustav),
1875–1961.   I. Howell, Alice O., 1922– Jungian synchronicity
in astrological signs and ages.   II. Title.
BF1711.H65   2006
133.5—dc 22
                                                2005037440

5 4 3 2 1 • 06 07 08 09 10

Printed in the United States of America

To all my teachers
especially M, C. G. Jung,
and my beloved husband
Walter A. Andersen (1911–1998)
and
to all those willing to welcome
the future in the Age to come!

CONTENTS

PART ONE

THE ASTROLOGICAL SIGNS

TABLES

PART TWO

THE ASTROLOGICAL AGES

The heavens declare the glory of God;
and the firmament showeth his handiwork.
Day unto day uttereth speech,
and night unto night showeth knowledge.
There is no speech nor language
where their voice is not heard.
Their line is gone out through all the earth,
and their words to the end of the world.
In them hath he set a tabernacle for the sun.

—PSALM 19:1–4

FOREWORD

by

SYLVIA BRINTON PERERA

Reading Alice O. Howell's book is like having conversations with the wise, "remarkably spry and cheery old woman" at the well in one of her stories. While teaching us about astrology, she pours for us a drink from the Source of many wisdom traditions, each of which, she tells us, represents "different emphases or approaches to one and the same thing."

In delightfully personal letter form, she opens the ancient ideas of the elements and the signs of the zodiac for us to see their relevance in our lives today. Teaching us to think symbolically about these, she helps us begin to find self-acceptance as we understand the patterns that mark the moments of our birth and continue to evolve through our lives. Then, moving from individual to a societal and global scale, she gives an overview of the evolution of consciousness represented by the astronomical constellations of the Ages unfolding from Neolithic times to our own era.

The astrological symbolism applied to the Ages lays out patterns that can be seen to underlie individual development, pointing us toward a vast perspective in which we participate both collectively and individually. This is an ancient vision once held by the caste of seers who watched the stars and sought to keep human activity attuned with celestial events. Today it is held by people of many professions who are aware of the archetypal field patterns in which all life is organized.

This view overcomes the literalism of fundamentalist thinking. Lacking capacity for symbolic understanding, like the millenarians in 1000 A.D., its contemporary adherents anticipate the actual end of life in the natural world. Remaining at an early, concretizing level of psychological development, they take literally what all spiritual traditions reveal through parable to open our minds to new levels of comprehension of the wonders of what are both beyond words yet also present in daily life. Fearing the literal end of time, they are unable to see that each Age represents a phase in the evolution of the structure of cultures and the consciousness that sustained them.

Since we are poised at the end of the Piscean Age, at the threshold of the beginning of largely unknown developments— in what systems theorists would call the "chaotic state" between an old order and a new "basin of attraction"—we can perhaps appreciate the backlash of those who are growing defensively rigid at the current upheavals and are clinging to modes of power that are becoming outmoded. Like clients in therapy, who learn through repeated experience to expect to survive the turmoil of such transformations of consciousness, we can learn from Alice Howell's book that the Precession of the Ages marks an overall, analogous series of shifts in culture. We can even find hints about the kinds of relationships and consciousness that are already emerging. Born in an "interesting time" (to invoke the well-known Chinese proverb), we can then take our destined places as participating witnesses in the present global, societal, and individual upheavals that mark the birth of a New Age.

PREFACE

L'amor che move il sole e l'altre stelle.
—DANTE, *Paradiso* 33.145

It might interest you to know how this book came to be written. Twenty years ago I was invited to write a text on the therapeutic applications of astrology. By then I had forty years of experience with the subject. I encountered a writer's block, not wanting to write another "cookbook" approach. Months passed. Then I had a dream and in the dream I was writing letters to a Jungian analyst called Sylvia Perera. I had met her perhaps three or four times and had read her wonderful book *Descent to the Goddess*. I plucked up my courage and telephoned her, as dreams of this sort have to be obeyed. Sylvia's response was one of delight and encouragement. The result was my first book, *Jungian Symbolism in Astrology,* which dealt with the archetypal processes of the planets in the outer world and the inner world of the psyche. (Sylvia has very kindly provided the foreword for the new edition of this book.)

The second book, originally titled *Jungian Synchronicity in Astrological Signs and Ages,* followed; it was first published in 1990. This revised and updated edition is in response to an urgent need in light of the prevailing devastating myth of "End Times" supposedly coming in 2012. In it I hope to offer an explanation and a comforting alternative! I have chosen the new title from the Nineteenth Psalm—"The heavens declare the glory of God"—because for millennia astrology has been the key to uniting religion and science. When it was discarded during the Age of Reason, religion lost its proof and much of science lost its sense of the sacred.

In a science museum in New York, a genealogical table of the sciences lists astrology as the mother of them all. Today astrology, viewed as a symbolic language of archetypal processes, unites every level of manifestation, as I hope the following chapters will demonstrate.

There appears to be an objectively observable coincidence of the *nature* of the astrological signs governing the *astronomical* Ages and the religious, mythic, and psychological expression of humankind in history: a truly discernible phylogenetic and ontogenetic pattern of sequence operating evolutionally through the collective unconscious both at the collective and individual levels. For the first time in history, we stand able to cooperate spiritually and consciously in the development.

When I was ten years old at a boarding school in Switzerland, I overheard a teacher ask another if she had heard that the world was coming to an end on June 10, 1933. Here it was already June 10, and it was also my roommate Vera's birthday! Before bedtime, I had shared the news with all the other girls on the floor. Shuddering, we agreed to meet in our dorm after lights-out to face the end together. I noticed a gathering tension and excitement as well as sympathy for Vera. At about 9:30, one by one, we assembled silently and sat somberly in our pajamas on the four narrow cast-iron beds in our dorm. We whispered our fears, apologized for our meanness, and hugged little Vera.

As luck would have it, an absolutely terrible thunderstorm broke out, causing us truly to panic. We clung together crying, began to pray incoherently, and the lightning lit up the terror on our faces! Then, as is the way with storms, the noise receded, the rain stopped, and the moon shone brightly through the departing clouds. You can imagine the uniform reaction I was to suffer at the hands of my classmates! Needless to say, this is a lesson I have never forgotten.

Now today there is again a rising collective fear gathering about various prophecies of the end of the world: for some it is called the End Times, and involves the Rapture of all good evangelical Christians, the appearance of Jesus in the sky, the Battle of Armageddon and the horrible end of everyone else—a collective myth somehow reminiscent of the power another myth had over the collective unconscious in Europe in the 1930s, when innumerable otherwise rational and decent Germans were brainwashed by Hitler without knowing what was happening. Today, it seems, there are thousands of rational, decent Christians unconsciously falling victim to the same power of a myth.

The problem this time has to do with several ancient prophecies other than the New Testament, namely the Mayan calendar, which states according to scholars that we are in the last *katun* (cycle), ending in 2012, at which time we can wake up to a new way of living in concert with one another. For another instance, according to the Vedic astrology of India, which uses the sidereal zodiac of the constellations, Rahu, the Vedic point of destiny, will be reactivated during the last months of 2012, helping consciousness to change for the better. All these pointers to this significant year do seem to indicate an end, but it is not the end of the world; it's the end of the Age of Pisces and the beginning of the Age of Aquarius! For those of you who are sick and tired of hearing about the New Age, cheer up: we have 2000 years of it ahead!

As I am writing this, a new space capsule is poised to further explore space, and a global concert on behalf of ending poverty in Africa is taking place with millions attending in one form or another. The Age of the Common Man is coming! Not without pain and fears for those invested in certainty. "We are the world" is Aquarius in a nutshell. For any skeptics, only observe the recent voluntary gatherings of individuals almost everywhere to make peaceful demonstrations for change. In Europe, instead of conquests costing millions of lives through history, nations are begging to become part of the EU. There seems to be a paradigm shift pointing to the intangible unity of the human race rather than the outward dissimilarity of cultures and religions. The pendulum will swing, no doubt, until we can honor and appreciate rather than blame our differences. Power needs to be guided by wisdom and love. I call this the Milkstool Principle.

The confusion for the evangelicals may well have come about because of two Greek words in the New Testament that have been interchanged, conflated, and mistranslated: *aion* and *kosmos*. *Aion* refers to an eon, age, or era of time. *Kosmos* refers to the universe or world, a matter of place. So the "end of the world" may really be referring to the end of an Age; that is, we are facing the end of a period of time, not of the world itself. This shows how words can be used for different purposes.

Possibly people in high places are even using the alleged "end of the world" to excuse global warming and are trying to overlook the destruction of the environment as a way of hastening the Second Coming. They fail to realize that this Second Coming is the evolution of consciousness to the reality of the indwelling Christ (also known as the Atman, *purusha*, Divine Guest, Light) within each of us: the realization that all humanity is One—that the same Light shines through each of us; the same fire burns on every candle. But just as light falling through a crystal breaks into a spectrum of colors, so energy displays the infinite variety and beauty of the world of manifest appearances. We are truly opening to the idea of a holographic universe in which each part of us contains the whole. All in One, One in all. Mathematically, the number 1 is hidden in every number: $1 \times 1 \times 1 \times 1 \ldots$ will always add up to ONE.

It is my hope to offer the reader "proof" of an unfolding evolution of consciousness that suggests a sacred purpose of awesome dimensions revealing itself in the immense mystery of the cosmos of Creation. Indeed "the heavens declare the glory of God." And perhaps Dante is right, as he said in the epigraph cited at the beginning of this section: "It is Love that moves the Sun and the other stars"!

A.O.H.
Monterey, Massachusetts,
2005

ACKNOWLEDGMENTS

I would like to express my deep love and gratitude to my late, kind husband, Walter A. Andersen, for his constant and caring support, patience, and helpful efforts in the original preparation of this book. Also to my daughter and son-in-law Elisabeth Holden Howell and Alan T. King, without whose daily help with my physical infirmities I would be unable to live another day in my home. Will Marsh, Glynis Oliver, and Nicky Hearon are my extra-angelic messengers and hands, as a stroke has rendered my right hand useless. May they all be blessed! Again a most special thanks to Sylvia Brinton Perera, to whom these letters are lovingly addressed, and who offered so kindly, both in my dream and in reality, to be a stand-in for the reader; to my friend and editor Richard M. Smoley, to my old friend Sharron Dorr, and to Nancy Grace. None of this would have transpired without the initial recognition and encouragement I received from analysts and friends, the Rev. Brewster Y. Beach, Dr. Edward F. Edinger, and Dr. Edward C. Whitmont. I should also thank Marc Edmund Jones, with whom I first studied in 1944 and Dane Rudhyar, who inspired me. My heartfelt thanks go to the many who have expressed such a lively interest in both the work of C. G. Jung and the serious and dignified development of analytical astrology.

NOTE TO THE READER

This book consists of two sections. The first is an informal explanation of the twelve astrological signs, the impeccable logic that underlies them, and their value to a therapist as a diagnostic tool as well as a guide to self-acceptance and fulfillment. The individual chart is to the psyche what DNA is to the body — a description of how a person is *likely* to process experience. The second section concerns the majestic unfolding of the evolution of the collective unconscious. The tables between the two sections are for a handy reference to anyone unfamiliar with the basics of astrology.

PART ONE

THE ASTROLOGICAL SIGNS

With our eyes open,
we share the same world;
with our eyes shut,
each of us enters his own world.
        —HERACLITUS

There be three things which are too wonderful for me,
yea, four which I know not: The way of an eagle in the air;
the way of a serpent upon a rock; the way of a ship in the
midst of the sea; and the way of a man with a maid.
        —PROVERBS 30:18–19

God never does the same thing twice.
        —MARTIN BUBER

—1—

THE RING OF QUIDDITY

Dear Friend,

O ctober 25, 1980, was a rather remarkable day. It was a
wedding day, and the bridegroom and the bride were
both crowned with white hair. To tell the truth, it was
one of the happiest days of my life! I am only sorry that you were
not there, but I had not yet met you. Despite the protest, at first,
by one of my children that it might be unseemly at our age to
have a big wedding, we had one. When I pointed out that all those
invited might be willing to show up at my funeral, so why not a
wedding?, she really had to agree. Well, we called it a "love feast,"
and friends and family all came bringing food. We were married
in an Episcopal church by three dear friends: two were clergyman,
one a Buddhist monk. Walter, my husband-to-be, had flown to
Long Island from California. Miraculously, we had met aboard
a ship on the Mediterranean while I was teaching a course on
Jungian symbolism and the collective unconscious as we visited
Italy, Greece, Egypt, Israel, Turkey, and Yugoslavia.

I wore a deep rose-red velvet gown with a crown of daisies
on my head and was attended by two little granddaughters,
who were flower girls, and a solemn grandson, who was the ring
bearer. Another dear friend sang the aria from Mendelssohn's

Elijah: "O, trust in the Lord, wait patiently on him, for he will bring thee thy heart's desire." I remembered first really hearing it on the radio some twenty years previously while mending my children's clothes and pricking my finger, which brought tears— a time when life seemed pretty hopeless indeed. It is so strange, isn't it, when we are asked to trust, how the ego interferes and tries to sort it all out, and we remain convinced that there is no way out of despair. I have experienced that quite often and can only say, numb as I felt, I did trust. Probably because, having met my teacher M when I was so young, I knew better than to deny the possibility of solutions. But I can confess it was hard, and it went on being hard for a long, long time. So this music on my wedding day filled my heart with special gratitude.

When the Buddhist monk began his blessings, we were on our knees and wondered how long the chanting would continue. I clearly remember Jessie, aged four, calling out in great concern, "Oh, Daddy, he doesn't know how to talk!" After the ceremony, we repaired to the reception hall, a medieval Norman building brought over stone by stone from France by J. P. Morgan. Some Irish musicians began to play the accordion and *bodhran*, the drum, and we danced jigs and reels till the lights suddenly went out. Huge iron standing candelabra were brought in, flares were lit, and we went into a sort of time warp. The whole event, in fact, felt like time out of time.

My reason for mentioning this is that, besides the wedding guests, all the elements attended. There was such a storm that most of the Eastern seaboard suffered a blackout! The wind howled, thunder and lightning boomed and crackled, and sheets and sheets of rain fell from black skies and swirled and eddied in huge puddles outside the church. I remember one daughter-in-law, up to her knees in water, writing "Just married!" in lipstick on our car. When we left for our honeymoon, we drove in utter darkness to Connecticut, and the next day the seas were so rough that the ferry to Martha's Vineyard was unable to sail. That's rough!

I was reminded of this when I began thinking how to start our next series of letters. I knew that we should begin with a discussion of the signs. How could we first approach them through the elements? Somehow the *coniunctio*, or inner marriage, takes place in the midst of the four elements, and, by golly, that's what really happened. So by hindsight, I see that the wedding must indeed have been blessed with more symbolism than I had realized. I never truly appreciated that until this moment.

What a pleasure to hear from you! I am so pleased that you are eager to continue your study of astrological processes and that you see how they relate to Jung's many-faceted concepts of the individual and, indeed, the collective psyche. I am so grateful that the former letters on the planetary archetypes (published as *Jungian Symbolism in Astrology*), merited publication and proved helpful to others as well. You should keep that book handy to refer to as we go along. It might help refresh your memory.

Maybe it would be helpful to give you a preview of what I hope to cover in this next series of letters, so that you can see the whys and wherefores of studying the elements and the signs before getting to the exciting but more transpersonal matter of the astrological ages. We hear so much about the "New Age" and do not appreciate the fact that not only is there a recurring cycle of ages, each cycle approximately 26,000 years long, but there is every historical evidence pointing to the fact that both the collective unconscious (as Jung called it) and the collective *consciousness* are in evolution, and, furthermore, that this evolution is repeated sequentially and psychologically in each individual. This makes it relevant to each of us. So I will try to explain this majestic unfolding in terms as clear and simple as I can find.

Also, I thought it might be helpful to you to include a small glossary summarizing basic definitions of terms (p. 257) so that you can refer to it whenever you feel uncertain of something we covered in the first series of letters. There are many excellent texts on astrology already in print, so the purpose of these letters is rather to emphasize two things: (1) the necessity for understanding within yourself and through your own body the various processes represented by the signs; and (2) appreciation of their equivalent within the psyche. After all, we are psychosomatic creatures, and Jung has pointed out that many of our individual problems can be worked upon within the psyche without necessarily being acted out in the physical world as "fate." This would include many illnesses having a psychological disturbance at their root—though not all.

I always like to remember that the word "cosmos" means beauty, the beauty of order and harmony. When you realize the way our solar system interconnects with the greater model of the ring of the twelve visible constellations, it takes your breath away. I think it would relieve much of the religious angst of the modern world to see at least a glimmer of patterned meaning or meaningful pattern to the unfolding of our history, both individual and collective. We have had to wait for a more general understanding of the collective unconscious and of Jung's other great contribution, the concept of synchronicity, to grasp this. (See Glossary, p. 257. Go on, try it!) But I think we are ready now, and, hopefully, a new understanding of astrology's function will be our guide. Each of us has to take on the task of seeing a spiritual reason for our individuation: it is our very uniqueness that represents our gift, our "widow's mite," to the collective. And the collective unconscious is the sum total of consciousness of all creation, ever there for each individual to draw upon deep within himself or herself. No wisdom nor love is ever wasted. Even our terrible sufferings are not wasted, for they go through the alchemical transmutation of pain into wisdom, leaving traces behind in the collective unconscious which may help others. This is the source of myths.

There is a deep reason why universal myths abide, becoming the ground of all religions of the world. As Jung pointed out, they are not "untrue stories," but rather are always true of the psyche unfolding in sacred time and space, always now and here. They are the literature of the collective unconscious. Myths can be seen as providing a "morphic reasonance" for the psyche. The biologist Rupert Sheldrake proposes that, with the gathering of a critical mass, sudden leaps occur in the evolution of species. Perhaps then myths provide a gathering place for collective wisdom, for all the human trials and errors, of each individual's suffering, failure, and triumph. Through the templates of universal myth, God willing, we may be guided and initiated, one by one, until the story of each age is completed. Thus, no one's love or effort, however small or seemingly insignificant, is ever in vain. Any one of us could add the culminating and critical drop of consciousness that might suddenly change us all for the better. Humanity, despite its rich differences in race, culture, and religion, remains a collective species. As we evolve into this new Age of Aquarius, the task is clearly to recognize this as a fact and to see that the new creative dichotomy will be that of the individual and the collective, that of the collective and the cosmos.

So, for me anyway, the essential message is a positive one: we can look up to the mystery of the heavens and see that they coincide and connect simply and naturally with the vagaries of our everyday life, giving it the meaning we so desperately seek and want to believe in. This connection may no longer be a question of blind faith: there is now a modicum of factual proof—scientific, practical proof. There seems to be a "menu"(!)—a sequence, something that the ego in us can "read" for comfort's sake but must always remember that we cannot control. We can now recognize it, savor it, and help to fulfill it. My glass of water connects me to all the water in the world; my little candle flame connects me to all the fire in the universe. But I need not aspire to control the totality of these elements. This would be hubris, and it seems typical of humanity sometimes to forget that.

I always remember my teacher M's admonition that the true purpose of astrology is a spiritual one, to help each individual understand those universal processes, called "gods" by our forebears, that operate both outside and inside us. Its deepest purpose is to reveal the *unus mundus*, the "one world," underlying our various graspings of reality. Alas, much of today's "astrology" remains a parody of this, which is all the more reason to persevere.

So let's begin without further ado. Just to refresh your memory, let me repeat a few basic concepts:

Natal astrology answers five elementary questions:

Who? Answered by the Sun, which generates its own system.

What about the who? Answered by the Moon and the other *planets* which reflect, in different ways, the light of the Sun.

How? Answered by the twelve *signs*, which modify the above and will be the subject of these letters.

To what degree? Answered by the *aspects* or geometric relationships among the planets, which will also be discussed.

Where? Answered by the twelve *houses*, which give us the locale in the outer and inner worlds and represent the stage sets upon which the drama of a lifetime unfolds.

As you know, the underlying premise of both analytical psychology and astrology is that we all subjectively experience the objective world, and in a fashion that is unique to each of us as individuals. Jung was concerned that we learn to do this more consciously, thereby fulfilling our deepest duty to God by helping the spirit to incarnate more fully in the manifest world, and, at the same time, to release the imprisoned splendor of creation through our consciousness. In more ordinary terms, he stressed the importance of self-acceptance, of wholeness rather than perfection, seeing the purpose of analysis as leading beyond the healing of neuroses to ongoing spiritual growth. For him, he said, the process of analysis was "maieutic" (note the four vowels!), in which the therapist serves as a "midwife" to the inner rebirth of the transformed ego, now able to function harmoniously in relationship to the inner Self, the mysterious center and totality of the psyche—the Christ Within or Atman, or as I like to refer to it, our Divine Guest. This reborn "divine child" is conceived within the individual mother soul (psyche) and its indwelling fathering Self, a divine spark, called by some the "scintilla." This process is said to be *contra naturam* (a reversal of nature's way), yet it mirrors nature's laws, for any new birth requires a *coniunctio* between feminine and masculine. Here it comes between a god and a virgin mother—a *theotokos* (god-mother) within the psyche of a mortal individual. Can you see how the symbolism of the human family is the closest the sages could come to expressing such a deep and loving truth? It is not the literalism that obtains here, but the clothing and personifying of a mystery in the simplest terms for our understanding.

To be such a midwife is a high calling for sure. Doubtless for many it is an unconscious one, very naturally forgotten in countless counseling sessions when two people confront each other to go over the seemingly endless and painful details of woundedness. We have all been there. Nor is this limited to analysis per se; it occurs between parents and children, teachers and students, priests and parishioners, doctors and patients, coaches and athletes—wherever one is seeking guidance and another is seeking to guide in matters involving the inner growth of character and personality.

Astrology fits into the picture in that it can provide a map, if you will, to an invisible world, the very "kingdom of heaven which is within." It can describe for us, not so much *what* our experiences are, but *how* we tend to process those experiences, to respond through projecting our own inner archetypal images in meaningful ways onto life and the people who surround us.

As I have said before, the chart is to the psyche what DNA and RNA are to the body: the template that patterns the way we consume life. We unconsciously use this template all the time, whether we believe in astrology or not. But we are given a blessing and a grace in the option to use it consciously and for its deepest purpose, something Jung called "individuation" as it applies to the Self in us, and which the theologians call "incarnation" as it applies to Christ in Jesus. This points to the concept of the Christ Within or the Atman. In this sense, the life of Jesus becomes a paradigm for Christians, a model of how to carry our *own* cross with faith in the powers of redemption. For every great religion there is such a model, an example of human life lived fully and simultaneously at both the human and archetypal level. They have become one. Moses, in the Age of Aries, was the poignant and heroic model for the collective birth of the ego, for, like the ego, he could lead his people to the Promised Land, yet he could not enter it. Viewed symbolically, he, like our own individual ego, had the task of leading his people (our inner throng) out of captivity, through a desert (a meaningless inner wasteland) to a Promised Land, a twice-born life. The closer to individuation any mortal comes, the more archetypally meaningful the events of that life are for the rest of us. Certainly we project upon such avatars, but it is because the highest in us resonates to the highest in them. It takes one to know one!

There is a story about Martin Buber, the great Jewish philosopher, that I have always loved. It seems that one day it dawned on him that if he ever got to heaven, the Lord would probably not ask him, "Martin, why were you not more like Moses?" but rather, "Martin, why were you not more like Martin Buber?"

This higher function of astrology is a far cry from Madame La Zonga's "Stellar Predictions" in your daily newspaper, but Madame La Zonga can acquaint almost anybody with their Sun sign, and so she serves a humble and mostly harmless role. I worry more about the astrology that is increasingly practiced by astrologers identified with their egos, i.e., their mental and controlling intellects, who think they have all the answers, chop-chop-chop. Both psychology and astrology are, first and foremost, lessons in wonder and awe of how much we do not know and may never know. Beyond the precious mind—and it *is* precious—lies the ineffable mystery of the heart. What one cannot put into words is where we truly begin. As Lao Tzu wrote:

Existence is beyond the power of words
To define:
Terms may be used
But are none of them absolute.
In the beginning of heaven and earth there
  were no words,
Words came out of the womb of matter;
And whether a man dispassionately
Sees to the core of life
Or passionately
Sees the surface,
The core and the surface
Are essentially the same,
Words making them seem different
Only to express appearance.
If name be needed, wonder names them both:
From wonder into wonder
Existence opens.

Astrology, mother of astronomy in ages past, gives us one great talisman as we venture into the unknown. It is the secret assurance that underneath the bewildering confusion of our lives there abides a cosmic order, a majestic and transcendent beauty so great that it bespangles the heavens with one sweeping arc, fearing not at the same time to miniaturize itself in the infinitesimal universe of an atom, or in the incoming gasp of a newborn infant or the outgoing gasp of one dying. The study of astrology should remind us that, though we share the process of creating, we ourselves and our wondrous worlds within worlds are created. We did not create ourselves. Even our bodies were created by our parents and theirs by their parents , and on and on—back to whom? Who created our psyches? The answer to that surely is a paradox.

I remember a conversation between an atheist and an agnostic. The atheist believed (an oxymoron to start with) that all creation and evolution were the products of chance.

"Even the human body?" asked the agnostic.

"Of course!"

"Even the human mind?" pressed the agnostic.

"Certainly," replied the atheist.

"Well, then," said the agnostic, throwing up his hands, "if that is truly so, of what value is your opinion?" Ha!

Anyway, what I am trying to say at the outset is that as Jungian psychology and its equivalents are intended teleologically to lead to spiritual unfolding, so, too, is astrology. It pays to remember that astrology began thousands of years ago when science (based on observation) was one with religion (based on awe). When the two split, astrology's role in uniting them was repudiated; religion lost its objective proof and science lost its sense of the sacred. However, the resulting polarity and tension may yet have a constructive outcome: a greater consciousness of how astrology might serve in bringing about a new and deeper awareness of the essential affinity of these two. The human race will live in deadly and daily peril until religion and science are reconciled and reunited, both within us as individuals and collectively on our fragile and lovely planet. The great trap for many religions today is the emphasis on "being good." Being good is the natural by-product, not the goal, of being kind and loving to the Divine Guest within oneself and others. As with innocence, the minute you try to achieve it, you lose it! A shift of emphasis seems to be required.

We need to remember that astrology itself is neither a religion nor a science. Like mathematics and geometry, it is simply a built-in characteristic of the cosmos as we know it. Dane Rudhyar defined astrology as "an algebra of life." To pursue its study for me is like reaching out into the darkness and void and touching the face of God, as I felt I did on that lightless night after my wedding. Once I wrote a little poem:

STARS

Each star
is a kiss
I would give you—
should others
wake to a starless night
you would be lying
in my arms
covered with light.

It is my intention to present the twelve signs to you in a different way, an oblique way calculated to help you integrate them into your own total being rather than just reading about them using your mind. But in order to accomplish this, I must ask you to memorize *by rote*, without even understanding them, the basics of the astrological alphabet—or scales if you are musically inclined. One cannot read or write without letters or compose without notes, so it is a reasonable request. You will find a set-off booklet, those pages with vertical stripes at their edges, set in the middle of this book (pp. 133–138). The glyphs and sequence of signs are essential. You need to learn them visually as well as orally, so that with ease you can picture, say, Aries and Libra as a polarity and know immediately what signs precede and succeed Virgo or Capricorn, etc. As I have mentioned before, the number of "facts" in astrology, compared to other disciplines, is very small and quite concise. However, the catch is that the permutations are infinite, so that these potential combinations and regroupings come up constantly in your practice. The universe simply won't stand still for a second while you pin up its hem!

By the way, you will remember the dream that initially gave sanction to these letters. I had been painfully blocked about how to write down my experience of astrology accumulated over forty-three years, and dreaming that I was writing you these letters released the flow of ideas so easily. I am grateful both for you and for the dream. Writing them proved to be an experiment of sorts: would it be possible to take lofty ideas and principles, normally dealt with in logical and sequential exegesis, and present them in an informal and intimate, and (as you remarked) feminine way, a way requiring a meaningful relationship, in this case, of friend to friend? From the response, the answer seems to be an unqualified yes! So consider these letters as a stepstool in a library enabling you, and hopefully others, to reach higher and more lofty volumes. Sometimes the gods and goddesses must envy us our simple human pleasures, which are the direct result of our limitations in time and space. They can't put up their feet and drink a cup of good hot coffee while reading of eternal verities; we can. So many in the world are reaching for higher consciousness, unaware and unremembering that the angels descend as well as ascend. It is only fair, therefore, that we remember them as we wait in line at the supermarket or bend over our desks in the office or walk the nightwatch on an aircraft carrier or with a child sick with a fever. The fair exchange would be to do it for the angels, in the same way that they in their dimension are doing it for us. We just might turn our mortality into a privilege, something as precious as the golden ring of quiddity.

It is good to be back in touch. I look forward eagerly to hearing from you soon.

Love ever,

ao

THE WORLD

I Saw Eternity the other night
Like a great Ring of pure and endless light,
*   All calm as it was bright,*
And round beneath it, Time in hours, days, years
*   Driv'n by the spheres*
Like a vast shadow mov'd, in which the world
*   And all her train were hurl'd. . . .*
                                    —HENRY VAUGHAN
                        Seventeenth-century Welsh poet

Our life is an apprenticeship to the truth that
around every circle another can be drawn; that there
is no end in nature, but every end is a beginning;
that there is always another dawn risen on mid-noon,
and under every deep a lower deep opens.
                        —RALPH WALDO EMERSON

Our psyche is set up in accord with the structure of
the universe, and what happens in the macrocosm
likewise happens in the infinitesimal and most
subjective reaches of the psyche.
                                    —C. G. JUNG

CHAPTER

2

CIRCLES, CYCLES, AND SPIRALS

Dear Friend,

The first time that I lectured at the C. G. Jung Foundation, quite a few years ago, I arrived carrying copies of this powerful poem by Henry Vaughan and a large cucumber. As I remember it, when the eyes of those in the class widened considerably, I told them how glad I was that they were not Freudians! After the laughter subsided, I reread "The World," as I would have you do, and asked them to imagine the humble cucumber as being circular and a symbol of time's ongoing eternity. Then I sliced it into thin pieces and gave each a slice, attempting to demonstrate our experience of time, which to the ego is the slice we are living and tasting, and which at the same time partakes of that "Ring of pure and endless light," the eternity wherein the Self dwells, that part of us not subject to time and space.

You may not realize how much personal courage it took for me, having been educated in Europe, to sacrifice my own ideas of academic rigor to do something so apparently crazy or silly in such a venerable milieu. But my task was to talk about astrology and its application to psychotherapy, and to do this in keeping with the nature of my subject, I needed to demonstrate that when we are dealing with astrology, we are binding, yoking, and connecting the loftiest, most universal and cosmic concepts and abstractions with the particular, the peculiar, and the deepest validity of down-to-earth daily life. Education, in general, tends to separate our heads from our feet, and too often it fails to help us find the most sacred truths displayed under our very noses in our daily lives and in everything in them. So as I sat in my kitchen praying for guidance and strength, the cucumber presented itself. I had several cucumbers on hand, so I sliced one and studied each slice closely. I found that the seeds are arranged in the most harmonious way; they spiral up the length of the gourd in much the same way that you might take a many-stranded necklace of small beads and twist it several times. In fact, it probably resembles a model of DNA/RNA.

By the same token, you could learn much from any grapefruit about how the two-dimensional horoscope represents a three-dimensional construct when you slice it into two hemispheres; its segments demonstrate our concept of overlaying the globe of the earth with longitudinal lines meeting at the north and south poles. I did not bring in the grapefruit, but I am not sorry about the cucumber because, *mirabile dictu*, it riveted everyone's attention, and we could polish off the proof with a minimum of mess.

What I am trying to say is that though we can study the cosmos with a telescope on the one hand, or with an electron microscope on the other, we can find the same affirmations in the normal scope of life. Here, too, we live in octaves of wonder, which, like the caduceus of Hermes, spiral up and down, in and out, in the most sophisticated simplicity. We live in a vibrational unity of color, sound, and visible and invisible worlds, hidden and enfolded, implicit, one within the other, all waiting for human consciousness and appreciation to reveal them. And if something is too awesome and overwhelming, nature provides the same lesson for us on a smaller scale in our daily environment. In fact, I firmly believe that it is one of the functions of the ego to step down the overwhelming nature of the cosmos, enabling us to live in the here and now of every day. It protects us within the psyche from the vastness of things. In this the universe is merciful. Rain comes down in drops and not all in one colossal SPLAT. And time comes minute by minute; were it not for clocks, we would measure it by heartbeats. The heavens arc and sweep in dependable beauty and majesty, and I am given time to try to unscrew the lid of a jar of marmalade.

The funny thing is that the screwing spiral of the lid and the hour hand of my analogue watch hint at a similarity of process. The cowlick on my grandson's head follows the mathematics of the galaxy. The little wisps of hair allow a moment of such tenderness. This is a wee galaxy I can cope with, and in its way, it is as great a miracle of creation. The one helps me to approach the other without quite so much fear of the unknown, of those limitless mysteries of infinite space and eternity. The wonder and mystery spelled out for us in kindergarten:

> Nor you nor I nor anyone knows
> how oats, peas, beans or barley grows!

Well, agronomists could teach us a lot today about how they do grow, but we could stump even them by asking how come they exist in the first place? Or why? Here science stops, metaphysics begins, and religions unfold.

But we have a precious key, which if given a chance, could help us understand a new way of uniting all of these in a harmonious continuum instead of a series of unrelated and clashing opposites. The key that astrology offers us is the language life speaks: *the symbolic language of archetypal processes.* Astrology teaches the grammar of that language; it teaches us that all nouns conceal verbs. They freeze, or slice, action and being through the simple device of naming them. By naming the phenomena of life—one of the first tasks of Adam and Eve—we gain control over them. A noun (*nomen*) is by definition a name. Behind this secret lies the reason for the awe we still address, unwittingly perhaps, when we pray "hallowed be Thy Name," or when a Jewish child is taught to leave blank the vowel in the name for G-d, because to name God ultimately is impossible, so even our label for the highest and deepest process of creativity can only be for what Jung called the *imago Dei*, the concept or image of God. For me, astrology describes the Tao of "what into how."

There are languages in the world which have no nouns. What we would call a carrot would be a "carroting," a house, a "housing." In such languages, which are primitive, the idea is not lost that, behind the carrot or the house, energy is moving; the divine is actively disguising itself through carroting and housing as mere temporary and perhaps playful attributes of a dancing world, or a terrifying one. Somehow "dying" sounds better to me than "death." In "dying," the verb, something active is taking place; by the same token living is concealed by naming death—the noun hides the verb. Notice that as I am "lettering" I am forced to convert all verbs into gerunds, which are classified grammatically as nouns.

Words, i.e., linear thinking, exclude the possibility even of describing the constant flowing of life, which is how the ruler of communication, Mercury the Trickster, tricks us! The only exception is poetry, where words deliberately evoke images, and in so doing make a poet of the reader. So you see, astrology, which is a symbolic language like mathematics, uses glyphs—we could say hieroglyphs (sacred signs)—to evoke images and to make connections instantaneously in a way that bypasses words entirely. These insights are then stepped down, transformed or "translated" into words, in the same way that integers and algebraic formulae can be talked about and written about.

There is a difference, though, in the way we perceive "12" and "twelve," because we use different hemispheres of the brain in reading them. Thus astrology offers a different way of "seeing" and "perceiving," and it yokes the seemingly disparate worlds of outer and inner into the *unus mundus*, so that they become one for an instant and profoundly meaningful. The outer event becomes metaphor to the inner world of the psyche. Astrology's time frame then becomes what Jung termed *synchronicity*. This is a very subtle but important point and one that bears repetition, so ingrained in the public mind is the idea of astrology's connection to causality. *A* does not cause *A'*; *A* and *A'* are really one but appear to be two. The sun in the sky (depicted by the Sun in the chart) is equal to the Sun in the psyche, "the kingdom of heaven within." This is a paradox, but we have to live and deal with it as a fundamental hypothesis. This is the way it works! And just as thousands of moons in puddles reflect the same moon, so the billions of suns carried in the hearts of the world's population and in the nuclei of every atom are inflamed by the unknown Sun behind the sun, that ultimate mystery we call Love and Life.

One of the loveliest traditions in Judaism is the idea that the consonants of the Hebrew alphabet were derived from looking at patterns of the stars, and that the planets are the vowels moving in and out of the consonants, thereby writing the endless story of life. To me both Hebrew and Arabic are among the most beautiful alphabets in the world, and I never fail to recognize them as I gaze at the fire licking the logs in our fireplace. How often can we read "Allah" or "Elohim" in the flames!

In this second series of letters, we will be looking at the twelve *constellations* and the twelve *signs* of the zodiac. In the first series we studied the planets as coincident with archetypal processes in the psyche. The signs of the tropical zodiac are to the planets as environment is to an individual. Just as we ourselves are subtly modified by our outer environment—more at ease in some places and with some people than others—so the planets we studied are affected by the signs they occupy at any time, including the moment of birth. The basic imprint or template of the psyche's individuality is patterned then, but it, like any growing organism, continues to unfold and unfurl into its own ever-living and ever-changing being throughout a lifetime. Though we cannot change the physical makeup of our genes, which is a given at birth, we can alter, adorn, strengthen, ignore, or allow to deteriorate what we started out with. Regardless, there will be certain inexorable developments, or we would remain toothless, howling infants at the age of fifty. We call this growth. Accepting and working harmoniously within the limitations and opportunities of the aging process of the body is reflected in the psyche as well, beautifully indicated by the cyclical nature of the solar system outside us and the individual one within us. Our body clock is matched with an interior one that is swept into far greater sweeps of time and timelessness. Like a great lemniscate, time loops through our days and turns them into years of meaning. Time changes its quality once we take it in. We can be young or old, as we choose. Space loses its quantity once we take it in. We can be here or there or out to lunch, as we choose. Many are confused about timelessness and space without space, until they realize we experience this nightly in dreams. There the whens and wheres are without measurable dimensions, and we do have some experience of an unattenuated life.

Remember this on any depressing or boring day, and it will make you feel extremely talented just knowing that you can remain yourself despite the fact that the following is true:

1. The Earth is moving at 1000 mph as it rotates on its axis.
2. The Earth is also traveling 66,000 mph as it orbits the sun.
3. The sun and solar system are whizzing along the edge of the Milky Way at 481,000 mph.
4. And the Milky Way is clocking 1,350,000 mph around a cluster of galaxies.

Add to this the fact that every single part of your body is in constant motion, and every atom in it is a minigalaxy dancing and whirling at incalculable speeds. And yet you remain you. Now, *that's magic!* Presto! Caramba! It makes me think of the two

English ladies driving towards a village. "Nice place we're coming to, wasn't it!" The word "cosmos" means beauty, and it is very comforting to know that its order is so constant. I only wish I could do as well with the things on my desk!

Back to the signs! We need to remember that there are two zodiacs, which like Ezekiel's wheels are one within the other. The outer zodiac is called the *sidereal* zodiac and consists of twelve visible constellations of varying width.

The *tropical* zodiac, which is the one used by Western astrologers, is only conceptual. It is an invisible circle of 360 degrees, neatly divided into twelve segments of 30 degrees each. This zodiac is traced by the *apparent* path of the sun. Since all the planets have elliptical orbits, and since astrology is not only geocentric but anthropocentric, and since we live not only on the Earth, but on a particular spot upon it at any given time, you can see that some incredible calculations were made by astronomers and astrologers over the millennia. My own personal impression is that if you could see the trajectories all manifest at once, the result would look like my ball of knitting wool right after the cat was through with it—only this cosmic cat knows exactly what it's doing!

Fortunately, there are many excellent texts that will sort all this out for you in a clear and understandable manner. Do not be overwhelmed or alarmed, please, or else accept the sense of alarm, as I have all along for sixty-one years when confronted by how much I know I do not know. I will try to concentrate on what little I have found out and what I have found helpful from the perspective of psychotherapeutic diagnosis, personal self-acceptance, and dealing with the rich language of myth, symbols, and images that connect the chart with the inner *temenos* of an individual psyche.

For me, the chart serves one purpose above all: it is the map of the individuation process. It is there as our guide in times of perplexity. Consistently, it will mirror to us what the lesson might be or may become if we do not seek to learn it; it will mirror our gifts and show where and how we might free them; and it can describe our inner subpersonalities and how their squabbles might be resolved; or how our self-doubts, anxieties, and sufferings might be transformed through seeing them as alchemical processes, sometimes transmuting pain into purpose or grief into wisdom. We are not to escape pain and suffering but to confront them with all the nobility of soul we have, until they yield up their treasures. Sometimes, by hindsight, we may end up being grateful for them—they have given us a leg up to further understanding. My image of this is Jacob and the angel: "I will not let thee go, unless thou bless me" (Gen. 32:26).

As a therapist you will no doubt perceive the problems of your patients even without astrology, since that other great key is at your disposal: the world of dreams and the wealth of the unconscious. But the chart, like an X-ray, can help pinpoint problems since, as I have said before, it describes the way we process experience. Also, I have found it helpful that the chart, properly used, can give the patient permission—and later a sacred mandate—to be who he or she really is. We need to share with a great sense of urgency that we are giving God another way of being in the world, in the totally unique opportunity of being ourselves. As Swami Muktananda put it, "God lives in you as you." After we have lived through a childhood of being exhorted to emulate others or some heroic model, this comes as an enormous relief to most people. And for one woman, as an analyst friend told me, the idea that she had a chart uniquely her own gave her an instant sense of worth—for some reason, she thought only important people had charts!

To summarize: at a person's birth, each planet will be placed in a different degree in a different sign in a different house from someone else's. (Occasionally two planets will occupy the same degree, in which case they are called *conjunct*.) What I hope to do is share the intrinsic essence of the signs by connecting them, as we did the planets, with the elements and the qualities they display in us. It is important to memorize these for convenience, but to understand what they actually mean in psychological terms must spring from an intrinsic level within you, so that at the drop of a hat you could form an "image" of the differences between a Mars in Aries and a Mars in Libra, or a Venus in Pisces and a Venus in Virgo. Mars is Mars, and Venus is Venus, you might assume, since they represent their own archetypal processes. But they will function differently in differing milieus and relationships. The "how" is what we are after. Remember especially that *there are no good, better, or bad signs!* All twelve are variations on a common theme and together represent a circle of totality. What distinguishes each individual is the drama afforded by the *planets in the signs.* If you look through a blue glass at a white teddy bear dressed in red, you will see a blue teddy bear in a purple suit. The blue glass modifies what is behind the glass. In the same way, a sign "colors" the way the archetypes will function. Mars in Aries will wield the sword of action; Mars in Libra makes the same action graceful, metaphorically speaking. He will be a fencer and turn the duel into a dance or a playful sport.

Now if I have muddled you, I beg your patience. You can view the perfect logic and harmonious consistency of the zodiac with absolute and total trust. By constant referral to it, rather than to texts or even my letters, you will connect what you already know with what is next to be known, just as a knitter knits into the stitch below. Even if you were a reader without a background in Jung, you would always have your own life experience to connect to these universals. Astrology is based on an observable and real phenomenon, the solar system; there is a knowable objective element to fall back on. The miracle of it is that astrology can connect that outer reality with an equally valid and real microcosm, that of the individual's inner psyche. Writing in *Memories, Dreams, Reflections,* Jung put it this way:

> Our psyche is set up in accord with the structure of the universe, and what happens in the macrocosm likewise happens in the infinitesimal and most subjective reaches of the psyche.

For that reason the God-image is always a projection of the inner experience of a powerful *vis-à-vis.* This is symbolized by objects from which the inner experience has taken its initial impulse, and which from then on preserve numinous significance, or else it is characterized by its numinosity and the overwhelming force of that numinosity. In this way the imagination liberates itself from the concretism of the object and attempts to sketch the image of the invisible as something which stands behind the phenomenon. I am thinking here of the simplest basic form of the mandala, the circle, and the simplest (mental) division of the circle, the quadrant or, as the case may be, the cross.

The two zodiacs, sidereal and tropical, are circular, the horoscope is circular, and the planetary orbits are elliptical. They are all mandalas of totality. As I have pointed out before, the circle is a perfect symbol for the unknowable nature of God because its area can never be known, since the nature of pi is limitless. And the Self, as Jung defined it, is the center and totality of the psyche. Since the psyche is connected through the personal unconscious to the collective unconscious, as an individual well is connected to the water table (as Ira Progoff so aptly puts it), that totality is potentially infinite. Symbols point to truths; they do not define them. Our charts in no way limit us or force us, since through greater self-consciousness we can alter the way we process experience. In so doing, as Jung has pointed out, the outer events change automatically as our view of them changes. Insuperable problems with no possible solution suddenly are either solved or outgrown; they fade away as we transcend them to focus on something new. The very obstacles in our path suddenly rearrange themselves into a stile on which we climb over the unclimbable wall. So there is no way we can blame the outer circumstances or individuals with the words "if only...!" Nor is there any way that we can blame our "stars" for our "fated" difficulties. Our free will always operates within the limitations of the given: we have the free choice to become conscious or to remain unconscious. When we elect to go "on the Path," we side with making the effort to understand. Then life begins to change and to acquire the numinosity promised us of old by the many messengers of Spirit. "God's grace is like an ever-blowing breeze," as Prabhavananda wrote. "All we need to do is lift our sails to catch it."

So meditate on circular matters and circular things: the eye, the centripetaled flowers, the gold coin, the glyph for the Sun. Think of the instant centricity of any light shining through fog or snowflakes, the concentric circles made by rain in puddles or pebbles in ponds.

How and when do circles open into spirals?

How do circles relate to spheres? How do circles relate to ellipses?

Why does Blake's "Ancient of Days" use a compass? Why is it symbolically important that, when you draw a circle with a compass, one arm must be rooted and at a still point while the other sweeps the arc of manifestation?

What is the sound of a circle? It is OM (A-U-M). When that sound is made, particles on a plate, responding to the vibration, group themselves into a circle and then begin to lift as if to make a sphere. (This was observed in an experiment conducted by Hans Jenny in Zurich. Jenny is a pioneer in an embryonic science called Cymatics, which studies wave phenomena.) Could it be that when this syllable is sounded, our invisible auras are temporarily ordered?

Have fun with bubbles and balloons. The bigger the balloon, the greater the surface exposed to the outer world. What in the psyche functions like the membrane of a balloon, touching inner and outer worlds simultaneously?

It has been helpful to me over the years to keep a notebook on these various symbols and to contemplate them. As we do the unconscious comes to our aid. Add to this the study of a mythological dictionary, and a whole world of universal motifs opens up: stories of girdles and balls and magic rings suddenly point to that hidden idea of totality. Perhaps now a list of "twelves" might be helpful:

12 signs of the zodiac
12 disciples
12 acupuncture meridians in the body
12 pairs of cranial nerves (24)
12 tissue salts
12 hours on a watch (24 hours in a day)
12 meridians on the two hemispheres of the globe
12 months in a year
12 inches to a foot
12 people on a jury
12 constellations
12 sons of Jacob
12 running springs in Helim
12 rivers flowing from the spring Hvergelmir (Norse)
12 loaves in the Sanctuary
12 stones in Hebrew breastplate (Old Testament)
12 stones on Hebrew altar (Old Testament)
12 oxen bearing brazen sea at Temple of Solomon
12 stars in bride's crown (New Testament)
12 foundations of Jerusalem
12 eons
12 Labors of Gilgamesh
12 Labors of Hercules
12 Olympian gods
12 *dii maiores* (Roman)
12 Buddhist *nidanas*, or states of emergence
12 saviors (in the *Pistis Sophia*)
12 Knights of King Arthur
12 deities on Ra's solar boat
12 gates of the Ming-t'ang
12 fruits on the Tree of Life
12 dynamic aspects of 4 x 3 (female & male) for Dogon and
    Bambara of Mali
12 spaces between knots on Druid's Knot

12 total of sides on two dice
12 Merry Men about the Oak King
12 Sacred Chinese Ornaments
12 Norse gods
12 episodes of Moses' life
12 exploits of Odysseus
12 Meistersingers
12 Paladins of Charlemagne
12 Tablets of Roman Law
12 Stations of Christ's Passion
12 sides to the dodecahedron

By now, hopefully, you can see the kind of finger exercises astrology thrives on. As silly as they may seem, they are the playful introduction to making those unexpected connections. The best hiding place for sense is in nonsense.

On a deeper level, of course, you will be reminded of Jung's own extensive observations of mandalas in dreams and his use of them outwardly in therapy. His own artwork is filled with beautiful variations on this theme. Much is being done at the moment in workshops around the world to explore the system. But this is nothing new, when you consider the rice paintings of the Hindus, the sand paintings of Native Americans, and the highly sophisticated thankas of the Tibetans.

As Jesus said of the Round Dance in the apocryphal *Acts of John*, "Not to join the dance is to mistake the occasion." So let's ring-around-a-rosy and realize what we are truly dancing!

Love ever,

ao

The whole universe is ever in his power.
He is pure consciousness, the creator of time:
all powerful, all-knowing. It is under his rule
that the work of creation revolves in its evolution,
and we have earth, and water, and ether, and fire
and air.

God ended his work and he rested, and he
made a bond of love between his soul and the soul
of all things. And the ONE became one with the one,
and the two, and the three and the eight, and with
time and with the subtle mystery of the human soul.
—SVETASVATARA UPANISHAD

The spirit of man is the candle of the Lord.
—PROVERBS 20:27

—3—

THE ELEMENTS
Four Levels of Being

Dear Friend,

I'm delighted that you can recite the sequence of signs backwards and forwards and round and round. Good for you! You will find that a tremendous time-saver. Truly.

Your questions always come at the right moment and help me to formulate my thoughts. You ask: *What is meant by the four elements, earth, air, fire and water, when we know now that there are so many others? Do the four still apply?*

Yes, they do still apply, but they are not to be considered in the same light as the Table of Elements of chemistry. In fact, none of the four appears as such in the Table of Elements, with the partial exception of H_2O. They really represent a basic quaternity of different qualities of being rather than quantifications of matter. Perhaps the simplest way of explaining this would be to quote a story told me by my teacher M many years ago.

We were down on Prince Street in New York in what he called his lab. This consisted of two rooms in a small and very old building in what then was considered almost a slum section of the city. It was the same building where Hermes, the first astrologer I ever met, lived on the floor above in an apartment smelling of Clorox and roses. M's lab had a meditation room in the front and a smaller room in the back with a daybed which served as a couch, a fireplace with a mantelpiece, two windows that looked out on a fire escape in the back, and a tiny kitchen set off by an old curtain. What distinguished the place was a beautiful heavy carpet hanging above the mantel, representing a turbaned master and his younger disciple. It looked Persian to me. And then there was the extraordinary combination of fragrances given off by the various essential oils he had in his possession. Rose, Siberian pine, lavender, narcissus—I couldn't breathe in enough of it. Occasionally this was cut through by the fierce aroma of a very fine Cuban cigar. M was a big, strong, white-haired man with an aristocratic beaked nose and a rosy complexion. Even then I knew how blessed I was in having met him.

On this day, he marched in ahead of me wearing a fine navy cashmere coat, a scarf, and a dashingly turned fedora. He strode to the windows and pulled up the shades exclaiming, "And the Lord said unto Moses, 'Let there be light!'" He always said that, and certainly there was light, never mind the history of it. I remember that we sat on the couch, and somewhere along the line I asked him the very same question that you did. He waved his hand at the Persian hanging on the wall, and said, "Dearie, let me tell you a story." So, being young and twenty, I curled up with my legs tucked under me and listened like a child. And the story went something like this:

Once upon a time there was a good man, a Scottish farmer who was going to market on a summer's day. (M knew I was of Scottish descent.) Since it was a fair distance and hot besides, he carried a leather water bottle, and he carried a bit of money to buy his family some few provisions.

Presently, he stopped by a clootie well, which was an old spring under the trees by the side of the road. Here thousands of "clooties" or colored strips of cloth were tied to every twig and branch, for you see, this was a holy well, a wishing well, and the clooties were each a wish tied there to remind the spirits not to forget. Suddenly, a remarkably spry and cheery old woman stepped forward, as he was making a wish of his own and filling his leather bottle with the clear sweet water that spurted from the spout. And the wish he was making was that he might learn a little more about God. No sooner had he tied on a clootie to a wee twig than up she spoke.

"Good morrow," she said. "I see you are making a wish the noo." (M's attempt at a Scot's burr made me laugh!)

"Aye," said the farmer.

"Well now," said she with a kindly wink, "I will ask you a riddle and if you can give me the answer afore sundown, I promise your wish will come true."

"Who are you?" asked the farmer, amazed.

"Surely, it's myself I am!" she retorted. "Now here is the riddle: What is there in this world that the more you give away, the more there is to be given away?"

Well, the farmer scratched his head and couldn't think at all what it was, but he touched his forelock politely and went on his way wondering.

Not long after, he came upon a little girl sitting by the roadside, all hot and "musted up" (as the Scots put it). She was crying because she was so thirsty. Without hesitation, the farmer stopped and shared his water bottle with her. And the child drank it all, almost to the last drop. She wiped her mouth and thanked him. The farmer went on, and he knew he had given away water, but now he had less, so it couldn't be that.

He walked on and almost stumbled over a poor old beggar who stopped him and told him a very sad tale. He truly believed in the man's misfortune, so he gave him all the money he had with him, but for a few farthings. So much for the provisions, thought he. Again, he had given away something, and he knew he had less and not more. So it couldn't be that.

On he walked, and he was almost to the town itself, when he was beset by a capering fool. One soft in the head, it seemed, because all he wanted was some air. "But there's air all about," said the farmer. "But I can't see it!" wailed the fool. "Och, quit your blethering," laughed the farmer, and he made as if to catch a handful of air and gave it to the fool, who almost fell apart entirely, so grateful was he for the gift! But the farmer knew he had given him nothing, so it couldn't be that.

When the fellow reached the market, his pockets were empty but for the farthings. So he walked about and causey-talked with his friends, and since he had so little money, he finally settled on buying a "pig in a poke." These pokes were rough little sacks that might hold a piglet, but sometimes only a kitten, which is why they warned not to "let the cat out of the bag." He picked out a poke at random. It rattled. It did not squeal at all. Shrugging his shoulders, the man set out for home, as it was getting late. He stopped finally to look in his poke and found at the bottom of it an old lantern, probably some trick of a tinker's. And in it half a mouse-chewed candle. Well, at least he had something, he thought. His wife might have some use of it.

He set off for home again, enjoying the soft and cooler air and the beauty of the twilight. The road just gleamed light enough before him, so that he could make his way. Then halfway back to the well, clouds from the sea rolled in, and it became pitch dark. A storm threatened. Now he was grateful for the old lamp, so he stopped to light it with his flint. He proceeded a little further when he heard several cries from the wee house of a small croft to the left. It sounded like the voices of women in distress. "Stop! Halt! Help! Hold up your light!"

Two young girls arrived first, followed soon by their anxious mother. All talking at once, they explained their predicament. One of the children had let the hearthfire go out. The father was away. Without fire, they had no light, no way to cook a supper for the father, who was bringing home the factor, the man who would report to the laird whose tenants they were. They might lose their croft! And on and on.

So our good farmer went up to the house with them and with his candle lit theirs, and they, in turn, lit their lamp and their hearthfire and put the kettle on the boil. And he could see their grateful rosy faces. Now there were at least nine sources of light in the house besides his own.

And he could see what a dear croft it was, and he knew the factor would be kind to them. The mother insisted on giving him some bread and cheese, and then he went his way.

Before long he came again to the clootie well and was not surprised really to see the old woman step out of the shadows. "Ah, 'tis himself again that's coming," she said. "And did he solve the riddle?"

"Aye, and I solved it, goodwifie. 'Twas the four elements, surely. The earth and the water I gave left me with less. The air I couldna give at all. But the fire, ah the fire, the more I gave, the more there was to give."

The old woman smiled wisely. "And did you get your wish, good man?"

"Aye," agreed the farmer, "I did that. For it is like love itself. The more it is given, the more there is to give." And touching his forelock to the Wise Old Woman, he went with a firm step towards home, knowing he was bringing his wife a treasure from the market. His old lantern, you see, for him at least, was now a magic lantern.

"How come?" I asked, still the literalist. M would not answer but waited for me to work it out. "Because the lantern had taught him something more about God?" I asked.

"Whenever some humble thing can teach us something, it becomes magic for us. That is the real good meaning of the word—it's not just tricks or sleight-of-hand or bugaboo stuff."

This little story taught me a lot, and it went on teaching me because I could use the image as an example of how you can learn to love people you don't particularly like. You could say that we are all flames of one fire enclosed in the lanterns of various bodies with various features. Taste and affinity lead us more naturally to one kind of lamp rather than another. But what is important to remember is that the identical source of light, name it what you will, is in every human being. Jung happened to call it the Self, but it goes by many names, and they all mean the same.

This particular story approaches the elements from the point of view of fire, but one should not get the idea that in the manifest world any one of the four elements is superior to the other three. They are symbolic of four necessary processes in this world that are continually interacting and are completely interdependent. One of the most essential basics in astrology is the need to think *symbolically* and *analogically* to make connections between different levels of consciousness. Thus we become more and more able to weave outer phenomena and events with inner significance and meaning, learning slowly but surely that they are one. The funny thing is that as you learn which of the signs are fire signs or earth signs, etc., you begin to intuit which element is likely to be preponderant in a person's chart, because there are psychosomatic clues. Very often, however, you are more likely to pick up on a person's rising sign (the sign on the ascendant at the time of birth), which describes the person's physical appearance and psychological persona, or what Jung described as the way we tend to deal with our outer environment.

This symbolism of the elements thus yields physical, psychological, and spiritual insights, as you shall see as we go along. As you know, the ancient Greeks got into all manner of debate as to which of the four was the primal element, and at one time a fifth element—ether—was put forth as a quintessence. This one was invisible and intangible. Today, with the help of physics, we can see what they were reaching for, perhaps, was a concept of "fields of energy." The important thing to remember today, in the astrological sense, is that like the four directions or the cross, this quaternity describes four ways of being, four different emphases or approaches to one and the same thing. The Four Gospels of the New Testament are a good example. Each of the

Evangelists has a traditional symbol derived, no doubt, from those of Ezekiel's vision of the wheel in the Old Testament. They represent the four "fixed" elements, "fixed" meaning the most stable expression of each element:

> Luke, the ox (Taurus, fixed earth): Luke's account of the life of Jesus is graphic and homely, down-to-earth.
> Mark, the lion (Leo, fixed fire): His account gives a journalist's story of the action in the life of Jesus.
> Matthew, the man (Aquarius, fixed air): This account focuses on the words and ideas of Jesus.
> John, the eagle (Scorpio, fixed water): John focuses on the mystical and emotional passion of Jesus' life.

In medieval monasteries, the monks would study the Bible sentence by sentence and attempt to interpret each through these four elemental ways. This is also the key to why so often spiritual teachers teach through parables or little stories. They stick in your mind better than abstract principles because they are clothed in images, and they can be understood on many, many different levels. We should be sharing with children, clients, and patients these ways of seeing, hearing, and interpreting such teachings. Symbols help us find insights at the factual, intellectual, emotional, and mystical levels. Dreams especially become personal parables for us, once we get the knack of seeing them that way, to be looked at on different levels. The elements give us so many hints for asking the right questions of our lives, our actions, thoughts, and intentions.

All the religions are replete with stories filled with "magical" import. The problem, as Joseph Campbell spent a lifetime trying to teach us, is that we tend too often to confuse historical events and symbolic messages. As materialists we tend to literalize and wish to fix events permanently in fact, which is an impossibility. Why? Because it is never really the fact but what we *think* is the fact that counts. Each generation, as well as each individual, will interpret "facts" in different ways. Culture really is a loose agreement of a large group of people concerning important "facts." For example, it is a fact that we use electricity. The fact that people 3000 years ago did not use electricity does not mean that electricity did not exist *in potentia*. We simply evolved to a level where it became possible to discover and use electricity. A prophet wandering in the desert prophesying refrigerators, turbines, and light bulbs would have evoked ridicule, no doubt. But it is a fact that electricity has always existed, only we didn't know it. By the same token, myths have always existed and astrology has always existed. Our attitudes to both have varied as the centuries have passed. Whether we deny, ridicule, accept, or appreciate the wonders that are "just so" in this world depends on our attitude. As children we are taught to take things literally, so, for the most part, we trade in our intuitive reality for the "hard facts of life." As Wordsworth expressed it so poignantly in his "Ode: Intimations of Immortality":

> *Our birth is but a sleep and a forgetting:*
> *The soul that rises with us, our life's star,*
> *Hath had elsewhere its setting,*
> *And cometh from afar;*
> *Not in entire forgetfulness,*
> *And not in utter nakedness,*
> *But trailing clouds of glory do we come*
> *From God who is our home.*
> *Heaven lies about us in our infancy;*
> *Shades of the prison-house begin to close*
> *Upon the growing boy,*
> *But he beholds the light and whence it flows.*
> *He sees it in his joy;*
> *The youth, who daily farther from the east*
> *Must travel, still is Nature's priest,*
> *And by the vision splendid*
> *Is on his way attended;*
> *At length the man perceives it die away,*
> *And fade into the light of common day.*

Alas, as we grow older, we meet with literalism more and more, not realizing that, in truth it paralyzes wisdom onto only one level of understanding. It gets stuck in the first two chakras, so to speak. The good intention behind this literalism, of course, is to build a secure and decent social structure. But by denying the unknown, fearing it to be potentially evil, fundamentalists of any persuasion try to destroy the indestructible, namely the archetypal world of the human psyche. As Heraclitus said, "Even cows have to be beaten to greener pasture."

Take an example from the Upanishads, a simple image: "There are two little birds in a tree. One of them eats the fruit, and the other one watches." Literalized, this little image remains what it is—a charming description of something that occurs all over the world where there are birds and fruit trees. So what!

However, if you interpret this image through the four elements, you open it further and further into depths of meaning that ultimately yield naturalistic, philosophical, emotional, psychological, and spiritual insights. Which kind of bird are you? Am I? To be one and not the other would be to participate without comprehension, or to comprehend without experience—oh dear! Can we be both sequentially? Simultaneously? Which is the introvert? The extravert? And so on. Ultimately, we come back to the wisdom of that first teacher who put the image into Sanskrit scripture thousands of years ago, who antedated Jung's concepts of Self and ego, explaining the watcher as the Atman, the Self, and the eater as *ahamkara*, the personal "I" or ego.

In closing, since you are way ahead in your studies, consider what processes lie hidden in that little image: How might you interpret it intellectually? Emotionally? Mystically? How would one bird feel about the other? About the fruit? What does the fruit represent? Using the image with one of your patients, how would he or she respond or identify with one or the other? Which seems more important, acting or observing?

The point I am trying to make is what a pitiful waste of symbolism and symbolic thinking it would be if a "fundamentalist"

Hindu came to you and said, "Those two birds did that in 510 B.C., in your reckoning, on a Wednesday in July. That's a fact!" He would be absolutely right. But those two birds are still doing it on every fruit tree on earth, every day in every year. That, too, is a fact. Which is more important? More meaningful?

Those two little birds are flying onto the page you are reading and into your mind and heart, perhaps evoking and enhancing a story you have already heard. They will continue to fly in and out of history, carrying their wise little messages. Blessed be the Master who first observed such a simple fact and freed it from its fixity in time and place, and symbolically set free its wings.

Happy flying, and my love always,

ao

Who then devised the torment? Love.
Love is the unfamiliar Name
Behind the hands that wove
The intolerable shirt of flame
Which human power cannot remove.
We only live, only suspire
Consumed by either fire or fire.
—T. S. ELIOT, *Four Quartets*

O Sun as you shine upon my heart,
so may my heart shine upon others!

This is the truth: As from a blazing fire, sparks
essentially akin to it fly forth by the thousands, so
also, my good friend, do various beings come forth from
the imperishable Brahman and unto Him again return.
—MUNDAKA UPANISHAD

According to the Pythagoreans, the principle of
individuality is the creative principle itself and that all
order, what the Greeks called cosmos, derives from it. The
Monad is also identified with fire, which is reminiscent of
alchemical symbolism in which the point (a version of the
Monad) is equated with the scintilla, a spark of light and
fire. Hence, the principle of individuality is the source of
both consciousness (light) and energy (fire).
—EDWARD F. EDINGER, *Ego and Archetype*

Someday, after we have mastered the winds,
the waves, the tides and gravity, we shall harness for
God the energies of love. Then for the second time in
the history of the world, man will have discovered fire.
—PIERRE TEILHARD DE CHARDIN

4

FIRE
Light, Life, Love

Dear Friend,

Today is a cold winter's day, so to write of fire might be heartwarming.

In Hinduism they speak of the three *gunas*, three ways in which energy manifests itself:

Tamas: slowly, inertly, fixedly.
Rajas: actively, powerfully.
Sattva: delicately, mutably.

In the Upanishads it is written of the Creator: "His first works are bound by the three qualities, and he gives to each thing its place in nature. When the three are gone, the work is done, and then a greater work can begin."

This applies to the four trinities of the elements as well. Each element has a *fixed*, a *cardinal*, and a *mutable* sign. These signs share the element but manifest it in different ways. A simple example in nature would be water as ice, as fluid, and as vapor. All are water, but in different conditions.

There are three fire signs in the natural zodiac: (See Table E, p. 138)

♈ Aries the Ram, cardinal fire
♌ Leo the Lion, fixed fire
♐ Sagittarius the Archer, mutable fire

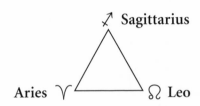

Each one shows forth the element in a different way. It is agitated in Aries, shines steadily in Leo, and is shared in Sagittarius.

To understand this better, you might meditate on the properties and underlying processes of fire and fathom why and how it was considered sacred, in virtually every culture, from earliest times. God, by whatever name, *is* the primal fire of life, of pure energy, and the other gods in mythology, representing different aspects of the One, become users of the fire—Hephaestus, Vulcan, Loki—or they become thieves of fire, such as Prometheus, who brings it to humankind. So the *processes* connected to fire are different at different levels, yet alike. At the very highest it is sheer energy, and at the level of physical manifestation it flickers atop our candles and flames out of wood.

The story in my previous letter emphasized the generative process of fire. One flame generates countless others without being diminished. It is like the sun from which all fires and light, life, and heat come. All flames leap sunward as if to return to their source, as spiritually do we. Fire is the only element of the four actively to counter gravity. At another level, the same process is hidden in every seed that grows, from which in turn myriads of others, down the centuries and generations, have the potential to spring. At another level, it is mythologically linked with energy (nuclear fire) and lightning, the attributes especially of the supreme gods of the Age of Aries: Indra, Zeus, Thor, and Lugh.

(We'll look more at the Age of Aries in chapter 16.) The sun just *is*. Were it to be extinguished, within minutes our entire solar system would be plunged into darkness. In astrology the sun has an affinity to the fire sign of Leo, of which it is said to be the "ruler." In this way, you might begin to see how astrological kinships arise. You see a connection of Leo the Lion to the "King of Beasts," to supremacy, natural leadership, and superiority. And Leo follows its ruler as the sign associated with the heart (ruler of the body) and the back and all those things we discussed when we studied the Sun in *Jungian Symbolism in Astrology*. The sign thus becomes the home of the Sun, and by extension, since it is the fifth sign in the zodiac, it rules the Fifth House in the natural zodiac, which happens to govern an individual's *creativity*: physical children, love affairs, and artistic endeavors. The quality of fire in Leo is "fixed," that is to say, it shines steadily and with natural inborn authority and generosity. The Sun never takes back its rays. It shines on all, "the just and the unjust," and this is the essence of the sign.

When you begin to place the different planets in that sign, each will react to the essence of Leo differently and according to the psychological process it represents. For example, a person with Saturn in Leo may have to deal with issues surrounding love or authority *perceived* in a negative way: either lack of love in childhood or, in some cases where love was given, the child could not receive it, convinced inwardly of its own unworthiness. The key is love, or suffering through resentment and anger, especially if Saturn should afflict the Sun or the Moon by difficult aspect. Jupiter in Leo would be just the opposite. Here the person is resplendent and able to "shine" on one and all. The individual's nature will tend to be optimistic, generous, and such a person will be able to *display* himself or herself.

Remember, I am not implying causality but am simply saying that this describes the way the person will be likely to process experience. Psychologically, Saturn in Leo yields "the Emperor," the actor, the one who projects himself a little larger than life, a ham, if you will. The danger here would be a tendency to inflations and deflations: life is not just a story—it becomes at least an epic.

I had a friend, an accomplished astrologer, with this configuration. Sixty years ago, we were walking down Fifth Avenue in New York, and he was boasting about his prowess. I teased him about his conceit, whereupon he stopped and turned to me and said, "Alice, if you really knew me, you would know that I am the *humblest* man of your acquaintance!" "See?" I grinned. He strode off furiously, no doubt aware of his Leo propensities.

If all this sounds too complicated at this stage, don't worry! It will make sense as we go along. My purpose here is simply to begin to demonstrate the way that the signs show "how" the planets will most likely function.

The sign your Sun is in determines whether you are a Virgo, a Scorpio, a Capricorn, and so forth. So in interpreting a chart, one would look immediately at the location of the Sun. Its essential nature of "being" and "creating" will be modified by every other sign but Leo. Leo is home for the Sun, just as Cancer is home for the Moon. Wherever the sign of Leo appears in your chart, which could be in any of the twelve houses, the Sun will be the "ruler" of that department of life, and you will take a special interest in matters pertaining to that house. For instance, if you have Leo rising and its ruler, the Sun, is in the Ninth House, you would be interested in understanding and expressing matters concerning philosophy and religion; in the Fifth House, in children and creative expression, and so on.

Psychologically speaking, one's essential and deepest identity springs from the Sun because it is the only true star in the solar system as well as in the psyche. All else reflects that inner light. The entire system of both zodiacs is generated by the Sun; the planets, including our Earth, orbit that center. Only the houses take their measure from the Earth. It is helpful to point this out to a client who is feeling overwhelmed by a complex or a depression. Either of these may temporarily eclipse or adumbrate that inner light, but they can never annihilate it. Even the ultimate suicidal destruction of the body cannot quench that light, any more than darkness alone can extinguish a candle. Some might see a resemblance here to Jung's idea of the Self, for the Sun in the chart is a focus: the entire chart, that unknown area of the "circle," points to the unfathomable, unlimited mystery of the totality of the individual psyche. Like the therapist, the astrologer can describe but can never define the psyche.

Although mythologically fire was generally thought to be phallic and masculine, *hermetically* it was considered to be androgynous: its flame was masculine, but its light was considered feminine. Perhaps this explains the fact that in some cultures, whose languages discriminate gender in nouns, sometimes the Sun is masculine and the Moon feminine (French *le soleil, la lune*), or sometimes reversed (German *die Sonne, der Mond*). In Gaelic both are feminine. This is interesting because symbolically "light" is associated with consciousness and illumination. She is the "woman clothed with the Sun," the *anima mundi*, and her light is the light of nature, of Holy Wisdom, Hagia Sophia. This intimate relationship of masculine and feminine in fire and light is the primal and ultimate *coniunctio* where each is the other, one in power and delight. Thus the element is also associated with a cosmic and creative love, God's love, which is "beating in our heartbeat twenty-four hours a day."

Masculine and feminine waves of sunlight

As you know, the myth of Sophia, holy feminine Wisdom, says she cocreated the earth with God, and in a playful moment playing hide-and-seek with God, she hid in matter as drops of light. Our task as human beings is to "re-member" her through our collective consciousness, the so-called "anamnesis of Sophia."

We take fire so for granted in our lives. All we have to do to make fire is to reach for a matchbox or a lighter today, but not so many years ago we needed a flintstone, and before that a stick and stock. Often this fire-making was ritualized, as in making a sacramental or need-fire. Here the sexual symbolism (which relates it to the planet Mars) obtains. A pointed stick was churned or drilled into a hole surrounded by flammable substances, dried moss, leaves, etc., to provide a virgin fire. In many cultures this virgin fire was generated on certain holy days after all other fires were extinguished. The tradition lives on in the Roman Catholic Church, where the old flames are extinguished after Good Friday and the Paschal Fire is lit at midnight between Holy Saturday and Easter Sunday. It is a ritual reenactment of what is happening in the cosmos every spring when the Sun enters the Sign of Aries at the vernal equinox. The movable feast is set for the first Sunday after the first full moon after the spring equinox. It is very moving to participate in this rite and to experience through the night the vigil of awaiting the glory of the rising sun.

It might be interesting to look at this powerful and magical ritual more closely. It involves a triple-branched taper (not unlike the trident of Shiva), flint and tinder, and a huge Paschal candle capable of burning for forty days. After the church is plunged into total darkness, a virgin fire is struck from flint by the priest standing at the west porch, and coals in a censer are lit. From these one branch of the taper is lit. The taper is mounted on a reed. (It is interesting that, in the myth, Prometheus gave fire to humankind hidden in a reed.) The *lumen Christi*, the light of Christ, is hailed. A second branch is lit when the procession reaches the middle of the church, and a third at the altar. The people cry out *"Deo gratias!* Thanks be to God." The taper is then carried to the great candle, and the following prayer is intoned to what may be the most ancient music in Christendom, the *Praecomium*:

> Rejoice now all ye heavenly legions of angels! Celebrate with joy the divine mysteries. . . . Rejoice, O earth, illumined by this celestial radiancy: and may the whole world know itself to be delivered from darkness, brightened by the glory of the Eternal King.

The prayer goes on to praise the night and darkness, because only when we have gone through the Dark Night of the Soul—our despair—can we begin to distinguish the very source of light, which Jung called the Self or the Christ Within and the Hindus call the Atman. After the great candle is incised with five nails and incense, the ceremony continues with the lighting of the great candle. "Which fire, though now divided, suffers no loss from the communication of its light." Then acolytes, taking a light from the Paschal candle, move about lighting the candles on the altar and elsewhere till the church is filled with light.

Nor is this the end. In another highly symbolic rite, the great candle is taken to the baptismal font and plunged into it three times, each time more deeply sanctifying the water. And the priest sings to God,

> Who makes this water fruitful for the regeneration of men by the arcane admixture of his Divine Power, to the end that those conceived in sanctity in the immaculate womb of this divine Font, may be born a new creature, and come forth a heavenly offspring: and that all who are distinguished either in sex or in body, or by age in time, may be born into one infancy by grace, their mother.

For the ancient Egyptians, the Sun was swallowed by the sky goddess Nut every sundown and was born fresh from her womb in the morning. Even today, for the Pueblo Indians and devout Hindus and countless others, the rising sun is a daily rebirth, to be assisted by the prayers of the people. Jung tells the touching story in *Memories, Dreams, Reflections* of his encounter with a Pueblo chief.

> As I sat with Ochwiay Biano on the roof, the blazing sun rising higher and higher, he said, pointing to the sun, "is not he who moves there our father? How can anyone say differently? How can there be another god? Nothing can be without the sun . . . the sun is God. Everyone can see that."

An anthropologist discovered that the Pygmies in Africa worshiped the sun as God as it touched the horizon but considered it to be just the sun the rest of the day. Oddly enough, a Japanese scientist called Maki Takata discovered that at the instant of sunrise, there is a measurable change in the speed of chemical reactions in blood proteins. (Similar things happen during an eclipse, sunspot cycles, and magnetic storms in the earth's atmosphere.)

Now the Sign of Aries the Ram is the first sign in the zodiac, and so by extension it rules both spring and dawn or any fresh beginning. The Sun is said to be *exalted* in Aries for this very reason. The term "exalted" denotes the place where any of the planets is happiest, where its process can be expressed most fully and harmoniously. You will see the list of exaltations on p. 135. So the fire sign of Aries, which is ruled by Mars, has a lot to do with the primal fire on earth. The quality of this fire is *cardinal*; it is an uprushing, active fire and vital force. It is one of the signs in which Mars is able to function in complete accordance with his competitive nature. Archetypally, Mars is the Mortal Hero, the loyal knight to the king. A man with Mars in Aries will be comfortable with his masculinity, and a woman may tend to have a strong and healthy animus or masculine side. The subtle difference between Aries and Leo is that Aries wants to be first, to win the race, while Leo rules and the battle is won. The Sun is the King, authority, father; Mars is the Prince, the warrior, the son, archetypally speaking.

At this point I can almost hear you asking: But how come, then, not all Aries are competitive? And I know a Leo who is a downright scaredy-cat. The answer again is that the planets, their positions, and their aspects do not always coincide with the essential nature of the sign they occupy. But deep down and perhaps unexpressed, all those born in Aries are concerned with themselves; it is almost a reflex for them to refer everything back to themselves personally. The motto of the sign is "I am." The timid Leo is miserable and angry with himself for failing to shine and others for not recognizing his true value, something the Cowardly Lion in *The Wizard of Oz* demonstrated to perfection. When someone's essential nature is thwarted, he or she becomes depressed or angry and then projects this out negatively upon others, as you know.

From what you have studied already, do you think Saturn would be comfortable in the sign of Aries? If you think not, you are right. Saturn rules ends and not beginnings, and so it is often hard for people with Saturn in Aries to get started; they never feel ready. I sometimes show clients a cartoon of a man lying in bed reading a book called *How to Get Up in the Morning*. Or I make a client laugh by saying you have to write an introduction to a preface to a prolegomenon before you can write the first sentence. Art Carney in "The Honeymooners" used to try to write a letter. Every time he would put the pen to paper, he would stop to smooth the paper over and over, till Jackie Gleason slammed him on the back and shouted, "WRITE!"

It might be interesting to ask yourself what your very earliest memory of fire was. In my own case, I remember that just after my fifth birthday, while we were still in Berlin, I was given an *Adventshäuschen*, a decorated four-sided open paper house with twenty-four little closed windows. A candle was lit and set inside it each evening, and we sang carols and then guessed what object might be hidden behind the little window for that day. Then, as the windows were successively opened, the candle light shone through the toys depicted: a drum, a top, a doll. It made a deep impression, and I wonder if this was the first time the image of matter containing an interior light was to impress me. My own Sun in Scorpio is in the Ninth House of religion, so this luminosity of the world comes quite naturally to me.

My second impression of fire came only a few months later in Athens at Eastertide. I was taken at night to witness a religious procession of monks and priests on their way to church. They carried flares and sang in those deep male voices that characterize the Greek Orthodox choirs. I remember the fear, awe, and fascination with which I clung to my father's neck as he held me up to see better.

Oddly enough, it was also in Athens that I stood on a hotel balcony and watched a fire burning a building directly across the little park. It is an element I certainly learned early on to respect! Strangely enough, forty years later, when I found myself back in Greece, I wrote a poem with a fire motif:

EARLY MORNING ON POROS

This morning
I was up before the radiant god
he hid behind the black-green mountain
and I watched the golds sway and shift
as he covered his nakedness

not because of me, surely
but because of that old widow ahead of me
the one with the stiffed bowed legs and dusty shoes
picking her way through the puddled street
on her way to church
preferring to forget certain matters.

I watched her make the sign of the cross three times
before she went into the darkness
unaware, it seemed, of the uninhibited
stations of the sun.

I watched her light a candle
in the dark womb of holiness
borrowing fire from fire
and she spoke my prayer and shamed me.

When she came out
The Nameless One had risen shining no other
*   comment than light,*
and we both shared the named reflections
relieved of supplication, blind to memory.

We stood then on the stone steps again
in the freshly lit air
staring vacantly across the silent bay
both of us like cows
milked and stripped of love —
*   the calm cattle of Apollo.*

Getting back to the fire signs, it is in Sagittarius that fire becomes mutable. It changes subtly to the aspiring fire of the return trip to its source. The creature of Sagittarius the Archer is the centaur, Chiron, who ran a school for heroes. Imagine Hercules, Achilles, and the like all together in sixth grade! Chiron is the archetypal coach, and, indeed, the sign rules sports. The centaur is half-horse, half-man, and he carries a bow and arrow pointed at heaven. So the sign rules our animal, human, and spiritually aspiring natures. Sagittarius is ruled by Jupiter, and Sagittarians love both teaching and preaching. The sign's affinity is to the Ninth House, which also rules athletics and travel. When we travel inwardly in the psyche, we tend to have long thoughts, the sum of which becomes our philosophy of life.

In keeping with the idea of seeing how the signs modify the planetary processes, try imagining each planet in different elements, to get the feel of it. Then each element as fixed, cardinal, or mutable. Try Neptune, for instance. Its entrance into the sign of Sagittarius in the late 1960s coincided with a great revival of interest in religion and spirituality, and when Uranus later joined it there as well, we had a good deal of radical changes: i.e., what we now call the "New Age" approach. Cults and gurus (some genuine and some not), meditation, the use of hallucinogens for altered states of consciousness, even jogging (Sagittarius rules the thighs and running) were connected to getting "high." The musicals *Hair* and *Godspell*, the phenomenon of Woodstock, the peace movement were all part of it. The backlash of fundamentalism and televangelism, with their successes and some shocking failures, were all developments coinciding with these transits. As you know from studying Neptune and Uranus, they can bring both fanaticism and a kind of craziness when our collective consciousness is not ready for them. But the good that has come out of it is that so many, for one reason or another, have forever refused to settle for mere industrial materialism; a whole generation born at that time is out there insisting on something more. Currently, as I write this in 2005, Pluto is transiting Sagittarius, and the nightmares of unresolved historical religious confrontations are still on full and frightening display: the fundamentalists of *all* the major *exoteric* religions are at ideological, if not actual, war with one another.

I cannot refrain from pointing out a potential solution, a very simple and hopefully prophetic one. Each of the founding avatars spoke of the "One Way." This is has been interpreted as a noun. But if seen as a verb, it points to the same "One Way" (as a process!) within each of us as individuals! The same inner method of surrendering the ego (who we think we are) to our Divine Guest (who we really are). Krishna, Moses. Buddha, Jesus, Muhammad, and others all discovered that "One Way." Blissed, they sought to bless the people of their time and culture. Exoteric religions followed with institutions, rituals and rules which, in many ways, became concretized. And fixation on concretizations can become idolatry! Yet the mystical or *esoteric* aspects of each religion seem to agree: Vedanta, Kabbalah, Gnostic Christianity, Sufism all offer the same message: The same wondrous Light shines through each of us; the same fire is on every candle. Even the so-called pagans among our forebears celebrated the rebirth of the sun at the Winter Solstice, when Sagittarius yields its fire to Capricorn's earth for physical manifestation. The Christian Christmas was deliberately set to replace the Roman Saturnalia. And no one can deny that Santa Claus and Jupiter are interchangeable archetypes, generously bestowing gifts of optimism and joy.

As Neptune and Uranus, the two trans-Saturnian planets, moved into Capricorn, an earth sign (in 1984 and 1988 respectively), ecology, crystals, and the translucency of matter opened up a new area of fascination. And, again, in the midst of all the seeming fanaticism and craziness, some new ideas unfolded. A much greater attention on the human body was just one example. All kinds of old methods of healing were given another look: acupuncture, kinesiology, chiropractic, craniosacral therapy, etc. emerged and the whole field of alternative medicine opened up. Negatively, the insidious spread of drugs and AIDS gave us a challenge that we still have not met.

Since then, Uranus has transited Aquarius (in the 1990s), leaving a trail of mostly peaceful revolutions behind it. Neptune entered the same sign in 1998, bringing a vision of freedom for all but also a danger of fanaticism Imposed freedom is an oxymoron! The opposing sign, Leo's shadow process of domination is lurking.

We need so badly to heed the lessons of history, to see how every really new idea is considered a threat to the status quo, until the subscribers to the new outnumber the old; then it becomes fashionable, acceptable, and eventually institutionalized. So it was with Christianity, or with heliocentrism in astronomy, or accepting the existence of an undiscovered continent or of the reality of the psyche. Now we are again at the edge of new experiences. I think Jung's advice was very sound. If something emerges from the human unconscious, we should not instantly reject it. We should try to understand it and ask ourselves its meaning. This is where astrology and alchemy owe him such a great debt. He looked at them in a new way.

My best advice is always keep an open mind and a good crap detector!

In conclusion, the three fire signs constitute within the psyche those processes dealing primarily with inner vitality, creativity, and our relationship to the spirit or lack of it. Since every chart will contain these three signs, no one exists without these factors. According to their positions in the houses (which are dependent on *birth time* and *place*) and the position of the various planets and their relationship to one another, the limitless variations of human individuality are played out. The Creator, in repeating, never really repeats. It is a paradox.

Before closing, let me suggest that you turn now to Tables B and E and fix in your memory the three fire signs, their rulers, and their planets of exaltation. You will notice also that certain other planets are said either to *fall* or to be in their *detriment* in these signs. This means that if a planet is in its exaltation in a sign, it will "fall" in the opposite sign. Thus the Sun falls in Libra, with the beginning of the autumnal equinox, which we call the "fall." At this time, the Sun appears to be on the wane and the days are getting shorter.

Venus, the ruler of Libra, is in her detriment in Aries, which means her intrinsic nature cannot be expressed so naturally there. She is like a pretty young girl who finds herself in a motorbike shop. So she will have to change her clothes and her seductive ways accordingly.

Anyway, have fun and play with the images as they arise for you. As we personify them, they become human for us, suggesting all kinds of archetypal yet everyday situations. Let me know how things go.

Love, as ever,

ao

As water parts and flows around obstinate rock
so to yield with life solves the insoluble.
To yield, I have learned, is to return.
But this unspoken lesson,
this easy example,
is lost upon men.

—LAO TZU

Listen! you hear the grating roar
Of pebbles which the waves draw back and fling,
At their return, up the high strand
Begin, and cease, and then again begin
With tremulous cadence slow, and bring
The eternal note of sadness in.

—MATTHEW ARNOLD,
"Dover Beach"

Inside this clay jug there are canyons and pine mountains,
    and the maker of canyons and pine mountains!
All seven oceans are inside, and hundreds of millions of stars.
The acid that tests gold is there, and the one who judges jewels.
And the music from the strings that no one touches, and
    the source of all water.

If you want the truth, I will tell you the truth:
Friend, listen: the God whom I love is inside.

—KABIR, "The Clay Jug"
(version by Robert Bly)

5

WATER
Fluctuation, Femininity,
Fruition

Dear Friend,

You ask, Why are you planning to discuss water when the next sign after Aries is Taurus, an earth sign? Well, I could just as well have discussed earth, especially since earth, of all the elements, is the one that gives form to life. Without earth, we would have no containers for life. My reason for taking up water is to introduce another basic way of looking at the zodiac, through the *quantitative* aspect of the three quaternities. In my last letter we looked at the *qualitative* aspect of one of the four elements, fire. You see, there are three *quadruplicities*:

Cardinal: the four elements at their most active;
Fixed: the four at their most stable;
Mutable: the four at their most flexible.

Each of the three quadruplicities forms a cross of elements, and in a way you could say that they are the "stuff" acted upon in life, which in turn conditions us.

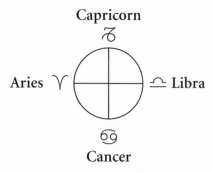

Capricorn

Aries — Libra

Cancer

You will see that Aries is the first cardinal sign, and the next is Cancer, a water sign ruled by the Moon. You will notice that all four of these in sequence are 90 degrees apart, i.e., in the *square* aspect. The cardinal signs mark the equinoxes and solstices of the year. The elements themselves, as you saw from the letter about fire, are all 120 degrees apart, which is the *trine* aspect. There is an easy confluence in this: the earth signs for instance, all three of them, have earth in common. They understand each other. However, the quadruplicities form situations like intersections in a provoking pattern. Collisions, frictions, and spontaneous combustions are possible and all too probable. In the psyche any planetary processes that square one another coincide with inner conflicts, and sometimes complexes and neuroses. As Jung said, "Thank God for our neuroses!" It is thanks to them that we learn to confront ourselves and are forced, frequently through exasperating circumstances, to grow.

I remember lecturing at the East Meadow Grand Rounds of Psychiatry on the uses of astrology as a diagnostic tool. After the lecture, two doctors came up to me. One, with a smirk, asked what was to prevent parents from deliberately timing the birth of their children to avoid any complications of character whatsoever. Before I could say a word, the other doctor told a cautionary tale of two friends of his who had done just that. They had been astrologers and had plotted the perfect child, one who would never have to face any problems. And they got what they wanted:

the child was born so severely retarded that she would never have to cope with anything. The experience had been so ghastly that the parents renounced astrology and became born-again Christians! All I could think of was my teacher M's warning to me never to use astrological knowledge to control others.

If your chart or those of family members, friends, or patients are beset with "squares"—and few are not—be grateful. They will force issues up to consciousness where, at long last, matters may be resolved. Difficult aspects guarantee an interesting and challenging life within the psyche. All too often we coast on the easy aspects and do not use them to their fullest potential. Later, as these ideas become easier to manipulate, you will see how very often a square, a T-square, or a grand cross is eased by another planet which shows the way to a solution.

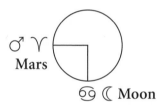

In *Jungian Symbolism in Astrology* I pointed out that all aspects partake of the nature of the first one formed in the natural zodiac. This first square between Aries and Cancer is the primal one. The tension is not only of the elements in question, but of Mars and the Moon, their respective rulers: the archetypal tension between mother and son, masculine energy and feminine caution, irritation and anxiety. Fire and water have a dramatic effect on each other: fire can boil water; water can extinguish fire. Fire needs air to burn; earth needs water to be fruitful; water needs earth for containment. So, looking at the natural zodiac, you will notice that all the way through the complementary elements are opposite one another, while the challenging or frictional ones are square. It follows, therefore, that when the archetypal processes of the planets are in elements that square one another, friction is likely to be present. Remember that when speaking of archetypes; they are the personification of universal, hence divine, processes (verbs). So for "Mother" read "mothering," and so on.

I described the possibility of a mother complex at some length in my *Jungian Symbolism in Astrology*. The psychological impact is this: wherever you see planets aspecting each other from Aries to Cancer, issues having to do with frustration and thwarted independence are possible; and wherever Mars and the Moon are square (or conjunct), feelings of being thwarted or irritated by the maternal are likely. For a man, issues would surround his masculinity and, depending on the signs involved, his temperament might be irritable, impatient, abrupt, or resentful towards the feminine. In a woman the relationship to the personal mother or the experience of mother figures could be difficult or annoying, regardless of their own intrinsic natures. We are dealing with the way the archetype of Mother is projected onto these women. Mars square or conjunct the Moon is not as traumatic as Saturn in such a configuration, because the nature of Mars is to challenge, fight, argue, or harangue, not to deny. But this aspect may point to a negative mother complex.

The fire signs all involve action, positive or negative; the water signs involve emotions, expressed in three generally different ways, as we will perceive further on. So squares generate affect—emotional reactions. When planets in water signs are squared by planets in fire signs, the emotions become "heated," the ego becomes hot and bothered. And, just as in traffic when we have to stop at red lights and go with green, the emotional traffic in the psyche usually learns to adapt by going with one leg of the square or the other, finding that to go full force with both leads to "crack-ups." Once a person learns this, he or she may habitually favor one planet and repress the other. Psychologically speaking, whatever we repress into the unconscious will be projected onto other people and life in general. Thus we will mysteriously attract outer situations and people that constellate the very problem, and we end up frustrated and mad at ourselves, knowing full well that when we fight ourselves nobody wins. (Note the word "constellate." It literally means "with the stars.")

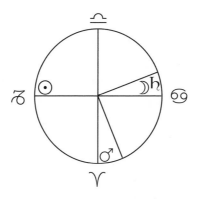

I can think of an extreme example of a man who has Mars in Aries in the Fourth House (home/mother and the natural house of Cancer) exactly square his Moon conjunct (within 2 degrees) Saturn in the Seventh House (marriage/the other), the house which reveals our likely projections. Since he has Capricorn rising and its ruler, Saturn, is conjunct the Moon, the ruler of the sign (Cancer) is on the cusp of the Seventh. Not only does he say he hates and is disgusted by his own personal mother, he projects a cynical and sadistic view upon his wife, having made her a surrogate mother. Since relating to any mother sexually is a form of incest, he suffers painfully from Don Juanism in a perpetual and fruitless quest for a valid anima figure. Psychologically, his constant blaming everything on others reveals a profound self-hatred and disgust. Analysis for him would hopefully reveal that his problem is with the archetypal Mother and not with the individuals who have already suffered mightily from his cruel denials and caustic treatment. I have run into this client occasionally over the years, and the litany of blame continues unabated. Teasingly, I suggested he mark on a pad each time he blames during a single day. By now he surely has added an astrologer to the list!

Should the squaring planets be Moon and Venus or planets involving Cancer and Libra, issues of the inner conflict of the Mother and the Hetaira (the courtesan) might be present. A man might tend to split his anima between them, with the result that he might turn his wife into "Mother" and look for sex and fun outside of marriage—a very old saga indeed. A woman might have a conflict between inner identification with the maternal and the seductive and be unable to express both simultaneously. As the French say, a woman is either *femme-femme* or *femme-mère* (a feminine woman or a maternal one).

Now suppose the woman becomes a mother herself. If she consciously identifies with the Moon, she may project her repressed sexuality (Venus) upon her own daughter or daughter substitutes, such as students or employees. This would be unconscious, so that the daughter may find herself "acting out" her mother's unexpressed sexuality, and/or the mother may unconsciously live out her Venus side vicariously through her daughter, while at the same time consciously expressing disapproval of the daughter's behavior. On the other hand, should the mother identify with her Venus (Hetaira) side, mothering her children would be a burden, and she might leave them to fend for themselves, while she concentrates on their father or on a succession of lovers.

You may wonder if this is inevitably so. The answer is that it is *likely* to be this way, but would only become apparent if acted out. One of the archetypal patterns in the past was for such women not to marry at all and become spinster headmistresses or teachers, venting their suspicions and frustrations on the young girls in their charge. Some of these women became veritable bitches who turned into old witches (negative Venus or negative Moon).

I remember an incident in my own life—one of many, I night add—when as a teenager I was in a boarding school in New England. In a copy of *The World's Almanac* I had found that for a dollar I could get twenty "Little Blue Books," so I selected them from a list of perhaps a hundred. They had titles like "Twenty-five Best-loved Poems," "Mathematical Oddities," "World Capitals," and the like—just the kind of thing that appealed to my Moon in Virgo. So I sent away, noting that for an order of twenty I would get two bonus surprise booklets. Several weeks later I was summoned to the headmistress's office, where I was confronted by a thin-lipped dragon with rimless glasses. On the desk was the opened package of "Little Blue Books." My surprise bonuses lay on top. They were, if I remember correctly, "Fifty Ways of Kissing around the World," and "Twenty Positions for Love-making"! Nothing could convince this gimlet-eyed woman that I had not deliberately ordered pornographic material. (Well, I really hope she knows the truth by now.) Her projection onto me lasted throughout my time at the school. As I had a highly idealized and romantic view of love and sex, pornography really had never entered my mind.

I guess one can only have compassion on such a warped outlook; it must have been hard, after all, year after year, watching so many fresh-faced young girls eagerly looking forward to a fuller life. What I found hardest to forgive was that she threw the lot into the wastepaper basket and, stubborn as I am, I had to reorder them during the holidays. In fact, "Mathematical Oddities" resurfaced among my papers, fifty years later. I do not know this woman's chart, but I know my own, and I have Moon square Venus myself. Life has shown me almost every variation possible of that aspect. Knowing that I have it has greatly helped me to cope with it and to have compassion when I see it in other people's charts.

I am going into this kind of detail in order to show you how the configurations of the chart allow us to bridge outer events and the psychological perception of them.

You might wonder how much it helps to know these things. My answer would have to be, a great deal. For this reason: when something outside constellates a difficult aspect in the chart, one can stop and say, "Aha! This is the way I am feeling, and I know I am being the usual stupid old me." But now I know I have a choice. I can *name* the factors in my chart and, by so doing, as in the story of Rumpelstiltskin, I might break the spell. How? If the situation is extremely painful, by offering it up with prayers and tears. If it is not too painful, by laughter and saying to myself, "There you go again. Typical old Moon square Venus!"

I know that I no longer have to be driven to act out the whole business all over again. As Jung has pointed out, complexes can be worked through, but "not until they have been drunk to the last drop." The funny thing is that when you think you have worked through the problem, then you find yourself counseling others with the same problem. I always remember what Dr. Edward C. Whitmont told me. "No sooner have you mastered something than you will attract a patient or client confronting much the same situation." It seems to be an axiom of psychotherapy, and I wager you as well as many others have had the same experience of dramatic irony. As you lean over dispensing some words of wise counsel, part of you is saying to yourself, "Are you listening, dear? Do you hear what you are saying? Don't forget that you need the very same advice." Ah well, it's a great life.

Now, back to the elements. The three water signs are:

♋ **Cancer:** cardinal water
♏ **Scorpio:** fixed water
♓ **Pisces:** mutable water

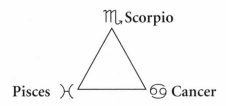

All four elements have their positive and negative expressions. I did not dwell too much on the destructive aspects of fire as they seem so obvious: anger, rage, tyranny, pomposity, or in the case of lack, a wan kind of weakness, Milquetoasty cowardice. I remember a cartoon of Mr. Milquetoast sitting in a convertible at a stop sign. He and the car were covered with cobwebs. He was waiting to be told to go!

The basic key is action (Aries) in balance (Libra). Too much or too little of any element in a chart can indicate problems. For instance, the lack of any planet in a water sign might indicate a difficulty expressing emotions, an inner dryness. This configuration sometimes surfaces in alcoholics, who drink in order to dream or float or connect to their own unconscious. People with many planets in water signs have no such difficulty in terms of the unconscious. If they become alcoholics, it is to escape the superabundance of their emotions, to deaden the burden, which never works.

With water, the shift is clearly to the emotional. If fire has to do with our life itself, water has to do with our birthing and our bodies (which are mostly water), our food, our planet Earth (which oddly has almost the same proportion of water to land as the human body has water to flesh). Water is affected by the Moon; there are instruments that can measure the tide in a cup of tea. Sap rises and falls in groups of trees simultaneously; the whole earth breathes, inhales and exhales the vapors of our atmosphere. Rains fall and trickle into rivulets and brooks; rivers flow majestically to the oceans, there to evaporate again. There are tides in the soul as well, and the Moon, which never ceases its motion, transits daily through our charts and gives us our own biorhythmic mood swings, our monthly "menstrual periods," their onset and cessation. The joys and excessive agonies of adolescence come when the progressed Moon has opposed its own place for the first time, and both boys and girls begin to integrate and function in their emotional body (sometimes called the astral body). Then everything is heightened and exaggerated, but at the same time it becomes passionately and vitally real and important. Nobody really understands us; we fall into reveries, fantasies, despairs; we "moon" about and cling to our peers. We are separated from the bright, intellectual curiosity of our childhood and from the rational common sense of our elders. It is as if we become a different species, we get "swamped" by our feelings, "drown" in our sorrows, and are lost in a "fog." Our behavior is considered "lunatic" (from the Latin *luna*, "moon").

Think back to your own adolescence and to that of your children. From the parents' perspective, it's as if the children go into a tunnel at thirteen and don't reemerge for another seven years. Parents can do nothing right, generally speaking, and yet this is part of the rejection and separation necessary to develop the ego of the child. Parents need a great deal of love and compassion, and patience is required. In Scotland hundreds of years ago, they came up with a sensible solution: parents exchanged adolescents within the clan, because the children were far more willing to learn from adults other than their parents. This knit the families into the clans at a warm, loyal, emotional level.

All these phenomena have to do with the element of water and the waves of feeling that come over us.

The religious rite that we associate most with water is, of course, baptism. The ideas behind it are symbolic of all three water signs: the birthing of emotion in Cancer, its transformation and purification in Scorpio, and the aspiration to agape or transpersonal love and compassion in Pisces. To demonstrate that these ideas exist potentially even in the unconscious of a child, let me share the following true story about myself when I was seven years old.

We were in Rome and I was in the care of a superstitious Balkan nurse, who repeated to some other nannies in the park that hair and nails were known to grow on corpses after burial. I was curious to see if this could be true and, reasoning that a doll was lifeless, cut off all its hair as an experiment. The doll was new and extremely costly, so I was scolded so severely that I sought to make amends by fashioning a kerchief to cover the doll's head. Looking for suitable material, I found the perfect thing in my mother's bureau drawer and without further ado took scissors and cut out a sizable piece.

I was already in trouble because I was not eating at meal-times. The nurse had tried bribery on the one hand and terrible stories of starving little Indian children on the other. Things came to a head when my mother was to go to a ball and found her gown missing a large piece in the front!

I (a Scorpio, with Pluto in Cancer, and the ruler of my ascendant in Pisces) felt that I was too wicked to live, and that I should kill myself. Not being too sure what that involved, I got into the bathtub as it was almost full, and taking a deep breath, held my nose and totally immersed myself. I listened to the roar of the water and imagined that I, the wicked one, drowned and the soul of one of those "good little Indian children" came into my body. I rose up with a big splash and imagined looking at everything with new eyes—the pretty tiles, the fluffy towels, my own pink toes. I felt truly renewed, fresh, newborn. The only problem was that, so convinced was I of my new identity, when the nurse continued to scold me, I hotly denied having done any of those dreadful things! My parents were ready to send me to a psychiatrist, I'm sure, and only my wiser grandmother, the widow of a clergyman, was able to explain baptism to me, and that I had carried it a bit too far in this case. The funny thing is that to this very day, whenever I am deeply troubled, I find that after taking a bath and submerging myself to rinse my hair, I am also psychologically renewed.

In the Orthodox Jewish tradition, women also take a ritual cleansing bath, the *mikvah*, after their menses ceases. The women go to a special bathhouse to bathe in a pool that must be fed from a natural spring. There they follow a meaningful ritual that is especially refreshing. My own mother would announce spontaneously to me that she was going to take her "B.o.B.," her Bath of Baths. She would not have known the connection to a *mikvah*. In India, renewing takes place everywhere on a daily basis, as men and women wade into the rivers to make their prayers to the rising sun.

In alchemy, the process is call *solutio*, cleansing and dissolving in water. The same root appears in the *lysis* of the word "psychoanalysis." It suggests the loosening and dissolving of complexes within the psyche through therapy. Water symbolism is prevalent everywhere: from the rivers surrounding Eden to the threatening floods of the Bible, in the Styx or river of death, the waters of Lethe or forgetfulness, and the "water of life," *aquavit*, or *uisge bheath* (whiskey). The miracle at Cana, when Jesus turned water into wine, has a psychological significance because there can be no "spirits" without water, though there is plenty of water that is not wine. The "living waters" are that transpersonal love, the Piscean *agape*, which Jung suggests is essential to healing, growth, and individuation.

In dreams, water usually refers to the unconscious. I remember my own recurring nightmares of terrifying tidal waves throughout my adolescence. After meeting my teacher, I had my last dream of this kind: The biggest wave ever was towering over me. I confronted it, and in a split second it turned to a cliff of rock, and I could see green grass growing on top of it.

The water signs have three ways of dealing with feelings. Turn to Table C and refresh your memory about the body parts ruled by the twelve signs. Therein lies a very important clue to the nature of the signs, because the way each sign functions is allied to the way the body system contributes to the whole organism. Cancer rules the womb, the stomach, and the breasts, so Cancer's processes are protecting, life-giving, nourishing, supporting. Its traps are fear, control, and not letting go. It deals with positive "mothering" and negative "smothering."

Scorpio, co-ruled by Mars and Pluto, rules the genitalia and has to do with sexuality, birth, death, and resurrection, all processes pertaining to transformation. Planets posited here trigger emotions that run very deep: Scorpio can evoke passion, tenacity, hidden strength, and reserve. There is no such thing as a shallow Scorpio. So you can imagine how Cancer and Scorpio would modify any of the planets. Take Mercury, for instance. Can you see that "communication" in Cancer would be muted and soft-spoken, and the person might find listening, absorbing, and digesting easier than chattering and nattering on, which would be characteristic of Gemini, an air sign? How would Scorpio affect Mercury? It might give the person a penetrating, perhaps caustic or sarcastic mind, and even a scatological tongue, but also a tendency to want to get to the very bottom of things, to uncover the truth.

Take Mars in Cancer. Think about it. Can you see that the rough, aggressive male energy can get swallowed up in the "mother"? So the fire turns to steam, and anger turns to resentment, and should other difficult factors be present, the person might develop "acid" (Mars) "indigestion" (Cancer), or even ulcers. The United States is a Cancer nation with Mars in Cancer, and some would say that Mom is our goddess and our icon is the mandala of an apple pie! So a great number of American men continue as *pueri aeterni* (eternal boys) who have difficulty escaping the archetypal mother.

How can we find the positive image for this? I would use the metaphor of a soup kitchen. Here the energy could find expression in providing shelter for the homeless or actively working to nourish others. Often Cancerian people are drawn to working in restaurants or nursing, where the energy flows outward to protect and nourish others. If you refer to Table B you will see that Mars "falls" in Cancer. This means that it is the most difficult place for Mars to be, so greatly is its intrinsic nature modified. Mars, on the other hand, is exalted in the opposite sign of Capricorn. Here the archetype becomes *homo faber*, man the maker. All that energy is put to hard and constructive work, and things get built, accomplished, and manifested in the outer world, often the business world. In fairy tales and myths, it becomes the smith, the one who with hammer and anvil becomes the maker of weapons, tools, and other essential things, even cauldrons (Cancer). The gods Loki and Vulcan were smithing gods.

Pisces, the gentle, mutable water sign, is ruled by Neptune. Venus is exalted there, and Jupiter co-rules it. The effect of Pisces on all the planets is one of dissolving. It is the sign most associated with compassion, martyrdom, pliancy, mysticism, music, poetry, weakness, self-pity, self-sacrifice. Its greatest strength is in adapting, as water will to the shape of any container. Mars in Pisces wouldn't hurt a flea and would fight only for peace and the underdog.

I know a man who has both Sun and Mars in Pisces. During the Vietnam War, he was at a university. He disapproved of the war but refused to take his student deferment. He was drafted, won status as a conscientious objector, and became a medic. However, he refused *not* to go to Vietnam; he wrote senators and congressmen to expedite his being shipped over because he wanted to make right what he felt so many were making wrong. Taunted by his army buddies for not carrying arms, he was given little to do. Finding free time on his hands, he offered his services to a Vietnamese civilian hospital (Pisces rules hospitals). He became invaluable to them, and his own reward was to discover his vocation. When he returned to the States, he completed his philosophy major and entered medical school. Today he is a doctor and psychiatrist.

That's Mars in Pisces! The only planetary process that has a really difficult time in Pisces is Saturn. Here the emotions are inhibited, and the person may have difficulty in expressing feelings.

Psychologically speaking, Pisces is also associated with the unconscious, as is its natural Twelfth House. Pisces is water in its oceanic dimension, and you cannot see to the bottom of it. People who are born under that sign are quite comfortable float-ing in a boundless way. They are not threatened by chaos. (It is the opposite sign of Virgo — a highly practical one — which needs definitions and containment and feels great frustration at being unable to fold up a cloud and put it in a drawer!) Sometimes, however, the very adaptability of Pisces becomes its handicap because decisions are so difficult. Pisceans can then become "wishy-washy."

I have a dear friend who is a Pisces with Virgo rising and Jupiter and the Moon in Virgo. At times she is one of the fussiest individuals I have ever met—"The Princess and the Pea" would be her story—yet at the same time she is kind, intuitive, and deeply spiritual. Her lovely watercolors run into one another with nary a definitive line. She confesses that the Pisces-Virgo polarity drives her sometimes to distraction.

Neptune, the ruler of Pisces, is associated positively with mysticism and self-sacrifice. The icon of the Crucifixion is probably the highest image for the sign, and we will meet these characteristics again when we study the Age of Pisces.

In the body, Pisces rules the feet. Its glyph shows two fishes swimming in opposite directions, hinting that the last can be first, and, indeed, the chart can be read backwards esoterically. Here the Twelfth House would become the First.

The negative Neptunian aspect of Pisces is associated with lack of boundaries, illusions, addictions, and delusions, so that the container of sensible Virgo is much to be sought after. Just for fun, here are a few questions:

Would Pisces love music? If so, why?

Which planets in Pisces would enjoy poetry?

Which planet, do you suppose, was discovered at the time of Impressionism in both art and in music?

Whose music better describes this planet, Vivaldi's or Debussy's?

Which artist, Albrecht Dürer or Monet?

Would this planet also rule ether, discovered at the same time it was? Why?

Can you see the polarity of Pisces-Virgo in pointillism?

Ah well, Neptune also rules sleep and dreams, and I think that it would be sensible to follow this direction, since it is quite late. In any case, I wish you good night and "sweet dreams!"

My love to you,

ao

*In the beginning God created heaven and
earth. And the earth was without form,
and void; and darkness was upon the face
of the deep. And the Spirit of God moved
upon the face of the waters.
And God said, 'Let there be light"; and there
was light.
And God saw the light, that it was good: and
God divided the light from the darkness.
And God called the light Day, and the darkness
he called Night...
And God said, Let there be lights in the firmament of the heaven to divide the day from
the night; and let them be for signs, and
for seasons, and for days, and years:
And let them be for lights in the firmament of
the heaven to give light upon the earth:
and it was so.
And God made two great lights; the greater
light to rule the day, and the lesser light,
to rule the night: he made the stars also.*
—GENESIS 1:1–5, 14–16

*Cleanse the thoughts of our hearts
by the inspiration of thy Holy Spirit.*
—THE BOOK OF COMMON PRAYER

6

AIR
Idea, Intelligence, Intellect

Dear Friend,

It's strange—I really had not intended to integrate the aspects into my letters so quickly, and I am amazed and delighted that this has not been too confusing. Somebody once observed—possibly it was Marc Edmund Jones—that the aspects themselves, in a way, reflect the processes of the planets. Just for fun I will list them here:

0–8°	= conjunction	= Moon	immediate
60°	= sextile	= Venus	facilitating
90°	= square	= Mars	frictional
120°	= trine	= Jupiter	creative
180°	= opposition	= Saturn	balancing
150°	= quincunx	= Uranus	transformative

The aspects are determined by the geometric angles formed within the circle of the chart according to the degrees separating one or more planets. You are already familiar with two of them, the *trines* of the elements and the *squares* of the quadruplicities (cardinal, fixed, and mutable). Angles are important in nature.

When rivers meet at 120 degrees, there is a natural confluence. If you force waters to meet at 90-degree angles, there will be turmoil. The branches and twigs of trees and plants tend to grow out of the trunk at harmonious angles of 60 or 120 degrees. To make fire with a stick, it is best rotated against a block at 90 degrees. Friction causes heat.

As for the conjunctions, their effect depends entirely on the nature of the planets involved, as with people. Some have a very strengthening and positive effect (like a good marriage), and others suffer from a dampening effect. It does not take too much imagination to distinguish the effect of Jupiter (expansion) conjunct Mercury (communication) from Saturn (limitation) and Mercury. The former's positive result would be great mental capacity; the negative, too much scattering of words. The latter aspect would make for a deep and focused mentality, if positively placed, or a reluctance or difficulty in personal communication.

Scientific experiments conducted years ago by RCA showed that radio reception on Earth is affected by the relative aspects of Jupiter and Mars, with poor reception and static when they are square.

The aspects answer the questions *to what degree?* and *in what manner?*, i.e., intensely, harmoniously, or with difficulty?

You can see that the twelve signs, in and of themselves, form within the circle the most beautiful designs, patterns found in nature, in flowers, and in the depictions of the chakras. The most astounding revelation for me was a photograph of sound made by Hans Jenny in his work on Cymatics. There a perfect twelve-fold diagram was formed on a metal plate by particles responding to a certain tone. We live in a wondrous world, and sometimes it seems that we are on the edge of more and more discoveries of the subtle world within our material one. I remember M cautioning me to keep a balance between gullibility and scepticism—"always an open mind and a healthy crap-detector!" For me, William Blake's remark says it best: "What is now proven was once only imagined."

You are now familiar with the four trines of the elements and the three quadruplicities. Today, in looking at the third sign on the cardinal cross, we come to Libra the Balance, which is an air sign. Libra is opposite Aries and makes the first 180-degree opposition in the natural zodiac; thus all oppositions take their basic meaning from this primal one. What does it imply and what would be its psychological import?

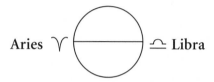

Aries ♈   ♎ Libra

The sign Libra is ruled by Venus and is the place of exaltation for Saturn; it is the detriment of Mars, and the fall of the Sun and of the year. So already we can infer quite a bit about Libra, even without any planets in it. It will be a lovely and harmonious place, social and affectionate, but somewhat debilitating to swashbuckling masculine energy. In mythology, there are many examples of heroes stumbling upon gardens of delight and falling prey to lovely maidens. Gilgamesh's sojourn in Dilmun is an example or Tannhäuser in the Venusberg ("the mount of Venus"). On the other hand, the untamed hero is subjected here to the civilizing influence of the feminine. A cartoon of two young mothers describes it. One mother says of her young son, "He must be growing up. He combed his hair for the party all by himself, but he wet it with his water pistol!"

Libra forms our first axis, our first experience of the tension of opposites and of the need for the *coincidentia oppositorum* that Jung spent almost a lifetime writing about. It is a place of realizing separation and experiencing the need and yearning for reunion. It contains the deep mystery of the *hieros gamos*, the sacred marriage. Above all, it deals with the basic issue of relationship. You will remember that the process of Venus is relating.

The horizontal axis in the natural zodiac, which is expressed through the houses, divides the chart in half. The upper half shows the planets above the earth at the hour of birth; the lower half, those beneath. So the lower six houses, and the signs and planets therein, have to do with our individual growth; and the upper six houses, and the signs and planets within them, have to do with the social application of what we have learned. The big news—TA-DAH!—is that the "I am" of Aries encounters someone else's "I am" in Libra, which would be the "not-I" or a "Thou"! For every infant born and toddler growing, this discovery that one is not the sole hub of the universe comes as a great shock.

The sign of Libra and the other two air signs of Gemini and Aquarius will help us deal with how we relate, communicate, and serve our community and the world in society.

♊ **Gemini** the Twins: mutable air
♎ **Libra** the Balance: cardinal air
♒ **Aquarius** the Water-Bearer: fixed air

You can think of it this way: We breathe in (Gemini); oxygen and carbon dioxide are exchanged (Libra); and we breathe out (Aquarius). Metaphorically, we experience; we become wiser; we form concepts and share with others (Aquarius). Since the air signs have to do with mentality, you could also speak of the trinity of intelligence (Gemini), judgment (Libra), and intellect (Aquarius).

Gemini deals with relationships that are given us, ones we did not necessarily choose: siblings, neighbors, people that happen to be around. Libra deals with one-on-one encounters, chosen partnerships and/or open enemies or opponents, as in chess games or duels. Aquarius has to do with our giving ourselves to friends, society, or community. In terms of C. S. Lewis's kinds of love, they are *philia*, *eros*, and *agape*: friendship, passion, and unconditional love.

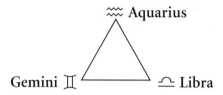

Gemini ♊ ——— ♎ Libra

Aquarius ♒

Libra marks the great divide spoken of in the first five verses of Genesis. Can you see how the diameter of the circle of totality, that horizontal line, symbolically explains that the One was made two so that creation could be made manifest? Even at the most basic level of energy, it is a dance of duality, of both waves and particles. So can you see how logical it is that the Sun and Mars, whose astrological natures are basically healthily self-centered, and whose fall and detriment occur in Libra, have to make a radical adjustment upon confronting not only a "Thou," but Venus as well! So by virtue of what Libra represents, you could say that Adam meets Eve and God creates two by the strange device of Adam's rib. Perhaps that myth was the best way they had of making it clear symbolically that we started out One, became two, and have been yearning to reunite ever since.

Light cannot know darkness, not even its own reflection, without "another"; this is excluded from the omnipotence of any solar god. So it was with the help of a feminine consort, Holy Wisdom, that the Creator was said to have created the wonder of our manifest universe. This also is in the Bible and in the Judaic tradition, but somehow was conveniently overlooked for the last two millennia by patriarchal Christian thinkers. In early Christianity this Holy Wisdom was called Hagia Sophia, the third person of the Trinity, which I discussed at some length in my book *The Dove in the Stone*. According to Jung, the only clue to that femininity is Sophia's emblem, the dove, the bird sacred to the goddesses of old.

The sign Libra introduces the need for wisely and harmoniously "balancing" those sensitive issues surrounding all I-Thou encounters, such as the subjective and objective worlds, and in our daily lives matters dealing with partnerships, marriage, diplomacy, justice, proportion, beauty, and art—in short, the aesthetics of relationship. Virtually every projection that we make is in essence a marriage encounter, because we are forming within the psyche a relationship, for better or worse, that will reveal something potentially meaningful to us. (As an aside, I could even say that keeping a journal, or setting down one's thoughts on paper, forces what is within out into the objective world where we can then relate to it in a new way.) Whenever this *coniunctio* occurs, there is a potential conception. Out of the yoking of the two, a third—a "brainchild," some new idea, even an aha!—is made possible, and thus we grow. This form of writing or sketching or drawing mandalas is a Gemini device and a fine therapy. Letters such as these are also ruled by Gemini, and I confess that as I write to you, all kinds of new ways of putting things occur to me. It is my relationship to you (Libra) that gives birth to these thoughts. For me writing a book rather than letters would be an I-Them exercise, not the same thing at all. And I have learned now that it is quite easy for readers to identify with "My dear friend." So you see how, in principle, the air signs help each other out.

Psychologically, you can see the tremendous importance of the sign Libra and its element of air, and how much you can learn from placing the various planets there to find how they are modified. Actually, no planetary process suffers much from being in this sign. The worst that can be said is that it can coincide with a certain amount of self-indulgence, procrastination, laziness, and pursuit of the ephemeral. Venus, or Aphrodite, the goddess of love, certainly has been the "downfall" of many a hero. Even today's heroes bog down in dilly-dallying or flirtations and affairs. But the consequences don't come until later in Scorpio, where guilts have to be confronted. Libra teaches Mars to leave his weapons at the door, take off his helmet (Aries), wash, and say please and thank you—not to satisfy his mother, but to woo his fair lady. Libra civilizes us, helps us to become social animals. At the most profound level, Dante's *Divine Comedy* and Goethe's *Faust* express the temptation, the beauty and love, the tragic dimensions possible, and the final transforming revelation that the feminine (Libra) can bring to the questing mortal hero (Aries).

Can you see how Tai Chi, the Scottish sword dance, and fencing all balance the Aries/Libra polarity by making these martial arts graceful? A man I knew engraved (Mars) copper plates (Venus rules copper) for wedding invitations. Yes, he had Mars in Libra!

Air is the most volatile and, in some ways, the most extraordinary of the elements. "It bloweth where it listeth." As we know from watching the daily weather reports, it moves around the globe, propelled by the Coriolis force of the earth's rotation and the highs and lows of atmospheric pressure. Actually and poetically expressed, we might be inhaling what a Swedish child or a Chinese farmer exhaled last week. We truly breathe a million breaths with every breath. I remember being mind-boggled at discovering, in one of my son's boyhood books, that since atoms are continually being dispersed *through time* as well as through space, it is a mathematical probability that we could be inhaling an atom that once went in and out of the lungs of Jesus or Genghis Khan or Napoleon, to say nothing of any of our brothers and sisters of the human race, the animal kingdom, the vegetable kingdom, and now more increasingly the mineral kingdom! The element air makes the "brotherhood of man" (Aquarius) a fact and a necessity as we confront the terrible threats of nuclear leaks and acid rain.

At a deeper level, all this is implicit in the word "spirit," which comes from *spirare*, to breathe. The link between breath and consciousness is shown by the air sign Gemini, which rules both hemispheres of the brain, the nervous systems, and the lungs, as well as the tongue, arms, hands, and fingers. In our first series of letters, I wrote at some length about Mercury (Hermes), the messenger of the gods; of the inner messenger in the body; of his winged hat and feet, symbolizing the speed of thought; of his function of communicating; and above all about his potent symbol, the caduceus, which today reminds us not only of DNA/RNA, but also of the *ida* and *pingala* surrounding the *sushumna*—which, according to the Hindus, constitute the subtle currents in the spine through which the powerful force known as *kundalini* rises.

Air circulates oxygen and carbon dioxide, and our consciousness depends on their balanced intake and flow. Too much or too little oxygen can cause us to black out or even to suffer brain damage. The work of Dr. Stanislav Grof with holotropic breathing, which I have witnessed personally, is astounding. It demonstrates that certain breathing techniques can dramatically alter consciousness, bringing contents of the unconscious to the fore. But this technique should be practiced only under strict supervision. The same warning applies to certain kinds of yogic breathing.

For most of us, breathing is a natural and automatic process. We can ignore it or pay attention to it calmly and deeply as we pray, meditate, or just go for a walk. Joggers can get high on breathing. Lord knows, if breath is so important to our consciousness, then how precious is the clean air that we breathe! To pollute it or to alter it by sniffing drugs is, through terrible ignorance, to misuse the most precious gift of all: the breath that gives us life as we are born, sustains us while we live, and which we surrender with our last exhalation. How can we not see this!

Psychologically speaking, planets in Gemini reveal how we are likely to deal with our surroundings and the ease with which we communicate our thoughts rather than our feelings. Archetypal twins, brothers, foes who become best friends or rivals fill eight pages in my dictionary of myths. They range from Gilgamesh and Enkidu and Jacob and Esau to Abbott and Costello and Laurel and Hardy. It's as if you can't think of one without the other, like comedy and tragedy, big and little, and on through all the dualities upon which consciousness depends. Unfortunately, as both Jung and Edward F. Edinger, author of *Ego and Archetype*, have pointed out so eloquently, with consciousness came the split into good and evil, and with it our concerns about shame and guilt and painful choices.

Gemini rules the *puer aeternus*, the eternal Peter Pan in the psyche, and issues surrounding *puer* and *senex*, the boy and the old man. It also rules children, games, books, newspapers, riddles, and puns, and all the Tricksters in the mythologies of the world. It is the sign of the Miraculous Child, the Divine Child: little Krishna stealing the butter, the infant Mercury stealing Apollo's cattle, little boy Jesus preaching in the Temple. Gemini's position in the chart or Mercury's location and the aspects it receives will reveal the state of the Inner Child of your patients.

Mercury, the ruler of Gemini, is androgynous or hermaphroditic. As such, he is the *passepartout* or Cupid uniting the planetary opposites as we unite our shoelaces by crossing them:

Sun——Moon
Venus——Mars
Jupiter——Saturn
Uranus——Neptune
Pluto——?

When Saturn occupies Gemini, it is safe to say that the Inner Child is crying out for recognition, no matter how old or young the person may be. The hurt is hidden, and to speak of it, despite the confident persona of the one before you, may open the floodgate to tears. Often such people were not touched enough physically as little ones, and they may need to learn to play again and be given permission to be silly now and then. Rather than heavy analysis, I would recommend sand-play therapy. For me, the most wrenching example of Saturn in Gemini is Hans Christian Andersen's story "The Little Match Girl." There is a little orphan hiding in those psyches with Saturn in Gemini.

We also find the Gemini-Sagittarius polarity in all those sports (Sagittarius) that involve two opponents or opposing teams: tennis, basketball, polo, hockey, football, soccer, etc. In each case, one side aims to get a circular object into the opposing side's territory; and the teams are distinguished by different names, uniform colors, etc. It has been seriously suggested that the ancient origins of such ball games were religious, having to do with the opposition of light and darkness struggling for the sun, or the struggle of good and evil. We see this still on New Year's Eve and Day (Hogmanay for the Celts) when a ball (sun) descends in Times Square to mark the transition of the year, and the entire nation is glued to climactic football games, with spectators' emotions running high. The fact that today such games involve so many people in "play" is wonderful. Edinger has pointed out that the word "play," as in sports or in drama, offers a safe alternative to combat which is still archetypal in essence.

I know that to be true firsthand. My grandmother and mother used to play a deadly game of cards called Russian Bank. Part of the fun was being free to make horrible and insulting remarks. They positively growled, so they could never play in public. My mother then played the game with me in the same spirit, and I with my own children and grandchildren. It is one time when absolute equality is the rule, and a fine way of letting off steam. I highly recommend such games to my clients.

Aquarius is the fixed air sign. Here the element is vast and as wide as space itself. I am always reminded of the French poet Francis Jammes's "*Tout est vain qui n'a pas le grand calme de Dieu*" ("All is futile that has not the great calm of God"). The sign confers detachment, intellect rather than Gemini's bright intelligence, and an affinity for abstractions and concepts. It thinks globally, no, cosmically; its difficulties are with details and individuals per se rather than with groups, communities, and countries. Ronald Reagan, an Aquarian, was particularly described as being this way. Mars in Gemini loves to debate and argue: it fights with words. But Mars in Aquarius gets excited only over principles and concepts, bigotry or inhumanity. Saturn in Aquarius becomes an architect of dreams.

Have you noticed by now that the shadow side of a sign is shown by the opposite sign? In the Aries-Libra axis, the problems have to do with egotism and altruism: "Love thy neighbor as thyself" applies here, which could be more accurately expressed psychologically as meaning, "Love thy neighbor's Self as thine own Self." Unfortunately, the saying gets a pious spin, implying that it is more Christian to love your neighbor *more* than yourself, as if your own ego were meant and not the Divine Guest in you. So we stack the cards in front of our neighbor and lose the game by subtly engineering our own defeat. This, in turn, leads to hurt and resentment. The lesson is plain in Libra's balance: we are to be just, play fair, and deal the cards evenly. One for you and one for me. This is why Saturn is exalted in Libra. Here Saturn shines as a wise judge, and this is the wisdom of the Sun's exaltation in Aries. It is the Divine Guest, or Christ within each other, the Atman whom we are to serve fairly in relationships. If God dwells in me as me, then God surely dwells in thee as thee.

The Aquarius-Leo axis has to do with monarchy and democracy. Leo, the king or queen, to be the best of rulers and the wisest, must first and foremost serve the people (Aquarius) with love, power, and wisdom. And Aquarius must remember that every other individual is a king or queen in his or her own right, to be honored and recognized as an individual, not a cipher in some social security system. Not just a group holding hands, but "hugs to the left and hugs to the right" (Leo). As viewed from the vantage point of the New Age of Aquarius, this is the mandate: to search for and find God in our midst, within ourselves, and within each other. And beyond that, to find Spirit within our created precious and fragile Earth and her family, the solar system. It is a huge task, and we are only just beginning. But for the first time in history we are moving towards it with considerable consciousness of what this means.

The Age of Aquarius is almost upon us, and as Uranus transited its own sign during the last decade of the twentieth century, enormous changes came to pass: individuals amassing peacefully to overthrow tyrannical regimes; the formation of the European Union with a common currency; global conferences on the environment, trade and economy. The proliferation at an enormous speed of computers, wire-free phones, space travel. And also the global impact of 9/11, the Iraq War, the spread of AIDS, the hijacking of identities, Google, and on and on. It will not be long before everybody ends up being everybody! Uranus, as the higher octave of Mercury has impacted the entire globe. Now that Uranus is in Pisces (where it will remain until 2011), let us hope it will concentrate more on peace. Neptune is also transiting Aquarius now (through 2012), which can have positive idealistic results or can coincide with fictional and delusional fanaticisms.

As far as I know, never have so many been aware of a paradigm shift as at the present moment. We surely must learn that life itself is a sacrament and then celebrate it.

I know that you do.

Love always,

ao

THE BODY OF GOD

God is the great urge that has not yet found a body
but urges toward incarnation with the great creative urge.

And becomes at last a clove carnation: lo! that is god!
and becomes at last Helen, or Ninon: any lovely and
    generous woman
at her best and her most beautiful, being god, made
    manifest, any clear and fearless man being god, very god.

There is no god
apart from poppies and flying fish,
men singing songs, and women brushing their
    hair in the sun.
The lovely things are god that has come to pass,
    like Jesus came.
The rest, the undiscoverable, is the demi-urge.
                    —D. H. LAWRENCE

Our grasping, acquisitive nature spoils things.
The beauty you leap upon dissolves under your dead
weight. Clutch the splendor of flame and you get burned;
pluck a flower and it dies; scoop water from a brook and
it flows no longer; snatch the wind in a bag and in it you
have dead air. The more determined you are to capture
life and hold onto it, the more life will elude you and
your own self-asserting effort imprison you. To enjoy
any living thing—fire, water, air, animal, vegetable,
human, God—we must let go of it. When we free it
from our grasp, we, too, become free. In detachment
is our liberation; and in our liberation the earth is
hallowed and God is glorified.
                    —WILLIAM MCNAMARA,
                        Earthy Mysticism

7

EARTH
Stuff, Structure, Stability

Dear Friend,

Your observation that fire cannot be cold, though the other three elements can vary in temperature, is a perfect example of astrological thinking. Sometimes something is so obvious that we overlook its implications. It got me to thinking about the other elements. I suppose you could say that water is the only one whose course is almost totally predictable: it will always seek the lowest level (like charity), will fill holes of varying depths until they are of equal level, will accept anything plunged or thrown into it, will part and flow around obstacles, and take the shape of its container. The essence of warmth and vitality is indeed characteristic of the fire signs, and the adaptability to life is true of the water signs. One can see why the ancients considered water a passive, yin element. I almost said "feminine," which today is a no-no, so I want to reiterate that the use of that word in astrology is not pejorative and does not necessarily refer to gender, i.e., women. In that respect, astrology follows nature and balances masculine and feminine processes fifty-fifty. Thinking otherwise is a negative projection. Men have feminine planets and elements and women have masculine ones, regardless of cultural history, and both are good and necessary.

So to speak of water as feminine and passive is not a sexist observation; it simply refers to the fact that in nature water and earth have functions different from those of fire and air. The only necessary distinction that the astrologer has to make is to determine whether a chart is a man's or a woman's, because what is manifested outwardly as gender is balanced inwardly by its opposite. Here Jung's concept of anima/animus makes perfect sense. I am hoping that, as we come to understand the element of earth, the strength, wisdom, and dignity of the feminine will come clear for both men and women.

There are three earth signs:

 as Taurus the Bull: fixed earth
♍ Virgo the Virgin: mutable earth
♑ Capricorn the Goat: cardinal earth

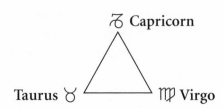

You could say that earth in Taurus is soil, in Virgo it becomes pebbles and sand, and in Capricorn it is rock. Each expresses something different about "matter," a word coming from *mater*, "mother"! Remember, mothers give form to life.

Earth in Taurus is solid, fertile loam. It is the second sign in the natural zodiac, following Aries, a fire sign. Coming in late April-May, its function is indeed to give form to life. It is to the seed sown in the earth what our body is to our psyche: the precious, living, nurturing container that tethers and roots us to our individuality. People who have Venus in Libra love flowers for their beauty; people who have Venus in Taurus love not only flowers for their beauty, but vegetables as well, and they have the patience and appreciation to grow them. There is a farmer hidden away in every Taurus, and a banker as well, who is but a farmer at another level. The process remains one of investing, trusting, and hoping much will grow from little. For every single grain of wheat, there is the potential for a sheaf. Remember this when we come to the Age of Taurus.

Taurus is *fixed earth*. It just stays put until moved or pushed. So the way it modifies any of the planets is to stabilize them. For instance, the naturally outgoing energy of Mars is grounded and turns to a stubborn endurance and resistance to pressure. Put Saturn there, and its conservatism, conformity, and heroic dependability can become almost unbearable. From the therapist's point of view, it is vital to understand that people with such configurations have two great fears: change and insecurity. There can be almost a paranoia concerning breaks in tradition or flexibility of views. They can become prisoners of their own opinions and the *idée fixe*. The one planet that defies this is Uranus, and the result is volcanic. Changes come like earthquakes, much to the consternation of others. Needless to say, Uranus is in its fall in Taurus. Venus and Jupiter and, above all, the Moon, which is exalted in the sign, are at ease here, because in this element they become fertile. Above all, Taurus is the most natural of signs: calm, dependable, friendly, comfortable with itself and with the natural world. The yearly full moon in Taurus is Wesak, the Lord Buddha's birthday as well as the anniversary of his enlightenment and his death. This seems to honor the great blessing of nature in the fullness of spring.

In the body Taurus rules the throat, neck, and quality of voice. Many singers are gifted with planets in Taurus. It is interesting to consider the opposite sign, Scorpio (Mars), which rules sex. With puberty, boys' voices change. In the past, to keep some boy sopranos just that, they were castrated. A very high, breathy voice in women is often a symptom of their being cut off from their own sexuality, and today there are programs of voice training to help both men and women connect with their lower chakras. The connection between money (Taurus) and sex (Scorpio) is well known to therapists and marriage counselors. Complaints about the former often mask problems with the latter. In fact, there is a parlor game in which you ask people to write down three personal observations about money. When they are through, you suggest they substitute the word sex for money. The results are hilarious.

In opposition to Taurus, Scorpio also rules death, and death activates last wills and the new distribution of money and property (Taurus). The entire business of marriage (sex) and dowries and land (property) is another polarity involving the signs. So in reading the chart as a diagnostic tool, these polarities can be extremely significant and helpful in understanding hidden fears or guilts surrounding these issues. The positive expressions of both lie in the capacity of Scorpio to "unstick" the stuckness of Taurus and with its deep emotions to water the soil of Taurus. On the other hand, Taurus brings a commonsense, down-to-earth normalcy to Scorpio's *Sturm und Drang* or times of doom and gloom. Can you see how helpful and informative these polarities can be?

In the body, Virgo, which is ruled by Mercury, governs the intestines, the discriminators, sorting out what will be useful and rejecting that which is not. The earth here is friable, and it is the time of harvest, seed, grain, and all things "granulated" into detail. Mercury, who is up to tricks and monkey business in Gemini, becomes sensible, logical, and meticulous, a veritable Aunt Polly. Things must work like clockwork (Virgo rules clocks and all measurements and accounting). The psychological problems here are of compulsion, scrupulosity, perfectionism, and a terrible fear of failure or being wrong or ridiculous. The faults are criticism, self-criticism, and an automatic tendency to make judgments. The two signs most gifted with worry are Cancer (fear of loss) and Virgo (fear of failure and imperfection).

Of course, the most beautiful archetype we associate with Virgo is that of the Madonna, the immaculately conceived Queen of Heaven (*immaculata* in Latin means "spotless"). This reminds me of how meaningful the Virgin was during the Middle Ages and the extraordinary discovery the observant Louis Charpentier recorded in his book *The Mystery of Chartres*. He found that, besides the great cathedral dedicated to Mary, there is a group of several other churches in the surrounding area also dedicated to her. He noticed as he looked at a map that it was as if the stars in the constellation of Virgo had been dropped onto the map of France. In continuing his studies of churches built at the time, Charpentier noticed that, despite the extraordinary accuracy with which they were built, their altars, which should have faced due east, were frequently off by a degree or two to the north or south. This puzzled him greatly until he realized that the altar of each church dedicated to a saint was aligned perfectly so that the sun would rise over the center of it at dawn on that saint's feast day. This might well have been one of the mysteries carried out by the unnamed fraternity of initiates at the time. It was a period of secret symbols and markings, about which Harold Bayley has written as well. Since Christianity arose with the Age of Pisces, its opposite constellation, Virgo, assumes a special significance, both for the Church and for the Age. A study of the symbolism of the Rose Window, the design of the oval yoni of the *vesica piscis*, the labyrinths and mazes make one wonder how much more is still hidden from us in such buildings and in the stones and stone circles of our forebears.

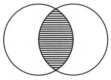

The *vesica piscis*

I remember M pointing out to me that geometry, which literally means "earth measurement," holds all the secrets of the universe for us, if we could but understand its symbolism. God geometrizes indeed. One of the great gifts of Virgo is to be able to recognize the logic connecting a flower, a shell, and a snowflake.

Virgo knows how to read the great book of nature. For any of the earth signs—and this is most important—the quest for meaning never ceases, nor is it satisfied by any conceptual abstractions. Answers have to make sense in every sense of that word. To find, for instance, that the Golden or Whirling Rectangle can be drawn with only a straightedge and a compass, and that the resulting logarithmic curve placed on tracing paper can then be placed over a chambered nautilus and fits—that is the kind of miracle and wisdom that all three earth signs can appreciate, as can the rest of us. Faith alone is very hard for earth signs.

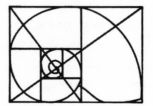

The vagueness and amorphousness of Pisces is threatening, as conversely Pisces can be impatient with too much exactitude. Virgo would be happy to say something is exactly the sum of its parts; Pisces would say it becomes more. Both are right, and they need each other. Do you see the polarity of opposites again? The two are highly important to psychotherapy as well, since Virgo analyzes and Pisces synthesizes. In fact, you have three related schools based on these processes: psychoanalysis (Freud), analytical psychology (Jung), and psychosynthesis (Assagioli).

So we come to Capricorn, the cardinal earth sign, which marks the winter solstice. It takes nine months to go from Aries through Sagittarius, and so the birth of the Child, the Savior in several ancient religions, is accomplished in Capricorn, the sign ruled by Saturn. If "the king [Sun] must die" on June 21 as the Sun moves into the sign of Cancer, he is reborn and made manifest in Capricorn. This is the process and the paradigm of incarnation, for Christians the Word made flesh.

If Taurus receives life as seed money, then Virgo counts it, and Capricorn builds and stacks it. All three earth signs are extremely practical, and many are involved with building, banking, and commerce.

Capricorn represents the outer limits and boundaries as well as the inner structures of our bodies and our manifest world. It rules the skin and the skeleton, the rock and the shell, time and death's leftovers—dust and ashes. But the glorious secret is that hidden away in Capricorn is new life. In its cave lies treasure. The essence of Capricorn comes out in Scrooge McDuck, the archetypal miser Silas Marner, or the wise provider Joseph in Egypt. It depends on your viewpoint. The process of Capricorn is to sober up and give a conscientious, constructive, practical application to each of the planets coming into its provenance. Mars and Saturn thrive here, but Jupiter and the Moon do not. Jupiter loses much of his bonhomie, and the Moon grows cold. From the therapist's point of view, a male patient will have processed the experience of the mother archetype as distant, absent or not cuddling. The issue is often depression and melancholy, an unnurtured ego, and self-loathing. In the case of a woman, though emotions run deep, it is at first almost impossible for her to express them cheerfully or easily. The stance of such people is defensive, and their childhood may even have appeared tragic in some way. For me the art of Käthe Kollwitz comes to mind.

Here again, by knowing the opposites we see that Cancer can come to the rescue. When the real or imagined suffering of such people is shown to have behind it a lesson in service and compassion, the lead can be transmuted to gold. People do respond to being told that they have an "alchemical task." Another helpful image is that of the diamond—pure carbon—buried deep in the mine, but which can be cut and polished to reflect the sun's light more brilliantly than any other gem.

It is my conviction that, in the next century, more and more attention will be given to the study of kundalini and the chakra system. Already acupuncture is an accepted medical practice. We know that it is based on twelve meridian lines in the body. We know there are twelve sets of cranial nerves. The study of the so-called subtle bodies has been going on in the East for millennia, and despite the scoffing of rationalistic Westerners, the concepts and vocabulary connected with such study are gaining ground. Paracelsus knew of these things, having probably studied in the East, and from time to time a few people like Mesmer and a group experimenting in France would look into the matter.

Concomitant with the discovery of Uranus (in 1781) and Neptune (in 1846) came a slow crescendo of interest in unseen forces: electricity, X-ray, radium, new theories of energy, radio, and so forth. What is true of our earth is also true of our bodies, and so we hear of auras and clairvoyants who can see and distinguish four different "bodies" for every one of us. That these should correspond to the four elements should come as no great surprise. It seems we have a physical body (earth), an etheric or vital body (fire), an emotional body (water), and a mental body (air).

Here is a strange experience I want to share with you. A woman I know went to see a Jungian analyst, a lady in her late eighties who had known Jung. When the younger woman met the older one, she had an instant sense of déjà vu. Here stood her old Tibetan teacher, whom she had known as a man. Not only did she recognize him, but she could remember what he had taught her—about how the five senses operate in the subtle bodies. That evening she got up the courage to mention this. "Well," said the analyst, "it is strange that you should tell me this. During the war, I was interned on the Isle of Man because I was a German citizen. I was very lonely, cut off from my family. One day I was gazing out to sea when I saw a vision of the Himalayas, the monasteries, and the *Potala* in all its beauty. I was deeply moved, and I heard the words, 'Know that you can come home to us at any time.' So in my imagination, I would frequently do just that."

That night the visitor asked the analyst if she had a certain set of unpublished notes on some aspects of yoga from a seminar given by Jung. She very kindly loaned them, and the student set the alarm for 4:00 A.M. to study them. To her surprise, they included a dissertation by a Dr. Hauer dealing with the function of the five senses in the subtle bodies. This is a good example of what Jung meant by synchronicity.

And here is another: As I was originally writing the previous paragraph, the phone rang. It was a friend telling me that Margit van Leight-Frank had died that day. Saddened as I was, I knew she had gone home. For she was the Tibetan teacher, and I the one seeking the lessons again.

Since then, Jung's notes on yoga have been published as *The Psychology of Kundalini Yoga: Notes of the Seminar given in 1932 by C. G. Jung,* edited by Sonu Shamdasani, in the Bollingen Series. Shamdasani is a head of the Philemon Foundation, dedicated to publishing the still-unpublished work of Jung, including his personal journal known as the *Red Book.*

Life is very strange and also very wonderful.

With much love always,

ao

The secret of the Philosopher's Stone is to look with the eyes
And see with the heart.
                              —PETRUS BONUS, alchemist

He asked the almond tree, "Speak to me of God."
And the almond tree blossomed.
                              —NIKOS KAZANTZAKIS

IMPRISONED SPLENDOR

Truth is within ourselves; it takes no rise
From our outward things, whate'er you may believe.
There is an inmost center in us all,
Where truth abides in fullness; and around
Wall upon wall, the gross flesh hems it in,
                              . . . and to know
Rather consists in opening out a way
Whence the imprisoned splendor may escape,
Than in effecting entry for a light
Supposed to be without.
                              —ROBERT BROWNING
                              Paracelsus

CHAPTER

8

SOME REFLECTIONS

Dear Friend,

Y ou ask, *Do the earth signs rule food?* Well, Cancer is the sign that has to do with cooking and preparing food, but Taurus rules the food itself. Food is food*stuff*, and we consume it all our lives. The so-called food chain is alchemy on a global level, because the plants absorb minerals, the animals and fish consume the plants, we consume them, and all along the chain there is a circulation of intake, transformation, combustion, and elimination. The interchange of life and stuff was a great mystery until we discovered that so-called inert matter is filled with energy. To some this implies that in its way it has consciousness, though this may be hard for many people to accept. In the East, this energy is called *prana*.

If you think about it, one of the most individuated and integrated of all creatures is a potato! I have given some of my highly agitated clients a potato to hold and contemplate. A potato is calm and complete, humble and unaffected by its dry and earthy exterior; yet it is moist, pure, and filled with goodness at its own level of being. Who could ask for more? And when I would see my husband relishing a plate of steaming hot mashed potatoes with a bit of butter and parsley on top, I'd find myself grateful to the spirit who came up with the design in the first place.

This constant natural recycling has been impeded by the invention of nonbiodegradable materials such as most plastic. We eat the earth, and we *are* the earth, and the earth before we came was made of the stars. So we are eating stardust, and our bodies partake of the stars as well.

I wonder if this extraordinary phenomenon of importing foods from around the world, so illogical otherwise, may not have a deeper purpose than we know? At the body level we are already becoming one world. Today, for instance, I have consumed a bit of Java, Brazil, and Vermont for breakfast. For lunch, there was Germany, Norway, Portugal, and Massachusetts, with India for tea. For supper, we may have some Alaska, Idaho, and California. I am wearing Korea, Scotland, Italy, Greece, China, Japan, Ireland, and Thailand, as well as the U.S.A. How about you? Upstairs in our meditation room I have a bowl with small stones gathered from China, Russia, Ireland, Easter Island, Finland, India, Iona, Greece, Ephesus, Israel, Egypt, and several of our own states; and I have dropped little stones from Rosecroft in as many faraway places as I can, or sent them with friends who are traveling afar. It pleases me to know that there are two pebbles from this place hiding deep in a sacred cave in China. It is a kind of United Nations of pebbles, and for all we know they may have their own broadcasting system! I know, I know—it's crazy, but it's fun, too, and harmless.

The funny thing is that whenever I mention it, I discover I am far from being the only one circulating stones. It is in the unconscious of Celts especially to carry stones and build cairns. I remember my father telling me that his friend, the newscaster Lowell Thomas, of Welsh descent, had a fireplace in his home built of single large stones brought back from his travels around the world.

What I have been learning all along, since I discovered "processes," is that you can find almost every process in the earth repeated in the human body, and vice versa: for instance, the branching out of trees, veins, rivers, lightning, dendrites, roadway "arteries," nerves, leaf patterns—they all follow a similar design. The earth, too, has her meridians, her aura, her power points, her breasts and pubic trees, her flesh and fruits, her springtime and old age, death, and resurrection. This vision lives in the place names of geography in many lands.

One of the most breathtaking descriptions of this phenomenon is in Eleanor Munro's beautiful book *On Glory Roads*. In it she describes the mythical body of Mother India, which lies stretched over the entire subcontinent. Her body is covered by that of the triple god of the Hindus, and where they made contact temples sprang up, so that even today pilgrims walk the trails of her nerves and veins, and they see in the great stone lingams the places of connection, the *coniunctio* of heaven and earth. They are partaking in a cosmic rapture that is determined by the cycles of stars and planets. Such a point of view may explain why the Indian people, despite poverty and deprivation, carry themselves with such luminous dignity. They are partaking daily in a symbolic life of grandeur beyond description. They sense their own divinity, in a *participation mystique*, on a daily basis. As I wrote in *Jungian Symbolism in Astrology*, my experience of the city of Varanasi (Benares) taught me that.

Paradoxically, as a people, Indians are richer than we are because their lives are given more meaning. All our Western psychological pathologies most likely have a common source: we have been cut off from the actual experience of God. Talking about divinity, reading about it, going through rituals from the neck up are no longer sufficient. In desperation, and for lack of that deeper reality, we in the sophisticated world of the West turn first to material things, status, and comforts, and then, when they fail or we have failed through our social position in a deprived inner city, we turn to addictions, to louder and louder music, to sex, alcohol, and drugs. We spiral down to a hell on earth entirely of our own making. It is so terribly, terribly sad. Having everything all the time leaves an aching void. When children grow up without parents acknowledging the Presence of something unseen, the projection goes to "idols," celebrities, and, in the absence of religions, to national or political isms. Personally, I am all for children growing up in any religion rather than none because when they become teenagers they have something to argue with and think about!

One has to ask oneself why all this is necessary. Moralizing is not the answer. I think the greatest service would be for young people to be taught the concept of karma simply as cause and effect, not as good or bad. In that way "virtue," at the most basic level, would become simply enlightened self-interest, not a bribe for an embezzled heaven or the result of fear of hellfire. Whatever we do to our fellow human beings, we do ipso facto to ourselves. If we lie, we trust no one else. If we steal, we fear for our own property. If we diminish the life of anyone in any way, we diminish ourselves. I truly believe that in the Age of Aquarius we will learn to say, "Love thy neighbor for he *is* thyself."!

I have also learned a great lesson from my computer: when I make a mistake, it does not tell me I have sinned (Virgo), it just goes "Boop!", telling me, "Not this way." Perhaps in the coming Age, parents will learn to say "That's a no!" rather than calling their children naughty or wicked and loading them with guilt.

Every so often people do reach out, and those in the helping professions such as yourself are there trying their best. How, I ask myself, can astrology help deal with the pathology of psychological suffering? Jung has described such pain as often resulting whenever the ego that we have worked so hard to develop becomes the be-all and end-all of our awareness. It happens when we identify with its rationality alone and cut ourselves off from awareness of that greater and ultimate center of our being which he called the Self, that Divine Guest within us. In astrological or even astronomical terms, this is like making the moon the center of our solar system. If we identify with the earth/moon, naturally we project the sun god as being "out there," distant, unobtainable, other. To recognize the sun inside of us is to recognize the immanence of spirit. But it need not end there with prideful inflation or solipsism, as the Church fears. It can have another result entirely: it frees one for the vision of this world and all in it as holy. It frees one to participate in creation by using our egos to become *conscious* of and reflect spirit. Jung and Teilhard de Chardin shared that insight, and for psychiatry—which for many of its practitioners is still very much an ego-centered preoccupation—the purpose of the healing of souls gets lost. To bring ourselves to realize and help anyone else accept even the concept that we have always had the potential for a direct experience, a peak experience, of the Self is to set ourselves on the path to healing.

This is nothing new; what *is* new is the amount of garbage that our rationalism has placed between us and a very simple truth. I had a dream a few years ago in which I heard a corollary added to Descartes' famous axiom, *Cogito ergo sum* ("I think, therefore I am")—it was *ergo scio quod Deus est* (therefore I know God is). Perhaps this is the ultimate purpose of consciousness.

In past centuries, as Jung has pointed out, the rich panoply and symbolic structure of the Church carried the projections of the people and made them feel safe. Protestantism forced many of these projections to be withdrawn, and collectively many were forced to look within themselves for what they had outwardly lost. Such a shift on a collective level is hard to imagine. But Jung felt that Luther led to psychology, because at the individual level so many—with the exception of mystics—were left feeling lost and insecure.

It is fascinating to me that it was in the late eighteenth century—precisely at the time of the discovery of Uranus and of the three great revolutions, the American, French, and Industrial revolutions, all enacted for the Aquarian vision of the common man—that the first inkling of Eastern philosophy and religion reached the Western world with its news of the Atman as the inner Self. With the Upanishads came the breath of a healing view from the other lobe of the earth.

But as a culture, we are still far from grasping this message. When Joseph Campbell was teaching the concept at a lecture not so long ago, one man was heard to exclaim, "Why, that's blasphemy!" Until we seek for the direct experience of that ultimate truth, which can only occur in one individual psyche after another, the agony and the angst will continue. The prophets, if you will, who tried to help at the turn of the century were a disparate lot, often ridiculed and rejected until understood. Vivekenanda in his way, H. P. Blavatsky and Anna Bonus Kingsford in theirs, to mention only a few, offered either a Uranian (occult) or Neptunian (mystical) alternative, and you know as well as anybody of the proliferation of religious and utopian cults in the world.

Along with the traditional ones, we now are witnessing a tremendous revival of fundamentalism in both Christianity and Islam. What I find interesting is the role of Jung, of Teilhard, Eliade, and Campbell in alerting us to the vital importance of what goes on inside of us. This interests me, not for egocentric reasons, but because the future of the earth depends on our understanding both the scientific ghosts that we have raised with nuclear warfare and the religious mythologies and political ideologies that are proliferating. There are so many, and they are so powerful, yet so misunderstood or left unexamined. Who could have imagined that not so long ago a writer, Salman Rushdie, could be condemned to death for heresy, or that one book, *The Satanic Verses*, could cause so many deaths? We might have relegated such an event to the Middle Ages. But there are people all over the world still willing to die or to kill for what they believe in. We need desperately to understand their mythology as well as our own. Literalism kills.

Forgive this long aside, but it is so essential to understanding how astrology could be helpful. On the individual level, it can point to where the block is, the problem, the complex, the despair, in short, the pathology. We have to be willing to work on ourselves. We have to be humble enough to believe that a solution is possible with consciousness on our side, trusting in grace on the other. We have to be willing to accept astrology at least as a hypothesis and not reject it out of hand based on totally ignorant assumptions. To deny it because we do not understand how it works is like refusing to live in a body for the same reason. In future letters, I hope to be able to discuss how astrology can give us insights even on the collective level. In discussing the astrological Ages, we will see that there is an evolution apparent in what Jung called the collective unconscious.

I am not talking about predictions at all; I am talking about understanding ourselves and our world in terms of that precious and fragile thing we call the psyche, individual and collective. The psyche is invisible, but we see its effects. Waves and particles are invisible, but atomic physicists see their effects. What we call God is also invisible, but we know that the unknowable and unnamable speaks in verbs, in universal ever-flowing processes. Throughout history we have personified them and called them goddesses and gods. Whatever names we give them, they are invisible, but we know them by their effects. Astrology is the language that can decode the mystery sufficiently to give us a glimmer of the great grammar of God. Then maybe we can see a little better, hear a little more, and accept the boundless love that is everywhere. It, too, is invisible, but we can feel its effects! The invisible is hidden in the visible, and to perceive it we need to develop the subtle equivalents of our senses, to grow into new dimensions.

Astrology really can help because it is the symbolic language of archetypal processes. It can link the light shining out of your eyes with the poet's "golden apples of the Sun, the silver apples of the moon."

Love always,

ao

To thine own self be true,
And it must follow, as the night the day,
Thou canst not then be false to any man.
    —WILLIAM SHAKESPEARE
       Hamlet

THE PRAYER OF A CANDLE

Dear—my Lord—use me!
Light the dull candle of my life
even if it be but to enlighten a dark corner
where one soul may find its lost coin,
its mislaid courage, its tarnished virtue—
Set the rude wick of my brain alight
in the rich fat of experience—
I would show of thy wonder and mercy
to the least and lowest of thy children.
      —A. GOODWILL

CHAPTER

9

PATHOLOGY AND HEALING

Dear Friend,

How can the chart be used specifically for healing? The answer to this has first to come out of the zodiac itself. As you may have observed by now, the three quaternities are potentially a source for friction within themselves. This friction serves a splendid purpose: it kicks the cosmic wheel, so to speak, and guarantees action in the world. Psychologically speaking, it guarantees challenges to an individual's inner growth. This was the ancient meaning of the Hindu symbol of the whirling cross, later perverted by Hitler.

positive  *negative*

Secondly, you have seen that the four trinings of the elements give us the harmonious foundation of ways of being with which to work.

Thirdly, and the topic of this letter, comes the consideration of the following: Each sign, when lived out of balance, is compensated for by its opposite sign. Each sign's virtue, when carried to excess, becomes its vice, which is corrected in turn by the virtue of the succeeding sign. So from the perspective of therapy, knowing the impact of each of the twelve signs helps one to know where to look for healing. We must never forget that the "twelve" symbolize totality, which in Jungian terms translates to individuation.

As an extreme example, to make it quite clear, look at the following partial and hypothetical configuration:

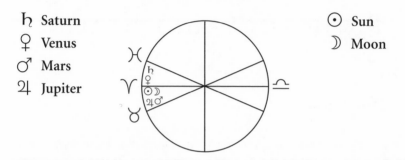

ℏ Saturn
♀ Venus
♂ Mars
♃ Jupiter

☉ Sun
☽ Moon

Here we have a "stellium" (four or more planets in the same sign) in Aries in the First House, with Aries on the ascendant (persona), Sun, Jupiter, Moon, and Mars. Let us assume it is the chart of a woman. You might approach it this way:

What is your first reaction? Will this be a sleepy, laid-back person? No? Why not?

What would bring this person, a woman, to be in your counseling room?

What is the opposite sign? (Libra)

What rules Libra? (Venus)

Where is Venus in the chart? (Conjunct Saturn in Pisces in the Twelfth House)

What process do Venus and Libra represent? (Relating and relationship)

What processes do each of those planets in Aries represent? Sun? Moon? Jupiter? Mars?

Would it help your patient to understand the following?

Her ambitions, competitiveness, and success make her come

across to others as someone admirable in terms of vitality and self-projection.

Yet she might be virtually impossible to live with because (1) she almost always judges others by her own standards and feelings; (2) she may consider any form of relationship in terms of a military surrender or defeat; (3) she may be highly impatient with others and most especially with herself; (4) she hides her own sensitivity and despises it as weakness, never to be expressed if she can help it.

She is wrapped up in herself and is considered selfish.

Could you see a potential for conflation of ego and animus and difficulty in differentiating the two? A quick trigger for resentment and anger? Difficulty with being objective?

Judging by the little depicted here:

Is she more likely introverted or extraverted?

Is she more likely a thinking or feeling type?

What archetypes come to mind? What mythological or historical figures? Joan of Arc? An Amazon? Lucy in "Peanuts" or Little Miss Muffet?

How would you justify your reaction astrologically?

How will she relate to her own femininity?

How would you use the wisdom inherent in her chart to help her? How could becoming more conscious of the way she tends to process experience enable her to make some changes?

I almost heard you protest that people cannot really change their intrinsic nature, but this is not what I am suggesting. To use a musical analogy, a single theme can have many variations. The same is true of the psyche and its outer manifestation of personality. When we are not conscious of the chart, it will tend to describe us as we express ourselves unconsciously. Like analysis, it is a helpful device for seeing ourselves a little more objectively, so that we can drive rather than be driven. It shows us how to make lemonade, as the saying goes, when we are handed lemons.

I sometimes use the image of a patterned knitted sock turned inside out. Any woman who knits one and any man who wears one will know that the wrong side appears to be a total mess. But as you pull the sock right side out by the toe, its beauty becomes more and more apparent. I suspect that most of us see only the mess, as long as we are identified with our egos.

The natural zodiac would suggest two remedies for our lady Aries: understanding the nature of the opposite sign of Libra; and understanding the nature of Taurus, the succeeding sign.

In the previous series of letters, we spent much time on Libra, so that it should be obvious to you now that the issues of fairness, of I-and-Thou, of sharing, of allowing rather than insisting, would come up in the chart. With so much Aries in the First House, this woman's way of relating to others would be to put herself in the other person's shoes and then react in her own way. Yet Aries will always respond positively by wanting to do something. Her challenge then is to learn to do nothing, to move from yang and fire into yin and her Venus (ruler of Libra) in Pisces, the gentle and compassionate water sign. She must learn to receive and allow. She has a Venus there (and I would show it to her), so drawing it out from under the denial of Saturn is her heroic task. She can put her animus to the task of rescuing the enchanted damsel from the dragon—or from the negative Old Man within herself. Her femininity and sweetness are imprisoned, and her life story, when you hear it, will tell you many reasons why. Her childhood will be her personal fairy tale. Like some Mahler symphony with movements of loud and bombastic fury, the music can change, and the sweet, redeeming melody of Venus (exalted, remember, in Pisces) will come floating up, as it probably has in dreams already. It is there. It just needs to be rescued through consciousness.

Supposing her Venus were in Aries or Taurus. Then you would use a different tack. How? By getting the image appropriate to Venus in those two signs.

We have considered all the polarities but one, and before proceeding, we should take a quick look at Gemini-Sagittarius. These opposites involve issues dealing with little and big, trivial and serious. Abraham Lincoln said, "The years know much that the days don't know." Gemini has to do with everyday environment, the hither and yon of life, or our busy daily thoughts. Sagittarius has to do with our philosophy of life and our religious stance which, like it or not, is the sum of our actual thoughts and deeds and not the grand theories we may pronounce. Too much Gemini and you have too much trivia, but too much Sagittarius and you end up with a lot of *theoria* and very little *praxis*. We are the sum of our thoughts in one way or the product of our deeds in another. This is reflected in the remarks of Jesus, "Wherefore by their fruits ye shall know them," and "For where your treasure is, there shall your heart be also."

Each of the polarities sets up a dialectic that is acted out in history as well, as we shall see in Part II. The important thing to remember is that all the polarities (oppositions) go back to the nature of the initial one of Aries-Libra; Mars-Venus (rulers); and Sun-Saturn (exaltations). And the issue is always what to do with confrontations of I and not-I, subjectivity-objectivity. When I teach astrology, I get two people to stand and face each other and spontaneously act out whatever comes to them: fight, ignore, tug-o'-war, dance, seesaw, back-to-back, hug, kiss, hand-in-hand. We see the polarity expressed in war (Aries); dance (Libra); in the sword dance; in duels and fencing; crime and punishment; and in "me and you." I often observe this in children who rush in and say, "Me and Tommy went to the movies!" It takes years until you hear "Tommy and I." It is not just a matter of grammar; it is a way of perception.

There is also a healing inherent in the naturally alternating electric yang and magnetic yin of the twelve signs. (See Table C.) I have not said too much about the system of progression in the chart. As the planets in the chart progress, they automatically trigger opportunities for making a shift in consciousness. The birth chart is not static; it is merely a seed pattern. An acorn has an oak tree enfolded within it, and to become an oak it progresses in its growth year by year. An acorn does not become a pine tree. So the chart unfolds through progression into becoming more and more of a description of one individual's psyche, not anyone else's.

Technically speaking, progression usually involves using a day for a year in the ephemeris. To understand your twenty-fifth year, you would set up the birthchart for twenty-five days after your birth date. By then, all the planets will have moved to other minutes or degrees, some more than others, depending on their speed of motion. Obviously the Moon, which travels the whole zodiac every month, will have moved the most rapidly, and Pluto, the slowest, hardly at all. I mention this here so you can calculate when someone moves into the next sign. For example, if you were born December 5, your Sun would be in 12 degrees of Sagittarius, and when you are eighteen years old, your Sun would move or progress into the next sign, Capricorn. Thus a subtle shift in consciousness would be open to you. At the utmost, you might have to wait thirty years for such a shift. The important thing is that our psyches have this built-in corrective measure, and so our Aries lady can eventually enjoy being an Aries both with a Taurus variation and, thirty years later, a Gemini motif. So the older we grow, the more varied and enriched we become—not only in life experience but in astrological potential as well.

So let us take a facetious turn around the merry-go-round:

The virtues of Aries are those of all fresh starts, the pioneering spirit, the courage, energy, and enthusiasm of setting forth, daring and ready for anything. Too much of this turns to the "vice" of reckless ruthlessness, selfish "me first!" and disregard of anyone or anything in its path. Anger, aggression, and a bullying feistiness could be a problem. The archetype of brave knight has turned into conquering soldier.

Taurus, fixed earth, steadies and cools Aries. Her virtues are form-giving fruitfulness, patience, fortitude, stability, traditionalism, which, carried to excess, become stubborn resistance to change, fixity, inflexible conservatism. The queen of spring has become the sacred cow.

Along comes Gemini and the trickster Mercury, who looks at all the would-be permanence of Taurus and lets a thousand monkeys run through it, all shouting, "So what, who cares!" His virtues are flexibility, seeing both sides of everything, keeping an open, eager, and curious mind; gathering, sharing, and communicating as much as possible. Carried to excess, this turns into shallow dabblings, indecision, inconstancies, puerile inconsistencies.

Then comes Cancer, and Mother Moon says that so far nobody has shown any caring or deep concern. Her virtues are loving, nurturing, protecting, and encouraging—"Mother knows best." But too much of this turns into possessive smothering, fear of emotional loss, and subtle and not-so-subtle emotional control, the archetypal mother-in-law, "*Ess-mein-Kind*" castrating female—witch mother instead of the good mother.

Then it is time for Father Leo the Lion to liberate us with masculine strength and regal patriarchal dignity. His virtues are wise dominion, generous benevolence, and goodness of heart. *Le roi, c'est moi! Noblesse oblige!* Too much power and his vice becomes inflated narcissistic conceit, and the archetype of the Good King turns into the pompous tyrannical despot.

Modest Virgo appears with her virtues of service, intelligent and practical attention to detail, helpful analysis from the secretarial sidelines. Too much of that turns into critical, calculating, fault-finding perfectionism and scrupulosity. The Faithful Servant has turned into a carping, fussy Prunefiddle.

Time then for a new message: it's not perfection that counts, says Libra, it's beauty. Everything must be pleasant, harmonious, and lovely. Weddings and receptions, dalliance and forgiveness. Eat, drink, and be merry, for tomorrow comes Scorpio! Too much procrastination or too much hedonism adds up to the vice of self-indulgence. Venus on the *chaise longue* eating truffles and saying, "Dahling, *do* join me..." has brought many a hero to his knees.

Just in the nick of time, Scorpio appears with his scowling message. It is not pleasure that makes the world go around, but passion. His virtue is to confront the heights and depths of reality, from the blood and gore of birth, to the dark shadows of lust and corruption, to the fearful maw of death. Scorpio's inner strength and courage will carry him and others through the dark valleys. Too much of this leads to temptation, to doom and gloom and guilts and self-castigation, sometimes to depression on an operatic scale. Sherlock Holmes can turn into Hamlet overnight.

Jovial Sagittarius comes to the rescue. Faith and philosophy, preaching and teaching, guiding others are what counts. His virtues are putting the mind on higher matters and getting out into the fresh air for some good exercise, or going on a voyage of adventure with friends or students. That's the way to go. Too much of this bonhomie, and the excess quickly yields a Fourth of July politician, a bombastic and inflated bore.

The virtue of Saturnian Capricorn cures this with a cool stare. Life is to be conducted soberly, conscientiously, wisely, and in an organized and professionally capable way—with decorum, structure, and no nonsense. Anything else would be immature. Too much of this and you get a lugubrious, melancholy miser contemplating eschatology—Shylock, a King Lear, an Eeyore.

The cure is instant Aquarius. "Why not? Who says?" And all of Capricorn's careful limitations are broken through by the happy-go-lucky, rebellious, open-minded, tolerant, anything-goes, original nature of Uranus. This wide-ranging, philan-thropic, space-minded, future-oriented virtue carried to excess results in scorn for detail, callous detachment, in depersonaliza-tion, to say nothing of lack of intimacy with other people. The result is an idealist or an idealist fallen prey to his own ideal.

Pisces picks up the pieces tenderly, with care and tears of com-passion, self-sacrifice, and love. An excess of Pisces can result in sentimentality and martyrdom, self-pity. "Poor Pisces!" Weakness, helplessness, and wallowing ensue. The cure obviously is Aries.

These exaggerated and irreverent cartoons are only that. Each person is a unique variation of all these combinations and permutations. Psychologically, though, the potential for certain types of pathologies will naturally show up in the chart. By that I do not necessarily mean serious neuroses or hurtful complexes; obviously there is a range of gravity in every case. Sometimes life itself provides a cure.

One has to avoid generalities, but I know that you are eager to learn as much as possible about the skills involved in a psychological interpretation of a chart. I can only humbly offer what has worked for me. I try to place myself in a receptive state and allow the chart itself to speak. I pay attention to the images that arise from the placement of certain planets in certain signs. Naturally, I pay close attention to the Sun, Moon, and ascendant (rising sign). I also look closely at the First and Seventh Houses, because the Seventh House will give a clue to what one tends to project.

If the person has come in distress, which is often the case, I look carefully at the placement of Saturn and the aspects it makes. I also pay close attention to the transits of Saturn and the trans-Saturnian planets, i.e., the weather report. As you know from my letters on Saturn in *Jungian Symbolism in Astrology,* I do not believe Saturn is malefic; rather it points to the Shadow aspect of the psyche, which needs understanding and ultimately appreciation, if not love. We all tend to process Saturn as the cruel judge, but the same planetary archetype positively expressed becomes the Wise Old Man. It's as if the voice telling you why you can't do something, when confronted with "I know why I can't, but could you tell me how I *could?*" answers, "I've been waiting almost forty years for you to say that. Come along now and we'll work on this together!" Then the crabby unloved Shadow emerges from the cellar of the personal unconscious and releases the energy that Jung tells us a complex entraps.

But it hurts to confront one's Saturn and to acknowledge one's lacks. It means sacrificing the idea of blaming others or outer circumstances for one's pain, and integrating one's own ignorance, stupidity, ill will, or whatever the case may be. This can be a harrowing experience. The only comfort is that in the end the rewards are very great indeed. When one refuses this opus, the results, alas, are often psychosomatic, so it is also wise to know the body system governed by the sign holding a person's Saturn. By the same token, functional illnesses, as opposed to organic ones, are often relieved when a person deals with them metaphorically within the psyche. In general, the most difficult ones are afflictions in fixed signs. On the other hand, someone like Helen Keller is a beautiful example of the triumph of the human spirit over the worst of odds.

The following is a list of some basic needs or issues people may have to deal with when their Saturn is placed in a particular sign. However, there are no hard-and-fast rules.

- ♈ **Aries:** attention, narcissism
- ♉ **Taurus:** security, inflexibility
- ♊ **Gemini:** communication, comparisons, inner child
- ♋ **Cancer:** someone to nurture, loss, anxiety
- ♌ **Leo:** approval, authority, love, lack of love
- ♍ **Virgo:** perfection, righteousness
- ♎ **Libra:** relationships, poor image, injustice
- ♏ **Scorpio:** self-worth, suspicion, guilt
- ♐ **Sagittarius:** giving, pomposity, respect
- ♑ **Capricorn:** structure, fear, selfishness
- ♒ **Aquarius:** freedom, depersonalization
- ♓ **Pisces:** praise, insecurity, emotional expression, self-pity

You, and several others, have asked if there are astrological signatures to such things as paranoia, narcissism, perversion, violence, criminal tendencies, psychoses. The answer is yes, but it would be pointless to discuss them in a letter, because such indications in the chart do not necessarily manifest in these ways; they are not just simply acted out. In fact, these aspects may fuel creativity and have positive outcomes. It depends very much upon the level at which a person is living the chart and on how the individual has handled his or her experience. Not everyone with Saturn/Moon afflictions has a mother complex; not everyone with Sun/Neptune afflictions is an addict. *Always start with the individual, not the chart.* The therapist is tempted to label the patient and forget that the Divine Guest is in residence defying such limitations. Forgetting this is our professional Shadow, and every time we treat another person as an "it," we diminish not only him or her but ourselves. All pathology, without exception, ultimately must call forth compassion. Karma is a fact, simply cause and effect, not a moral judgment. My own experience of good therapy is that I have been helped most by those who have fanned the light within me, even though it was well obscured, and who helped remove some of the obstacles that I had carefully placed in my own way by my ignorance, rebelliousness or obstinacy.

I am reminded of a helpful image from my youth: the bottle game. I remember someone assembling a slalom course of bottles at a beer party and calling for a volunteer to thread her way through them without knocking one over. You were given three practice tries, and then you were taken out the door and blindfolded. When you reentered the room, you tried to repeat the feat, having memorized the course. To shouts of astonishment and whoops of praise, I myself managed with caution and brilliant memory to run all twelve of the bottles. There was wild applause. I tore off the blindfold, only to find not a single bottle in sight. They had all been removed before I came in! This is a good example of karma—we undertake the course of life convinced that it has been set up to entrap us, but we have entrapped ourselves.

Well, this has been a long letter, and I trust it has not been too confusing. It staggers the mind a bit to try to put so much in such few words. I always have confidence in you that your intuition will meet me halfway and that, as I go along, certain images will spring to mind. I hesitate to fill in too many, because that would be the cookbook approach. I hope always to stimulate you to becoming an analytical astrologer in your way, being true to your own psyche and its way of processing experience.

Does that make sense?

Love, always,

ao

ZENITH

NOON

MC

10 9

11 8

12 7
DAWN ASCENDANT DESCENDANT SUNSET
1 6

2 5

3 4

IC

MIDNIGHT

St. Columba
by Kathryn Smith

NADIR

The Houses of the Horoscope

—10—

THE HOUSES

Dear Friend,

I just received your question, *What, oh what, are houses?* I had hoped to save that question for another series of letters, but I realize that it would be unfair to leave such an important feature entirely out of this series.

The houses are the divisions you see when you look at any horoscope: the wheel with twelve sections into which the planets are placed. The houses themselves always remain stationary, since they are arbitrary divisions of space. Picture yourself standing outside with a full view in all directions. You could look to the farthest point on each horizon (east and west), then look straight up and straight down. These four points would remain the same at all times of the day, even though the sun, planets, and stars would continually shift their positions relative to them. In the same way, the houses always remain stationary in relation to the eastern and western horizons and the highest and lowest points in the sky (zenith and nadir), and to other coordinates as well.

Here are three important things to remember about houses:

1. *They stay put while the signs move through them clockwise every twenty-four hours.*

2. *The planets move counterclockwise through the signs.* This means simply that, for example, if the sun is in 11 degrees of

Taurus today, it will be on the cusp of the First House (ascendant) at dawn where you happen to be. It will be at the midheaven at noon at 11 degrees, 15 minutes (true local time, of course), will set at the cusp of the Seventh at 11 degrees, 30 minutes this evening, and will be at the nadir at approximately 11 degrees, 45 minutes by midnight. (Each degree in the zodiac is subdivided into 60 minutes, just like the hours of the day.) But when it rises tomorrow on the eastern horizon, it will have moved to 12 degrees of Taurus. It will take a year to make the complete cycle. The Moon, however, will zap through the twelve houses of your chart every month. Don't let this throw you; it will be clear as you work with more and more charts.

3. *Always remember that aspects are formed in the signs and not in the houses.* Confusing this is one of the most common mistakes made by any beginning student; this is why I keep reiterating the importance of memorizing the essentials.

The houses form the stage on which the drama of life unfolds. They answer the question, *Where?* Unlike the planets and signs and even our geocentric view of the precession of the equinoxes through the constellations—all of which are generated by the central position of the Sun—*the houses are defined by the earth alone.* There are different ways of calculating them, which makes things extremely confusing. As you go along you will find systems called Placidus, Koch, Equal House, Regiomontanus, etc., each using different coordinates. They all have one thing in common: the quaternity of the intersection of a vertical axis with a horizontal one. Each of the different systems has its own rationale and shows a slightly different picture of the psyche. They are like dialects of the same language; the words are the same, but they sure sound different in different places.

It is not my purpose in these letters to go into the technical reasons for the different systems; there are many good books that discuss them. So I will limit myself to explaining why I choose to use the Placidean system and what the houses can help reveal from the point of view of the analytical astrologer or the Jungian therapist. I prefer the Placidus system because it shows "intercepted signs." This means that the signs on the cusps, which are those spokes of the wheel, sometimes stretch over two cusps, owing to latitude or season. In such a case, a whole sign can be sandwiched between two others in a house, like this:

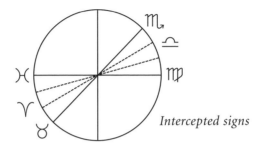

Intercepted signs

When this happens, the encapsulated sign does not "rule" or govern the external affairs of a house, since it does not touch a cusp. Therefore there is no "where" in the outer life for it to govern, and so the matters pertaining to those signs and the planets therein are kept within the psyche. Thus the person tends to lead a double life in that area—an outer one and an inner, secret one. It is like the lead hidden in a pencil or the ink within a pen, enclosed and only obliquely revealed to others. At the same time, the sign covering more than one cusp will have its ruler governing the affairs of more than one house, doing double duty, as it were.

Psychologically speaking, this seems significant to me, and I have always found it helpful in interpretations. The intercepted signs reveal the introverted attitude to the outer situation. Owing to the contradictory nature of the succession of signs, the introverted ones can set up quite a conflict of attitudes in matters governed by a given house.

For example, imagine a woman with gentle Pisces rising (i.e., Pisces on the cusp of the First House), whose persona is all kindness, pliancy, and compassion. Suppose that she has Mars and the Sun in Aries intercepted in the First House, and patient Taurus on the cusp of the Second. This can set up a tremendous conflict between the desire to flare up and out, in an Arian way, and never allowing herself to do so. Others perceive the woman as Piscean, and only she and her astrologer or therapist see the imprisoned and frustrated essence of Aries. If she is living this unconsciously, she will be in a constant state of frustrated resentment at always having to appear "nice," when she knows herself to be a seething wolf in sheep's clothing. She may well feel trapped in a sense of hypocrisy.

If one sign is intercepted, the opposite sign will be intercepted in the opposite house. In the case above, sensible Virgo will be on the cusp of the Seventh, and beauty-loving Libra will be imprisoned. So the potential for artistic gifts, joyous relationships, and such may all be shyly hidden away, while the woman lives a life of service to others, denying her own inner beauty and gifts. Clearly, her opus psychologically becomes liberating the totality of herself. The good news is that the potential is there; something is obviously present crying out for rescue and for a heroic (Aries) adventure in "coming out," in hatching those hidden gifts.

The X-ray of the Placidus system shows what could never be obvious from outer appearances. This is an opportunity for the astrologer or therapist to place the actual chart in front of the client and literally point to the planets imprisoned. They are there, right there, and this is what one needs to realize and to release. The effect can be quite astonishing.

Sometimes intercepted signs have no planets in them. In that case if, say, Leo was intercepted, you would look for the Sun and Uranus (ruler of Aquarius) in the chart.

If you follow this chapter, you will see the usual assignation of matters governed by the twelve houses. You will find that they correspond considerably to the signs and their rulers in the natural zodiac (Table A), just as your own real-life home reveals much about you to somebody who visits it in your absence. For instance, in my house, which is a warm and cozy place, there is one area that tends constantly to be overflowing with—guess what—books and papers. They tend to spread, innocuously at first, from my study into the living room, but then they crop up like mushrooms beside my bed, under my bed, and into the kitchen. What rules books and papers? Mercury. What rules expansion and overflowing? Jupiter. In my own chart they are conjunct. Since I have Sagittarius on the cusp of the Tenth House of profession, and Mercury is the ruler of the opposite sign, Gemini—which is on the cusp of the Fourth House of home—almost all of these books and papers are related to my work and interests in religion, mythology, philosophy, and other such subjects, or else they are connected to words, etymology, dictionaries. Snuck in between are the knitting booklets and cooking recipes, detective stories, and fiction that deals with foreign places. As you know, I was fortunate to have a very dear and patient husband with a high tolerance for literary endeavors. He had the Moon in Gemini.

From the Jungian perspective, the houses will show different nuances from those of the ordinary assignations, but you will see that they are related. For instance, the Second House, which rules our physical possessions, money, etc., in the psyche, relates to one's inner sense of value, one's feeling of self-worth. To have the Sun, Moon, or Saturn in the Second House will always raise questions involving these matters.

Over the years, I have observed certain things about the houses from experience, and yet I hesitate to make any firm and fast pronouncements about them. However, I can give you a little sampling:

First House. For me, this connects with Jung's concept of the persona, the mask or role we instinctively put on to deal with our outer environment. It shows how we tend to come across to others. Sometimes, as in the case of the Aries woman mentioned above, this can be misleading. Sometimes one has a clown persona who is laughing on the outside while the real person is crying on the inside. If, for instance, Saturn is conjunct the ascendant, there is much self-denial and disapproval. Whatever planet is in the First House will color the personality quite strongly, which may be a positive or negative factor in helping individuals express themselves completely. One of the most trying planets in the First House is Uranus, especially in one's childhood. It would be a boon and a help for parents to know that their child has this planet rising. Another difficult situation is Sun squaring the ascendant (cusp of the First House). These people feel that their exteriors and interiors just don't match, and they don't. Accepting this can be helpful. It doesn't have to be a handicap.

Second House. I have found that this has to do, as mentioned before, with inner security or sense of self-worth. You can see that, should this be miniscule, it might compound things in the outer life: a person who feels worthless has a problem in self-confidence in financial and other matters. The outer poverty such people fear may actually be an inner one.

Third House. To me, psychologically, this is the house of thought, the inner and outer communication of the psyche with its circumstances and the seemingly haphazard relationships within families, neighborhoods, etc. Its demon is doubt. Here Saturn (I mention Saturn not to single him out, but to point up the place where it pinches) will put a crimp in self-confidence in communicating, whether through the spoken or written word. Things build up in these people, but even when they are expressed the person is still dissatisfied. Obviously if Jupiter were posited there, it would be hard for the person to shut up, especially if Jupiter is in an air sign.

4

Fourth House. Psychologically, this house shows how we are within the privacy of our own psyches when we are all alone and not forced to relate to anybody. Someone once defined character as what we are when nobody else is looking. We tend either to enjoy our own company or to flee it. The opposite house, the Tenth, has to do with our self-image in the outer world of the public, so you could say the Fourth has to do with our self-image in the presence of God, where we come to rest within ourselves. The foundation of this is often based on the childhood experiences of mother and home. The cusp itself marks the nadir or lowest spot in the chart, but spiritually it is just the reverse. When we are most alone, we are least alone in the presence of the Ultimate.

5

Fifth House. This house is easy to understand. It is the natural home of Leo, the first trine in the fire signs, and so psychologically it has to do with our creativity, our will, our joy in giving ourselves to others—our self-expression. You can see that Sun, Moon, or Jupiter would facilitate this, and that Saturn might start out by telling us that whatever we create will never be good enough. The answer, of course, is that creativity moves through us—it is a divine process—and does not come out of us. The denial of creativity is at the heart of many a complex. Also, learning to let go of one's children or creative work—understanding that they must independently affect others without reflecting either glory or calumny upon their creator—that's another task!

Sixth House. Here a person is likely to define himself or herself almost exclusively in terms of work. An enormous amount of inner bookkeeping, brownie points, and weighing of souls takes place in this house. Tit for tat, giving to get, or guilt at owing, or just plain feeling overwhelmed by one's imperfections and all too keenly aware of those of others. This house often points to issues dealing with lack of forgiveness and dissatisfaction through over-comparing ourselves with others and through remorseless self-analysis. Such hidden miseries often manifest in health problems, many of which can be psychosomatic and therefore subject to healing through psychotherapy. Self-acceptance and above all a sense of humor can help.

Seventh House. I see this house, psychologically, as second in importance only to the First. It is the house of projection. Planets here describe what we admire or fear or envy or resent. In that way, it has much to do with either our dark Shadow or our light Shadow by which we project our positive values upon others in hero worship. It is also the house that points to what we long for the most and look for in others. Withdrawing these projections can be the work of a lifetime. The "ghostly lover," the supremely Beloved, dwells here for those with Neptune in the Seventh, or the ever-present "enemy" (Saturn) lurks, making one habitually defensive. Again, look to the planetary processes, always remembering that the chart only describes the way we are likely to process experience. I find two sayings helpful here: "it takes one to know one," and "it ain't necessarily so," depending on whether the projection is a positive or a negative one.

Eighth House. This is the house that Freud built—and Jung moved into. It governs our attitudes towards sexuality (*eros*) and death (*thanatos*); it shows our psychological ability to deal with the naked facts of life, the beauty and passion, the corruption and transformation of the corrupt. Here dwells the toilet bowl of the psyche, the place of confrontation of the personal unconscious and its guilts and shames. Shame can be an extremely helpful emotion. The good news is that consciousness of shame and the reasons for it can open the door to redemption. We cannot go up until we have touched bottom. It is curious how many "miracles" have occurred near festering and decomposing detritus, as we learn from the examples of Lourdes, Findhorn, the tales of Castaneda, and the Tantric practices of copulating or meditating in cremation grounds. It would seem that wherever things seem outwardly the most hopeless, there is where the redemption begins. This makes the Eighth House rich in meaning in terms of analysis and therapy.

Ninth House. This house reveals our philosophy of life, the basic premises we came in with and the capacity we have to further our dimensions of wisdom and religious expression. The signatures of Saturn and/or Uranus here, for instance, would show an enormous resistance to dogma per se, and yet a fascination with philosophy and the religious meaning of life. "The Hounds of Heaven" run here, and "O Love that will not let me go." Leo on the cusp of the Ninth or the Sun in the Ninth is the earmark of the priest or priestess, the monk or nun, the bodhisattva returned to serve humanity in some new way. Perhaps that is why so many of them are interested in "Jung" or the message he carried to this new age. I put quotation marks around his name because it is not just the man; it is the message that is flowing out, wider and wider, in directions he may or may not ever have imagined possible. He would loathe a cult in his name. "Thank God," he roared, "I am Jung and not a Jungian!" No, he counted on his message enabling us to be more readily who *we* are. I call that the Betty Crocker factor: you put in the eggs and milk and make it *your* cake!

Tenth House. Outwardly this shows one's profession, how we are seen by the general public, our reputation. Psychologically speaking, it shows our self-image and ability, or inability, to let go of it. This house points to where we are the most involved in the work of our incarnation and the most present in the world and preoccupied with its daily affairs. We may become famous or notorious or remain hidden and unknown; in any case, how we feel within ourselves about our achievements or their lack is shown here. Some of the most famous stars in the entertainment world, for example, have histories of dismal problems in the realm of relationships, drugs, alcohol, etc. Apparent success in the public eye, which is out of phase with their inner sense of failure, must cause them much suffering. Both Hitler and Mussolini had strong emphasis in their Tenth Houses, and both fell from great heights. It is a house loaded with paradox.

Eleventh House. This is the natural house of Aquarius and the psychological domain of our intentions and our ability to look to the future without getting lost in it. The lesson here is often that the ends do not justify the means because the means may create their own karma and end up somewhere else! So the wise balancing of means with ends becomes an important issue. "The way to hell is paved with good intentions." The ability or inability to survey and conceptualize is here, and the ability to plan intelligently. But also the Walter Mittys of this world find a home here. "I dwell in possibilities," to quote Emily Dickinson. This is a place for dreams of descent. The Eleventh House has much to do with committees, community, and politics. Can you see, for example, how having many planets in Virgo in this house might indicate a lifetime of community service or social welfare?

Twelfth House. This is the last house. If you remember that the signs move through the stationary houses, then you will realize that whatever sign or planets are in the Twelfth House will be the last to pass over the ascendant. So whatever is in this house will be what we come to as a last resort. If your Sun happens to be here, you will tend to be one of those people who says, "Who, me?"—the Piscean (twelfth sign) approach. If you have Mars there, the last thing you would want to do is fight. So psychologically speaking, whatever is in our Twelfth House will tend to be subliminal and difficult to access without real and conscious effort. It is so easy to forget our lost value, like money we hid away in a file, but which file? If you have difficult planets with difficult aspects in the Twelfth, chances are you will go around tugging your own portable cloud of doom. You cannot define it, yet you have a feeling of having to reckon with something, but what? The analyst with chart in hand can at least get an image of what it might be. I call this a "Cain complex."

This is also the house of gifts from the unconscious, the house of dreams, also of inspiration, the very source of invisible strength to the persona and one's sense of individuality. In therapeutic terms, the best way of getting to the contents of the Twelfth is through bypassing the conscious mind and letting whatever comes appear spontaneously in artwork, poetry, dance, sand play, improvisation, or active imagination. After the material has precipitated into the light, it is helpful to analyze or observe what came up. Over seventy years ago Jung worked with various techniques which he first applied to himself and then to his patients. He set the stage for some of the therapies which abound today: sand play, dance therapy, guided music imagery, and so forth. The famous Rorschach test would be another device. They all have in common the possibility of observing projections in action at any given moment. And this is what a chart can reveal.

I have written you before that I believe analytical astrology, like analysis, should best be practiced in the presence of the person involved, because we never know at what level the chart is being lived. In most cases, we are given the option of voluntarily working out a problem within our own psyches, in which case we do not have to inflict it outwardly upon others or act it out as "fate" in the metaphors of outer life. The great danger today, one that fills our headlines, is that the great majority of people are living out unconscious lives and drives, motivated more often than not by the values and delusions (Neptune) of what is supposed to be entertainment on television. As a society we seem unable to connect cause and effect, having perhaps ourselves grown up with the sensible notion that drama and detective stories provide a natural alternative and outlet for morbid fantasies. Astrology teaches us that anything Neptunian bypasses the conscious mind (ego) and goes straight to untamed and chaotic sources in the unconscious, and unleashes them. Instead of coming out in ordered beauty or fantasized terror, these dark urges are being acted out in blood, murder, death, drugs, and shootings that often have no basis in conscious intention. It is a madness seemingly as irrational as the frenzies and orgies of ancient history.

So far we are learning to cope better with Uranus, the first trans-Saturnian planet discovered. But Neptune and Pluto are still defying us and, until understood, will continue to confront us with processes which we are far from mastering. (But then Pluto has not made a full orbit since its discovery.) The message of the Twelfth House is that archetypal forces can be redeemed by us through our living, our art, and by the constant conversion of the inchoate, with the help of individual consciousness (First House), into creative order. The alternative is with us every day. The tragedy is the waste, the terrible waste of the privilege of consciousness and human incarnation, the simple dignity of the human condition. Neptune positive is the mystic, but when negative gives us the fanatic fundamentalist of any stripe. When Neptune was transiting Virgo, it produced the Granola generation with a whole new and healthy attention to proper and natural foods. However, a friend of mine with Neptune in Virgo rising tried to regiment and control her family so fanatically, they resorted to cheating whenever they left the house!

Well, we sure live in parlous times! Keep safe and well in whichever house feels best tonight.

Ever my love,

ao

TABLES

St. Columba
by Kathryn Smith

The Natural Zodiac

TABLE B: The Planets

Glyph	Name	Rules	Glyph	Detriment	Glyph	Exalted	Glyph	Fall	Glyph	Positive Archetypes	Negative Archetypes
☉	Sun	Leo	♌	Aquarius	♒	Aries	♈	Libra	♎	Father God Ruler, solar house	Tyrant
☽	Moon	Cancer	♋	Capricorn	♑	Taurus	♉	Scorpio	♏	Mother Goddess	Devouring Mother Witch
☿	Mercury	Gemini Virgo	♊ ♍	Sagittarius Pisces	♐ ♓	Virgo	♍	Pisces	♓	Divine Child, Messenger, Psychopomp	Trickster Demon
♀	Venus	Taurus Libra	♉ ♎	Scorpio Aries	♏ ♈	Pisces	♓	Virgo	♍	Love goddess Maiden, daughter	Seductress Siren
⊕	Earth									Mother Nature Body of Sophia	"Matter" only
♂	Mars	Aries Scorpio	♈ ♏	Libra Taurus	♎ ♉	Capricorn	♑	Cancer	♋	Mortal hero knight, son	traitor killer
♃	Jupiter	Sagittarius	♐	Gemini	♊	Cancer	♋	Capricorn	♑	teacher preacher	bombast glutton
♄	Saturn	Capricorn	♑	Cancer	♋	Libra	♎	Aries	♈	Wise Old Man Just judge	Cruel judge critic, Death
♅	Uranus	Aquarius	♒	Leo	♌	Scorpio	♏	Taurus	♉	Liberator Inventor	Mad Scientist Wizard
♆	Neptune	Pisces	♓	Virgo	♍	Leo	♌	Aquarius	♒	Mystic Sage	Drunkard Deluder
♇	Pluto	Scorpio	♏	Taurus	♉					Redeemer	Macabre Darth Vader

N.B. The Sun is a star, not a planet.
The Moon is a satellite of this Earth.

The asteroids are associated now with ♍

⚷ Chiron is a new body being studied, perhaps a comet.

TABLE C: The Astrological Signs

#	Glyph	Name	Quality	Element	Ruler	Old Ruler	Animal Symbol	Body	Saying	Process
1	♈	Aries	Cardinal	Fire	♂		Ram	Head	I am	Igniting, beginning, pioneering
2	♉	Taurus	Fixed	Earth	♀		Bull	Neck	I have	Forming, stabilizing, conserving
3	♊	Gemini	Mutable	Air	☿		Twins	Brain, nerves Hands	I communicate	Connecting, communicating
4	♋	Cancer	Cardinal	Water	☽		Crab	Stomach	I care	Digesting, nourishing, mothering
5	♌	Leo	Fixed	Fire	☉		Lion	Heart, back	I rule	Creating, life-giving dramatizing
6	♍	Virgo	Mutable	Earth	☿		Virgin	Intestines	I analyze	Granulating, analyzing, ordering
7	♎	Libra	Cardinal	Air	♀		Scales	Kidneys	I relate	Relating, justifying, harmonizing
8	♏	Scorpio	Fixed	Water	♇	♂	Scorpion	Genitals	I desire	Intensifying, transforming
9	♐	Sagittarius	Mutable	Fire	♃		Archer	Thighs	I teach	Expanding, sharing, benefiting
10	♑	Capricorn	Cardinal	Earth	♄		Seagoat	Bones, knees	I structure	Manifesting, structuring, achieving
11	♒	Aquarius	Fixed	Air	♅	♄	Water-Bearer	Circulation Ankles	I plan	Challenging, exploring, planning
12	♓	Pisces	Mutable	Water	♆	♃	Fishes	Feet	I synthesize	Dissolving, synthesizing, releasing

TABLE D: Fixed, Cardinal, Mutable Signs

The Fixed Signs

The Cardinal Signs

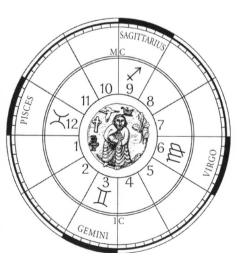

The Mutable Signs

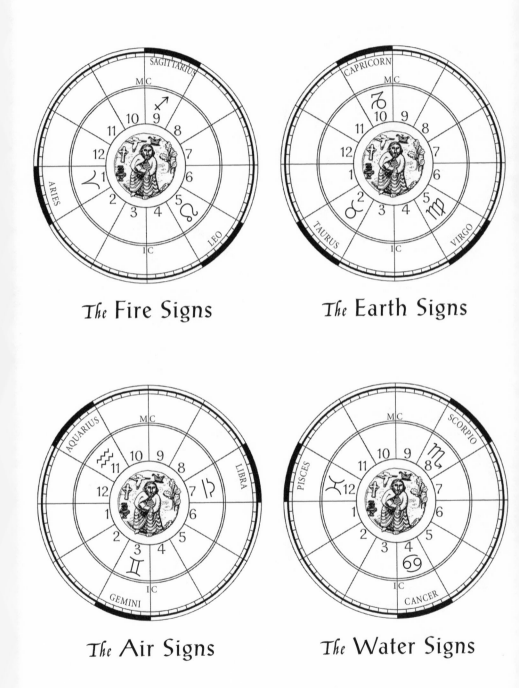

The Fire Signs

The Earth Signs

The Air Signs

The Water Signs

PART TWO

THE ASTROLOGICAL AGES

The individualized conscious man of our era is a late man, whose structure is built on early, pre-individual human stages from which individual consciousness has only detached itself step by step.

The evolution of consciousness by stages is as much a collective human phenomenon as a particular individual phenomenon. Ontogenetic development may therefore be regarded as a modified recapitulation of phylogenetic development.

This interdependence of collective and individual has two psychic concomitants. On the one hand, the early history of the collective is determined by inner primordial images whose projections appear outside as powerful factors — gods, spirits, or demons — which become objects of worship. On the other hand, man's collective symbolisms also appear in the individual, and the psychic development, or misdevelopment, of each individual is governed by the same primordial images which determine man's collective history.

—ERICH NEUMANN
The Origins and History of Consciousness

Behind every civilization is a vision.
—CHRISTOPHER DAWSON

In each age of the world distinguished by high activity, there will be found at its culmination some profound cosmological outlook, implicitly accepted, impressing its own type on the current springs of action.
—ALFRED NORTH WHITEHEAD

11

THE EVOLUTION OF
CONSCIOUSNESS THROUGH
THE ASTROLOGICAL AGES

Dear Friend,

We come now to a very exciting application of astrology, one I hinted at in my first letter to you. It has to do with human history and has enormous implications for us collectively as we move so precariously into what is termed the "New Age." It really does appear that creation from the beginning has had a discernible plan, and that at last, because of the new consciousness of the Aquarian Age, we are being given the opportunity to become aware of this—to see a glimpse of what this means so that we can cooperate more fully on the tasks of this age to come. This has never happened before. Never have so many been collectively *conscious* of the onset of a new eon. The enormity of this staggers the mind.

Before beginning, however, I would like to clarify two things:

1. The dating of the astrological Ages has been extremely confusing to many astrologers. The reason for this is the amount of empty space between the visible constellations in the sidereal zodiac, resulting in interfaces of several hundreds of years. If I could make an analogy, the problem is akin to determining the beginning and the end of a large but discernible wave in the middle of the

ocean. You can feel it gathering, you can see it crest and break, and you can feel the energy spending itself and intermingling with the next surge. But I think you would agree that determining the very moment such a wave begins is virtually impossible. For this reason, do not take my dates or anyone else's too literally. *What is of paramount importance is the sequence of development.*

2. You will notice that the sequence of the Ages runs in the *opposite* direction from that of the natural or tropical zodiac. The sequence of the equinoxes seems to apply to humanity at a collective level, while the forward one—Aries-Taurus-Gemini, etc.—applies to us as individuals in our personal lives.

The evolutionary sequence of the Ages repeats itself in the growth and development of every individual psyche, as well, and it is equally variable and subtle. Lest this seem confusing, let me use the analogy of our physical species. All humans have a common pattern of physical growth. We are born as babies, grow baby teeth, lose them, grow another set; all of us progress through puberty and on to physical maturity, slowly age, and finally die. This is the norm, no matter what continent we live on, what color our skin, or what race we belong to. However, there will be many, many variations on that general theme. So the sequence of the Ages would seem to pertain to the collective pattern of evolution of the collective psyche.

These Ages are of importance to psychotherapy, I believe, because some of us get stuck in one of the stages, for example identification with the ego (Age of Aries). Having such a cosmic paradigm in history, we can look up to the stars and see what came before, what is now, what comes next, and how and why. What is true so far out is also true for us far in. We are not without guidance, but it behooves us to look for it. As Jung has pointed out, the collective unconscious is always there, ready to heal us. But we need to deal with the bugaboos of our personal unconscious first, with the help of our ego as center of consciousness. And for this, we had to develop an ego in the first place.

So as we proceed, I beg you to keep the two cautionary

concepts that follow with you every step of the way. It is a matter of flow, rather than precision. We are watching the great river of time itself, winding in majestic cycles and carrying us along in a paradox where both linear motion and synchronicity are true at one and the same time. As with a record on a turntable, the needle is in one spot only, and yet the totality of the record lies before us.

Exploring all this requires a modicum of understanding in four areas: (1) the astronomical feature known as the Precession of the Equinoxes; (2) Jung's concepts of synchronicity and the collective unconscious, which he also called the "objective psyche"; (3) history and mythology, and a willingness to research them; (4) astrology used as a key to decoding the symbolic language of archetypal processes. That's not much to ask!

The hypothesis goes as follows: *There appears to be an objectively observable coincidence between the nature of the symbols for the constellations in the sidereal zodiac and the religious, mythic, and psychological development of humanity.* There is an observable evolution of the collective unconscious which synchronizes with the sequence of Ages named for the constellations hosting the point of the vernal equinox. Each constellation in turn hosts the point of the vernal equinox and gives its name to that Age; and each Age coincides, seemingly universally, with a religious mythos whose symbols reflect precisely its nature at the collective level, and also in a psychological development that is repeated in every individual to this very day.

To fully understand this, it might be wise to stop here and review a few pertinent definitions. This may seem a bit like school to you, but it is vital to get it straight before we go on.

What is meant by the constellations?

The twelve constellations of *visible* stars make up the circle of the *sidereal* (from the Latin *sidus*, "star") zodiac as seen from the Earth. These constellations are given the names of Aries, Taurus, etc., and they vary in width. They are like the fixed rim of a vault lock within which the dial of the *tropical* zodiac turns.

What is the tropical zodiac?

It is the ecliptic or apparent path of the sun, which is *invisible*. This *conceptual* circle is divided into twelve equal segments of 30 degrees each, called signs. They are named Aries, Taurus, etc., like the constellations. This tropical zodiac is commonly used by Western astrologers to set up individual charts or horoscopes. It is geocentric, earth-centered, since we live on the Earth. Astronomers today use a heliocentric, sun-centered zodiac, the sidereal one. Ignorance of the significance of the difference between the two causes much confusion. Scientists point to the discrepancy between the two zodiacs, not seeing that the very discrepancy is part of the greater plan and that it is the interaction of the tropical and sidereal zodiacs that determines these Ages.

What is the Point of the Vernal Equinox?

Imagine a great circle surrounding the equator out in space called "the celestial equator." Imagine another circle out in space, at an angle to the first one, that is traversed by the sun each day as it appears to move around the Earth (this one is called "the ecliptic"). The equinoxes are the two points where these circles intersect. This occurs twice a year, at the first day of spring (the vernal equinox—0 degrees of Aries) and the first day of fall (the autumnal equinox—0 degrees of Libra). The Point of the Vernal Equinox is a term for 0 degrees of Aries in the tropical zodiac.

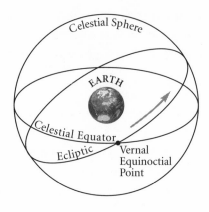

What is the Precession of the equinoxes?

The equinoxes slowly circle westward at the rate of 1 degree every 72 years. The moment of spring (0 degrees of Aries) occurs just a tad earlier each year (owing to a wobble in the Earth's axis), so that over the years the equinoxes appear to move backwards (clockwise) against the backdrop of the constellations. This is an *astronomical* fact. This clockwise movement is in contrast to the motion of the sun and planets, which go forward along the tropical zodiac of signs. Thus you have the wheel of signs containing the sun and the planets turning within the fixed wheel of the constellations—a wheel within a wheel (Ezekiel!). The precession of the equinoxes results in the Great or Platonic Year of 26,000 years (25,920 to be more exact), in which the Point of the Vernal Equinox (like an hour hand on a dock) makes a complete cycle around the sidereal zodiac.

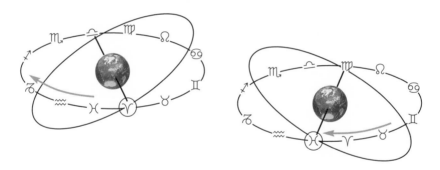

Since this is a highly complex matter, I suggest you read further in an encyclopedia. The easiest definition I have come across is: the precession of the equinoxes is the clockwise march of the intersections (equinoxes) of the ecliptic and the celestial equator around the sidereal zodiac of the constellations.

What is an astrological Age?

It is a varying period, a Platonic month, of roughly 2000+/- years (with a generous interface of several centuries to be considered), named for whichever constellation is hosting the Point of the Vernal Equinox. An example is the Age of Taurus. This phenomenon was discovered, *mirabile dictu*, by Hipparchus on the isle of Rhodes, around 200 B.C. (Hipparchus should be acclaimed as well for devising the system of lines of latitude and longitude; he also invented trigonometry and compiled the first list of chords. Quite a guy!)

What is Jung's theory of the collective unconscious?

This was Jung's concept of the transpersonal aspect of the human psyche common to all individuals in the space-time continuum; the common underground water table feeding all our wells, as the writer Ira Progoff puts it. It contains the archetypal images and motifs projected collectively in myth and symbol and unites us universally in the human condition. I believe astrology reveals that it is not static but discernibly evolving.

What is Jung's theory of synchronicity?

It is Jung's concept of acausal coincidences which take place simultaneously within the psyche and outwardly in the world. Since "neither can be explained by causality, it seems to be connected primarily with activated archetypal processes in the unconscious" (Jung). An example would be in the story of the analyst and the Tibetan master I told in chapter 7.

This concept of synchronicity, in contrast to our perception of linear time, dissolves the concretist fallacy of stellar "influence" on us. A does not cause A^1; rather A and A^1 are moving in unison, visible and invisible, as one. Whenever we perceive this apparent duality as one, we momentarily enter the *unus mundus*. This is probably the best explanation that we can come up with for the fact that astrology works through synchronicity. Like mathematics and geometry, astrology is inherent and discernible, a "just so," a given, built into this universe. And like mathematics, geometry, and music, it is human consciousness that has revealed it to us—the great wonder is mirrored by humankind. It is also interesting to note that all of these disciplines have measurement and vibration in common, and all are attributed to the feminine as part of the archetype of Holy Wisdom or Sophia. (She goes by many other names, of course.) In fact, in some enlarged decks of the Tarot created during the Renaissance, Geometry, Astronomy, and Mathematics appear as divine archetypes in their own right, like the Muses. Our words "mind" and "mental" go back through Latin to an Indo-European root connected to "moon" and "month," and to measurement.

Just about everybody has heard the expression "the New Age," and some are sick of it and think it's passé. But it isn't; it's just barely dawning, and we have two millennia more awaiting us. In the meantime, we can look at past Ages and learn a lot from them, not only about the synchronicity of myths and symbols, but also about the evolution of human consciousness and the human psyche.

The last time we entered a new Age was around the time of the birth of Jesus. By then, Hipparchus' discovery of the precession of the equinoxes must have been known by a few astronomers and educated people. It is even possible that the Apostle Paul knew of it. In his letter to the Ephesians he wrote:

> If ye have heard of the dispensation of the grace of God which is given me to youward:
> How that by revelation he made known unto me the mystery...
> Which in other ages was not made known unto the sons of men, as it is now revealed unto his holy apostles and prophets by the spirit;
> That the Gentiles should be fellow heirs...
> (Eph. 3:2–3, 5–6).

And elsewhere he wrote: "Old things are passed away; behold, all things are become new" (2 Cor. 5:17).

Since they were prior to Hipparchus, there is so far no way of knowing if the Chaldeans and Egyptians knew of the Ages. There is speculation that the ancient Egyptians might have known about them, since the number 25,920 appears in the measurement of the Great Pyramid. But as yet no definite proof exists beyond the indisputable fact that Egyptian symbols show each of the shifts from the Age of Gemini through the Ages of Taurus and Aries in their cosmogony, mythology, and architecture.

In any case—and this is the point—it is remarkable that these astronomical synchronicities occur in history with an almost symphonic regularity. As far as I know, no one with a celestial whistle blew it on a certain day and said, "Now this myth is out and this one is in." It just seems to have happened at the level of the collective unconscious, mysteriously and spontaneously, of its own accord.

Lest we think this is all theory, it might be well to remember how Jung first came upon the idea of the collective unconscious. He tells the story in his autobiography, *Memories, Dreams, Reflections*. There he relates a remarkable dream of descending through layer after layer of civilizations beneath his own house, until at the very lowest level he came upon two primitive skulls in a cave. Later he had some unusual patients, in particular a Swiss man in a mental hospital who kept pulling Jung to the window to see the sun moving this way and that. And the patient described the phallus of the sun and spoke of a solar wind. It reminded Jung of a passage he had read in a liturgy of Mithraism, an ancient mystery religion, which spoke of "the origin of the ministering wind" as something "hanging down from the disc of the sun . . . that looks like a tube." How could this patient, "a small business employee with no more than a secondary school education," have known this? It set Jung to thinking.

Dr. Stanislav Grof's book *Realms of the Human Unconscious* is filled with further objective proof of our access to this collective level of the unconscious. It seems we haven't even begun to appreciate the contents of our own psyches. Now more serious attention is being given to the phenomenon of past-life regressions under hypnosis. I believe that Jung himself was convinced of reincarnation, but as a scientist he would probably have restricted himself to saying only that anything emerging spontaneously from the human psyche deserves attention and study. Speaking for myself, I think one can better trust what comes out of one's own unconscious on these matters than what someone else tells us. Charlatans or well-intentioned psychics are all too ready to tell you who you were, which is not quite the same thing. Some may be right, but others may not be. It has to ring true or else be viewed as a metaphor. There is nothing wrong with skepticism combined with a truly open mind! Grof's work with holotropic breathing, which I personally witnessed at Esalen, has provided some profound insights, and Roger Woolger, the Jungian analyst, has been a pioneer in applied past-life regression.

Jung has suggested that, as soon as we make a conscious effort to deal with our personal unconscious and its suppressed or repressed and forgotten contents, the transpersonal level of the collective unconscious rises up to meet us, offering healing. It makes a reality out of the poetic phrase "God's everlasting arms," and it surely has something in common with the "akashic records" of Hinduism. The collective unconscious is a beautiful concept, because it works the other way, too. This means that absolutely nobody lives and dies without adding his or her two bits to the collective ocean of wisdom. And if you see it this way, it shows yet another purpose in everyone's uniqueness—our specific gift to the collective. Nobody else has lived our memories or seen life exactly through our two eyes. *Each of us, therefore, matters to all of us.*

Before going any further, I would like to say that this subject of the Ages is so vast that one could spend a lifetime researching and developing the concept. It is my greatest hope that sometime soon somebody will undertake this work in a systematic and scholarly way. To compress all of the history of religion in the last 12,000 years into a few letters is more than I can or hope to do! The life's work of Arnold Toynbee, Mircea Eliade, and Joseph Campbell could be studied to great advantage here, and I will attempt a bibliography for you if you are interested. The only thing that I feel competent to contribute is some sweeping strokes that hint at and describe what *could* be done. What is of particular interest to me are the implications of that sequence of psychological evolution that occurs collectively, to which I just referred, and which is repeated in us as individuals. This is a concept beautifully unfolded by Erich Neumann in two of his books, *The History and Origins of Consciousness* and *The Great Mother*, though the connection to astrology is not made.

It is also important to remember that a generous number of years, several hundred in fact, constitute the interfaces of the Ages, and it is virtually impossible to pinpoint a given moment for the beginning of any new Age. Nevertheless, one can recognize, in outer symptoms and manifestations, definite shifts in the collective consciousness of a period. I say *consciousness* here rather than *unconscious* because what is conscious in one Age will enter the collective unconscious of the following one, just as on the personal level there is a certain transmission of the psychic content of parents to the unconscious of their children (Grof). This is also seen in the way the inner child lives on in the old man and woman. I can vouch for that!

Since we have to begin somewhere, I will start with the Age of Cancer (c. 8000–c. 6500 B.C.). You may well ask why. It is simply because this is a prehistoric age from which a great many archaeological artifacts survive. It is contiguous with the Age of Gemini, at the end of which writing was developed and true history began. It also appears to mark a new wave of human evolution.

Today primitive people and aborigines are living in a world in which we have landed men upon the moon and unlocked the secrets of nuclear energy. It is possible that other sophisticated civilizations have come and gone, alongside primitive people, leaving behind only the barest hints in tradition and mythology and some exceedingly tough archaeological riddles which refuse to go away or yield an explanation. For instance, there are the enormous groundworks whose beauty and complexity can only be appreciated from the air: the Glastonbury zodiac, Stonehenge and Callanish in the Scottish Hebrides, the Nazca patterns in Peru, and of course the Great Pyramid at Gizeh, all of which point to a sophisticated knowledge of astronomy and construction, skills which are in no way commensurate with the general ideas of conservative historians. In fact, these constructions are an embarrassment to historians. There are many theories, some of which have been ridiculed and rejected, such as those concerning Atlantis or the Hyperboreans. Yet little by little, as science with its instruments of measurement catches up, these ideas resurface and require a closer look. The work of John Michell and the late Dr. Alexander Thom, both acknowledged scholars, simply cannot be brushed aside. My own feeling is that we need to keep that open mind and the crap-detector handy and always discriminate between what can be proved and what is still a matter of speculation. But we need to speculate more, because the discrepancies and unanswered evidence are requiring it. We need a "new history" as much as a "new science."

Let me share a tidbit as an example of what I mean. Back in the days of my studies with Hermes and M, I had occasion to go into a bookstore in New York, where I found a very small green pamphlet written by a Mrs. Maltwood. It told of her experience at Glastonbury in 1922, when she was doing research on the legend of King Arthur and his Round Table. She went up onto the high mound of Glastonbury Tor and gazed off into the distance. She thought she saw something extraordinary: the outline of a great figure in the earth. So intrigued was she that some time later she managed to have aerial photographs taken. To her amazement, despite the encroachment of the town, she found a huge circle, three miles in diameter, containing the discernible outlines of the twelve figures of the zodiac!

I filed this information in the back of my mind with interest. Twenty-five years later, I happened to be at Blackwell's bookstore in Oxford and was drawn to a bottom shelf where I found a bright yellow pamphlet on the Glastonbury zodiac. This one contained aerial photographs and more. It seems that instead of a crab for Cancer, there was a dog (dogs are ruled by Cancer). The photograph shows the clear outline of the dog's head and particularly its ear. The account goes on to say that the small triangular lake forming the ear was called "Earlake," but nobody really knew why. Furthermore, in the area where the figure of Virgo is stretched out, there is a place where traditionally over the centuries little biscuits and cakes were thrown for good luck (Virgo happens to rule all grains). Then, a few years ago, I read in *Time* magazine that the diaries of John Dee had been published. Dee was an alchemist and astrologer to Queen Elizabeth I. He was very much interested in the occult and studied with a mysterious Edward Kelly, also an alchemist. In his journal Dee writes that on a certain day he was initiated into a great secret: that the Round Table of King Arthur was laid out in the earth at Glastonbury!

Since this disclosure, Mrs. Maltwood's discovery, which as you can imagine earned short shrift at the time, has been the topic of serious research. The latest findings suggest that the legend of King Arthur may be the remnant of a very ancient myth involving the shift of the polar star. The name "Arthur" comes from the word for "bear," and so this may be an astronomical myth reaching far back into what we think of as prehistory. The fact remains that the circle can only be seen *in toto* from the air, just as the churches in France forming the constellation of Virgo can only really be spotted from the air or on a map. If you are interested in this sort of thing. I really recommend Francis Hitching's book *Earth Magic*, and the work of Keith Critchlow and John Michell. The latter are pioneers in the field.

In addition, in Britain researchers continue to study ley lines, the straight tracks linking ancient standing stones, churches built on pagan sites, market crosses, etc., crisscrossing Britain for miles and miles. Where two or more of these lines intersect, bigger stones or churches stand. You need only an ordnance map and a straight edge to find them for yourself. Many of the early medieval churches standing on these sites have a dragon carved on them. Could these indicate that the ancients thought these were special lines marking telluric (earth) energies? I have been in quite a few of these rather decrepit, neglected, and largely poorly attended little churches. I wonder what might happen if the local populace got word that attending their churches might cause them to be zapped by some extraordinarily fine energy! It might turn us all into believers on a different level. Gradually the idea of "power points" and energy centers is growing. What excites me is that scientists are becoming intrigued, not just psychics or people who are dismissed as crackpots. (Of course, astrologers often come under that heading as well.)

Much of this is just plain fun to consider. But underneath it all is the idea, which is gaining momentum yearly, that historians down through the ages have been highly selective in their reports. One cannot help suspecting that much information has been suppressed or altered. Could it be that from time to time true history was imparted only secretly from mouth to ear, out of mortal fear of persecution and death? One of the hopeful developments coming with the Age of Aquarius—a sign, by the way, known for its tolerance—will be a total reexamination and understanding of such material. It all needs demystification and fresh interpretation. Much in the descriptions of early Britain is based on Julius Caesar's impressions of Britons and Picts as uncivilized, ignorant, wild men. Perhaps, ahem, given the circumstances (he tried to invade the island, unsuccessfully), he did not get invited to meet the right people!

I hope that some of these ideas will intrigue you, as they do me. It's a great world, come to think of it!

With much love,

ao

*A recognition of the mystery of death,
and therewith, of life, marks the spiritual
separation of man from the beasts.*
—JOSEPH CAMPBELL
*Mythologies of the Primitive
Hunters and Gatherers*

*Yet not to thine eternal resting-place
Shalt thou retire alone, nor couldst thou wish
Couch more magnificent. Thou shalt lie down
With patriarchs of the infant world—with kings,
The powerful of the earth—the wise, the good,
Fair forms and hoary seers of ages past,
All in one mighty sepulchre. The hills
Rock-ribbed and ancient as the sun,—the vales
Stretching in pensive quietness between;
The venerable woods—rivers that move
In majesty, and the complaining brooks
That make the meadows green; and, poured round all,
Old Ocean's grey and melancholy waste—
Are but the solemn decorations all
Of the great tomb of man.*
—WILLIAM CULLEN BRYANT
"Thanatopsis"

—12—

LOVE AND FEAR
The Age of Cancer
(8000–6500 B.C. with generous interfaces)

Dear Friend,

W ell, here goes! I'll start this "lesson" with the traditional associations to the sign of Cancer:

- Its glyph is ♋, representing the claws of a crab or the
  breasts of a woman.

- It is a cardinal water sign, ruled by the Moon, and associated
  with the archetype of the Great Mother and the process of
  bearing, birthing, nurturing, protecting.

- It is yin and in the world rules containers, such as pottery
  and houses, whose function is Cancer's, while the materials
  are Capricorn's. This is a good example of polarity.

- Its opposite sign, Capricorn, ♑, is ruled by Saturn, and this
  is the sign ruling stones, skeletons, and all materials that
  outlast their inhabitants, such as shells, bones, teeth, graves,
  caves, and the basic material "stuff" of the world. It also
  rules archaeology and the passing and measurement of
  linear time. To look at any book on prehistoric times is to
  look straight at Capricorn. Not only is such a book full of

illustrations of bones, stone tools, caves, and arrowheads; but, history itself is ruled by Saturn, whose Greek name, *Kronos*, is close to *chronos*, "time," which gives us the word and concept of *chronology*.

According to most historians, the world that they describe in and around 8000 B.C. was in a Neolithic (late Stone Age) period. The artifacts found in Anatolia, the Near East, and Europe point to an almost universal worship of the Great Mother. Oddly enough, one of the most famous artifacts, the Venus of Willendorf, dates back to the *previous* Age of Cancer. But this more recent Age has provided us with evidence that, in all probability, people gathered together and formed a group soul, and there was hardly any individual self-consciousness. This is what Neumann equates with the "uroboric" phase in an infant as well, when such awareness as there is comes and goes, and the consciousness of the infant, like that of the collective primitive, is largely fused with that of the mother and with the environment, in what anthropologists call a *"participation mystique."* Neumann used the symbol of the uroboros, the serpent swallowing its own tail, as an example of a kind of uterine paradisiacal space that is enclosed upon itself like the Garden of Eden.

The great motif of the Age was that of womb and tomb, both symbolized by the vagina of Mother Earth, who gives birth to and takes back into herself the bodies of her children. At this period of history, anthropologists maintain, men probably did not know their role in procreation, so that the appearance of new little people out of the vaginas of women put them in special awe of the feminine. I should add that I think it still does, and not only men. As my own mother put it, "It's a good thing that my body knew what to do—why, I can't even make a decent cookie come out right!"

My own conscious experience of giving birth was of being seized by a power so much greater than my own that I could only witness it in astonishment. And being present at a death, I had the same sense of a great curtain of time sweeping inexorably through the room. Both experiences envelop the greatest paradox of majestic enormity and utter simplicity. At the one end, suddenly there on the bed is a wee, mewling miracle, all equipped with little eyes, eyelashes, and tiny, shell-like fingernails. I remember marveling that I, a woman, could somehow produce a son, so *other* in gender. The miracle of birth must always have evoked amazement that something that wasn't suddenly is; and at death, that something that was, isn't. From the physical standpoint, it seems so mysterious, yet so simple.

Artifacts from the Age of Cancer depict the feminine figure almost exclusively. There are many, many touching figurines, clumsily carved and out of proportion, and yet with a singular beauty, which perhaps contemporary art has helped us to appreciate. Like the sign of Cancer, they are mute and do not give us their names. But they speak, out of their breasts and incised vulvas and heavy hips, of the veneration for what they stand for: Mother Goddess. Sometimes she is enthroned and guarded by lions or cats, which hint perhaps at the previous Age of Leo, and sometimes her body is incised with depictions of animals, plants, and birds, frequently vultures (Capricorn).

It is clear that she was worshipped, and it is probable that in certain parts of the world this involved cannibalistic rites (Cancer). The good and life-giving Mother is also the devouring and chthonic one. Her archetype lives on today in Kali, the black Mother Goddess of India. Her feast day of Kalidurga is still celebrated with bloody animal sacrifice. I will never forget being in Kashmir on that day and seeing a man and a woman on either side of a huge goat, all in the back seat of a taxi on the way to the celebration. Psychologically, the Mother still remains a highly ambivalent figure today. Jung himself said of his own mother that he loved her by day and feared her by night. And since we live in a country (U.S.A.) ruled by Cancer, "Mom" is an extremely important figure, along with our mandala—apple pie. Yet as a Cancer nation, we send "care packages" to the world, feeding the hungry and restoring even our enemies, much as a mother would comfort a child after it has been punished enough.

During the Stone Age, burying corpses in the fetal position after sprinkling them with ochre was another hint at the concept of going back to the Mother Earth's womb. It shows evidence of a religious rite and an awareness of death, by setting the dead apart from the living. Animals do not dig graves. Whatever the rites and mythologies of that period, we know that they were basic—and lorded over by a dark, brooding, omnipotent, and definitely terrifying Mother Goddess; no sweet virgin here. From a psychological point of view, this awesome archetypal figure lurks in all of us in our unconscious collectively as uncontrollable Mother Nature, nurturing and life-giving on the one hand, and the Witch or the life-denying, death-dealing Mother, on the other. Later this complex archetype developed into a triplicity: Maiden, Mother, Crone, and into the three Graces or three Fates, the three Norns, and the 3 x 3 of the nine Muses, the nine Valkyries, and the number 9 being sacred to the feminine in Native American symbolism and in other traditions as well. It still takes nine moons to gestate a child.

As I have mentioned before, Cancer stands astrologically at the crossroads of the cardinal quaternity of signs, and it is the hero's task (Mars, ruler of Aries) to get past her. All the male puberty rites in the world have that one aim in common. If we today were wiser, we would see that there is still an underlying need for this ritual; its lack results in those street gangs where young males band together toting their death-dealing phallic guns. Primitive people are infinitely wiser, because with them it is the elders who initiate boys and guide them into bonding with the social structure of the tribe. With us, sports are an alternative, where Chiron is the coach (Jupiter's process): psychologically a highly important figure. But the kids in gangs have only their peers to look to; they have to invent their own initiatory rites, which all too often involve drugs, death, and destruction. Puberty rites surface more benignly in hazing in college fraternities. It is a wise country that satisfies this collective need with a brief mandatory military service or its equivalent, in which boys are truly challenged to become men. In Switzerland all men have to serve in the military, with an update of a few weeks every few years, and every man by law has to have a rifle. The solution to potential misuse is that no one has any ammunition, unless it is required! Switzerland is one country that has managed to stay at peace for several centuries, no small feat. Jung, by the way, used to enjoy his military service immensely. It got him away from patients and threw him in among men from all walks of life, to say nothing of time spent in a beautiful environment.

The roots of fear (Saturn) are perhaps to be found in the Age of Cancer. This influence is still with us collectively—as children, in our fear of the dark; as adults, in our dread of earthly upheavals, earthquakes, polar shifts; and in our prevailing insecurity about our Mother Earth and whether she will "punish" us. It is amazing how many such powerful ideas are among us and how many dire prophecies abound. Today, it is the "End Times." We have projected a collective Shadow upon our mother, the earth, because we have defiled and polluted her. One can only hope that the real shift will take place collectively, not at the poles or in Armageddon, but in our consciousness, so that we may be saved from ourselves. It is not nature we need fear, because nature is consistent, but rather us ourselves.

We can only speculate, through sifting the evidence, that somehow people in the Age of Cancer were making a big step from living entirely in the present to thinking about the future. They staved off starvation by gathering, conserving, and planting, by domesticating the dog and later the goat, the sheep, the ox, and the pig. The role of women in this time must have been central, and it is most likely they who came up with all sorts of practical and time-saving devices like pottery, bone needles, brooches, and pins. Towards the end of the Age came domestication of the horse, the invention of the wheel and weaving. Flint was mined, and not long ago in Belgium a miner was unearthed with his deerhorn pick in his hands, his fingerprints still upon it. Besides all the stone, horn, and bone artifacts and protovillage remains (Capricorn), metals and more sophisticated tools and weapons were developed toward the end of this Age. The use of copper goes back to around 6000 B.C., when it was employed by the lake dwellers in Switzerland.

These new technologies reveal much more conscious creativity and reasoning, characteristic of the incoming new Age of Gemini. And during this interface there appeared figurines of the Goddess holding birds, symbolic of consciousness (Gemini), or a baby (Gemini). *The significance here is that birds can fly away and babies grow up as separate people.* The uroboric state of unconscious group participation shows signs of evolving. Out of the Age of the Mother came a new myth, a new and exciting development that freed humanity to greater independence and to making choices. Before this incoming Age of Gemini, it looks as if we didn't have many choices at all. Survival depended on filling the most basic level of needs: food, water, shelter, and reproduction. We were at the mercy of nature, just as an infant is totally dependent on the nurturing (Cancer) process of parenting, feeding, protection, and transportation. Nothing in this world is more dependent than the human infant. Today much of our unconscious fear of the dark and, by extension, of death, is connected to this powerful Mother archetype and to the fear of regression and loss of consciousness. Psychologically, the new level in us is afraid of slipping back to the older one. Behind the fear of death is the fear of oblivion, of losing the identity we have worked so hard to acquire. We can only guess that at the end of the Age of Cancer a shift occurred that drove humanity collectively further in its progress. The quality of life had not changed much in thousands of years; ice ages had come and gone, Cro-Magnon had replaced Neanderthal, and people had responded daily to the challenges of an arduous and dangerous life. But a shift in the psyche, such as it was, definitely took place, because by the time of the sixth millennium B.C. a whole new era was at hand, and we would never be quite the same. A new kind of consciousness with the potential of individual choice was emerging.

Today, many thousands of years later, one wonders whether this issue of consciousness and choice could be connected to the ubiquitous drug culture. Using drugs, or alcohol to excess, is certainly a quick way of losing that most precious attainment of centuries and centuries: consciousness. Living in industrial cities of concrete and values of no-values, many are cut off from the feminine, the Mother, nature herself, with few rituals connecting them to the unseen "gods" or the divine. Could this be the reason so many in a whole generation, like lemmings off a cliff, are unconsciously driving themselves back into a uroboric oblivion? It is as if for them there is nothing left that is worth being conscious of. This, in my opinion, is what Jung warned us against: when we cease to live the symbolic life, we cease to partake in the life of the gods (the divine and universal processes that are the very ground of existence), and so we miss celebrating the divine sacrament of a daily life meaningfully lived.

I remember one teenager in particular, whose slogan was "So what? Who cares? This is ridiculous!" He was lucky: he outgrew it. Many today do not.

Well, I'm sorry to end on such a sober note, but the way things are, it is vital to look at both the positive and the negative or Shadow side of these Ages. Only by understanding the force of the chthonic element, the dark face of the goddess archetype, can we understand the powers that generate both enormous love and enormous fear within us. For millennia she has been worshipped, i.e., acknowledged. In the last few centuries, many in the West have failed to do this, at their peril. Those countries who rejected the "feminine" have made the greatest industrial and scientific advances. But we have gained a materialistic world and are losing our souls. Now with the clamor on all sides for a redemption of the feminine, there is hope. It is certainly understandable that this should trigger collective fears of castration and/or unconsciousness. The good news is that we cannot willingly return to that state if we use our consciousness to appreciate and celebrate *both* masculine and feminine. So many people who are opting out of the conscious state through substance abuse are falling back, through a kind of suicide on the installment plan, into the devouring mother of oblivion, not the restoring mother of a good night's sleep.

One can also wonder if a very deep collective unconscious memory from this era has affected the lasting dogma of the Roman Catholic Church: the exclusion of women from the priesthood. We know that in those cultures in southern Europe where the Mother Goddess was worshipped, male devotees were obliged to be castrated and to wear women's clothing. Could there be a hidden connection to the requisite celibacy, the wearing of frocks of priests upon their serving "the Mother Church"? And the statuary of bare-breasted priestesses holding snakes might still give popes the willies about having women handle sacramental objects. I wonder what you would think about this? It still affects their attitude to half the human race. And I still have problems with the old Church Father Tertullian's question: "*Habet mulier animam?*" Does a woman have a soul?

Well, the times they are a-changing. Stay tuned. Sweet dreams.

Love,

ao

Myth is a big secret everybody knows but no one can tell except through a story.
—NICKY HEARON

Archetypes are really verbs.
—A.O.H.

A little bird told me.
—FOLK SAYING

—13—

CONSCIOUSNESS AND CHOICE
The Age of Gemini
(c. 6500–c. 3750 B.C. with interfaces)

Dear Friend,

Your reaction to the psychological plight of those who "mother" today certainly is timely. One of the most important issues confronting us in this coming Age is the reemergence of the feminine and its *balancing* with the masculine—not just the "overthrowing of the patriarchy" we hear so much about. Perhaps the angry feminists and the women's movement have been essential to attract attention to the problem. But we are to move on towards another level of the feminine, which I believe to be that of Hagia Sophia, the archetype of feminine wisdom, who in myth was, with God, a cocreator of the manifest world, symbolized by the dove and the original Third Person of the Trinity. I have written at some length about this in *The Dove in the Stone.*

Hagia Sophia (Greek for "Holy Wisdom") today represents an evolution in our view of the feminine, and therefore of "matter" (*mater*) and nature. Hopefully she will offer a process for us to find the sacred in the commonplace in our everyday lives, for then we would be able to see "the Kingdom of Heaven which is spread upon the earth" that Christ spoke of. But in order for this to happen, men and women have to become more aware of that chthonic and scary dimension of the dark mother, the nameless one. For this reason we find a myth about "The Descent to the Goddess" emerging at the end of the Age of Gemini, the myth of Inanna going down to the depths to confront the cold and merciless hag Ereshkigal. In your book *Descent of the Goddess*, Sylvia, you describe a journey we all must make before we can continue on toward individuation. The going down into our darkness comes first. As Jung said, "One does not become enlightened by imagining figures of light but by making the dark conscious." This negative feminine archetype lives as the Witch in fairy tales and even more subhuman monsters in sagas. Beowulf's mother, Grendel, is one; Shelob, the spider mother in Tolkien's *Lord of the Rings*, is a modern version. In the Middle Ages the dark one often took the form of a fire-breathing dragon, whom the hero must slay before he can lay hold of the "treasure," whether the "Pearl of Great Price" or the fair Princess.

These myths and fairy tales are not untrue fabrications but, as Jung has pointed out, are true of the psyche, which is why they refuse to go away—and why they continue to fascinate us. Awareness of these matters can help women to be there in a new way for men, and for men to be there in a new way for women. But we have to be patient; we are still ending the Age of Pisces. We women need to understand *why* some men are still afraid of women having too much power. Thus they may too quickly turn strong women into "mothers," and such women can provoke a sense of psychological "incest" in their husbands, who then turn to the hetairas for comfort. It would be nice to call a truce, so we could stop blaming everything on the bad mother or the cruel patriarchal chauvinist and come to see how much a bit of mythology could help us free ourselves from these unconscious projections. The rediscovery of love might ensue. Until such time, the gap between what one person says and the other one hears may continue to cause us painful problems.

The great motif, then, of the Age of Gemini, which followed the Age of Cancer, was the emergence of a new consciousness, and with it came the first signs of organized religion (ruled by the opposite constellation Sagittarius). This is reflected in the artifacts of women now holding birds (Gemini) or infants (Gemini), both symbolic of something new; for, as I have said, both birds and children can separate from those who hold them. And religious temples and art and artifacts appear profusely the world over as is demonstrated by archaeology.

As Joseph Campbell has pointed out, this period of time also marks a split between the religious attitudes of those who began to settle and the nomadic tribes that continued to wander. (II, the Roman numeral for 2, points to the twin opposites in the glyph of the sign.) It was the farming settlers who were able to set up the first crude centers of worship (Sagittarius). They no longer relied on the direct and numinous experience of the tribal shaman or witch doctor (or later the prophets), but set up a priesthood to mediate the separation between the gods and humankind. If you stop to think about it, as soon as man became conscious, God became other and nature became other; as soon as we become aware of being subject, everything else becomes object. Duality (Gemini) and separation ensue. The *participation mystique* is over, and we humans stand up and walk alone, even as the infant, who had been mostly "out to lunch," takes its first faltering steps to independence.

These first steps into consciousness form the basis of two of the great myths of the Age of Gemini: the Epic of Gilgamesh, the world's oldest known story, and some of the myths in Genesis. The story of Cain and Abel, for instance, is one of rival brothers; "Abel was a keeper of sheep, and Cain was a tiller of the ground." Since the story is a Hebrew one, the shepherd Abel was the one who found favor with God, and it was he who was slain. For the nomadic Hebrews, the farmers were the bad guys. The same opposition was repeated in this country many centuries later with the hostility between the cattle owners and the farmers who wanted fences. This theme formed the basis for the musical *Oklahoma!* Previously, when the Puritans came to America and built houses with fences and stockades, the nomadic Indians were astonished; they had no concept of land as personal property. For them it all belonged to God.

To review quickly:

- The glyph of Gemini the Twins is Ⅱ, the Roman numeral II. The Roman archetypal twins were Castor and Pollux, and they are often sculpted and associated with horses (the opposite sign is Sagittarius ♐, the horse-bodied centaur ruled by Jupiter), as were their Hindu counterparts, the Asvins, twins born of the sun and a mare. The motif of the twin brothers, the rival brothers, or best buddies is found in almost every mythology imaginable, from Jacob and Esau to Roland and Oliver, from Hungarian mythology to that of the Native American.

- Gemini is a mutable air sign, associated with thought. Its ruler is Mercury (Hermes, Thoth, Odin), the messenger of the gods. It is a yang sign, though androgynous (hermaphroditic).

- In the body it rules all those systems involved with communication: the nerves, the bicameral brain, the arms, hands, fingers, tongue, and the faculty of speech. Its symbol is the caduceus (DNA/RNA, kundalini), and it rules intelligence and coordination.

- One important key to understanding Gemini is what I call the "switcheroo" process. By that I mean, for example, that in the body those things on the right side are ruled by the left hemisphere of the brain, and things on the left are ruled by the right hemisphere. The eyes receive images upside down, reverse them, and send the image from the right eye to the left brain, and vice versa. This "switcherooing" is the main cause for the confusions that delight the Trickster, causing a dilemma of levels in arguments, so that we are thinking and arguing at cross-purposes. Abbott and Costello (Gemini) used this over and over as a source for their humor, the "Who's on first? What's on second?" routine. Laurel and Hardy and Mutt and Jeff had similar conversations, where every question was answered with a Gemini response: now and then, sooner or later, more or less, yes and no. One can also add R2-D2 and C-3PO from *Star Wars*.

- In the world Gemini is associated with all things dealing with communication: writing, reading, newspapers, books, short trips; making mental connections, and most importantly a sense of humor—fun, games, puns, riddles, etc. In *Jungian Symbolism* I wrote extensively on Mercury, whose process can even be found in a zipper—because it can make one piece out of two, or two out of one.

- Gemini's positive archetypes are the Psychopomp (leader of souls) and the Divine Child; the negative ones are the Tricksters in mythologies, the scamps, mischief makers, all the way to Bugs Bunny and the Roadrunner in the "funny papers" (Gemini, Gemini!).

- Besides the caduceus, among its symbols are the masks of tragedy and comedy and all examples of pairs of things or opposites, all binaries and syzygies. (I don't get to use that lovely word very often!) The sign is also concerned with such opposites as mortal/immortal, animal/human, large and small, and on and on, and is typified in Punch and Judy or the black-and-white-clad harlequins and columbines, magicians, prestidigitators, and pickpockets.

- Gemini underlines the necessity of duality for consciousness to exist. Out of the opposites all new things emerge, and through their inward reunion (yoke, yoga) are born those attacks of insight that yield an "Aha!" Gemini triggers what Jung called the "transcendent function"—the wee tab on the zipper!

Most of the Age of Gemini remains prehistoric, so we can only speculate about how the progress was made. But there is no doubt today that by the very end of this Age and its interface, the idea of writing had emerged, appearing first in crude ideographs and pictographs and finally in full-blown cuneiform on tablets in Sumeria and hieroglyphs (sacred carvings) in Egypt. In India and China, too, pictographic signs were developing. In one fell swoop, prehistory became history, and humanity learned to communicate (Gemini) across space and, more importantly, across time.

I suspect we often forget that the first parts of the Old Testament were not written down until around 1000 B.C., at the time of Solomon. Certainly the tablets of the Epic of Gilgamesh so far discovered date mostly to the reign of the Assyrian king Ashurbanipal (in the seventh century B.C.), though there are fragments dating back to the middle of the fourth millennium B.C. However, it is likely that these, like the Pentateuch, were based on centuries of oral tradition and memorization. Certainly the themes in Gilgamesh and the story of the Garden of Eden both bear on the motif of consciousness and its consequences.

Studies have been made, even in the twentieth century, of the prodigious ability of people who do not read or write to remember things verbatim. Robin Flower, an anthropologist, made a study of the *seannachaids*, Gaelic storytellers, on the Blasket Islands off Dingle Peninsula in Ireland. He found that the old women and men would spin out their tales over several nights by the peat fire, and when asked to repeat them could do so word for word. Among the Celts of old, as well as the ancient Hebrews, were certain people who could recite genealogies by heart. Flower discovered that within a generation after the appearance of the first school on the islands, the ability to memorize to that degree was shortened until it vanished altogether. With the advent of writing, the old stories were set down and fixed, but they had been set many generations previous by a breed of bards and tellers of wonderful tales whose authors we will never know, since, like dreams, the stories emerged out of the heart and soul of a people.

The Epic of Gilgamesh is the great myth of the Babylonians, but evidence points to its origins with the Sumerians, a people who lived in Mesopotamia prior to the Babylonians and who flourished during the Age of Gemini. Abraham himself was said to have come from Ur, and according to the great Sumerologist Samuel Noah Kramer, the Sumerians were in contact with the Canaanites. So the potential dispersion of the myth and its contents has several possibilities. Gilgamesh and the biblical stories resemble one another in quite a few respects, notably the story of the Flood and survival in a boat and in the symbolism of a serpent stealing away the possibility of immortality.

Let's look at the Gemini motifs in Gilgamesh. Gilgamesh is an inflated young king, part god, part mortal, who is lording it over his people, helping himself to other men's wives, and generally acting like a spoiled, power-drunk brat. The people appeal to the gods for help. The Mother Goddess Aruru decides to fashion a rival for Gilgamesh out of clay, and so makes Enkidu, who is half animal and half man. Enkidu, one of the most lovable characters in mythology, is a nature boy who speaks the language of the animals and releases them from traps set by men. The villagers complain to Gilgamesh, who sets about subduing Enkidu. The result of several fights is a standoff, and the two decide without further ado to become best friends, going off together in search of adventure. Together they kill the monster Humbaba.

There is one touching episode in which the villagers decide to weaken Enkidu, the fearsome hairy monster, by sending a young prostitute to him. (I can just imagine the people relishing this part of the story!) Scared to death, the timid young girl goes into the dark forest to teach him the art of love. Instead of devouring her, Enkidu falls head over heels in love, and they dally for several days and nights. But after she leaves him, he finds that he no longer can understand the language of the birds and the animals. His grief is great. So here the feminine has drawn him out of his innocent unconscious oneness with nature and closer to human consciousness.

A goddess, who has watched Gilgamesh fight, propositions him, and he rejects her on the grounds that she destroys her lovers. In a rage, she lets loose a monstrous Bull of Heaven to rampage the landscape. Gilgamesh and Enkidu set off together to slay the bull. But Enkidu is mortally wounded, and Gilgamesh, stricken with grief, sets off on a quest for the cure for death. The ensuing tale has twelve episodes, and Gilgamesh is guided to find Utnapishtim, the Sumerian Noah who has survived the Flood, who tells him the story of the boat upon which he survived and the three birds he sent out to find land.

Humor enters the story as well. While visiting Utnapishtim, Gilgamesh brags that he never sleeps. To teach him a lesson, the wife bakes a loaf of bread every day and lays it by the head of our cocky hero as he sleeps for a week. Confronted by the evidence of stale and staler bread, Gilgamesh meets his comeuppance.

In the end, having learned the secret from his host, Gilgamesh acquires the flower of immortality from the depths of the sea and sets off for home to save his friend. Alas, overconfident, he falls asleep by the fire, and the serpent steals the flower. His mission ends in failure. He returns to find Enkidu's body dissolving back into the earth. He weeps for his loss and is forced to come to terms with the fact that he is not omnipotent. (Nor are we!)

I read this story, of which there are several variations, to a class of seventh graders. At the end, five of the children were in tears. It is an awesome experience to realize that a tale most probably 5000 years old is still as fresh as today in its impact and ability to move us.

This epic addresses, among many other matters, the following problems that are the essence of Gemini:

- The rivals who become friends;
- The challenging and rejecting of the Mother Goddess;
- The raising of consciousness by the feminine;
- The quest for reunion, the emergence of humor;
- The part-divinity of the hero and the mortality of the animal body.

In addition, the epic contains several "firsts":

- The first story of human loves (*philia* and *eros*);
- The first tragedy brought about through human hubris;
- The first conscious separation of the psychological functions of the sexes;
- Most important of all, the first book, and the first tale of a male hero with a name!

Naming things is a Gemini function—a task also given to Adam and Eve.

In the story, which I urge everyone to read, there is a new masculine rejection of the "mother," and a new perception of the feminine as capable of weakening the masculine. In an episode where Gilgamesh tarries in Dilmun and is waited on hand and foot by the lovely maidens (every man's fantasy), he almost forgets his mission. The humorous putdown of the hero by Mrs. Utnapishtim with her loaves of bread hints at a no-nonsense commonsense aspect of the feminine as well. The entire epic, of course, is a celebration of the male, specifically as hero, conscious of his own strength and independence—up to a point. Enkidu, being half animal and half man, is the mortal aspect of ourselves. This motif reappears with the myth of the Dioscuri, Castor and Pollux, one mortal and the other made a god. The brothers refused to be separated, so Zeus placed them together in the heavens as the constellation of Gemini. This same theme appears in the myth of Sagittarius (the opposite sign) as well, where Chiron, the immortal centaur, is wounded in the foot and offers his immortality to Prometheus. Zeus is touched and sets Chiron in the heavens as the constellation Sagittarius.

The Hindu twins, the Asvins, are also associated with the constellation of Gemini, one being dark and the other light, and also with horses and with healing, both associated with Sagittarius, the sign of the horse. As you know, there is a whole cycle of myths having to do with the horse cult. It appears in Greece and also in

Norse and British mythology. The horse sacrifice is one of the most ancient of all. To this day when we say the word "pony," we refer to the horse goddess Epona.

As Jung and Edinger have demonstrated, the story of Adam and Eve is also a story of consciousness and the price it exacts from us when we acquire it. During the Age of Pisces, the Christian era, the blame has been placed upon both the serpent and Eve (i.e., the feminine) for dragging us down into original sin and exile. The tree upon which the apple hung was called the Tree of *Knowledge* (Gemini) of Good and Evil (opposites). One bite, and Adam and Eve knew shame and guilt, lost their innocence, and were banished from Eden lest—and here many of us forget the clincher—they reach out and eat of the Tree of Life and become as gods and "live forever." Thus the first tree becomes a Tree of Death. The second, a Tree of Life, could we but taste of it, would confer upon us the immortality of the gods. Humans would become "one of us," as the Lord God says.

As we move into our own Age of Aquarius, we are beginning to see another way of interpreting this mythos. The Tree of Life is a universal symbol, an *axis mundi* in terms of the earth, but also in terms of our bodies. Thanks to the age-old wisdom of the East, we are learning more and more about the Tree of Life within our own bodies—the spine and the serpent of energy coiled within us called kundalini. The spiraling dual energies of the *ida* and *pingala* are ruled by Gemini (nerves) and enhanced by breathing (Gemini) in meditation. In the esoteric teachings of all the religions, the positive feminine is that which ascends—Shakti, Shekhinah, and Sophia, "the Holy Spirit." So it is this aspect of the feminine which, through Mercury's process, has the power to unite the opposites and draw us closer to awareness of our own potential immortality. The flower of immortality may well be the Third Eye. Its place has borne the mark of Cain for millennia. The mythos hints that it is through this process that both Adam and Eve are redeemed. Without their story, we would not have the promise of an inner rebirth.

Consciousness is a terrible burden as well as an incomparable privilege. We suffer agonizing choices in our awareness of sin and guilt. Further on, with the development of an ego, we risk identifying with it and rejecting the Creator who gave it to us in the first place. That is the original sin of pride! Human evolution leads to a point where we need to substitute gratitude and awareness of the Giver for pride. We keep forgetting that we did not create ourselves, that we only *cocreate* ourselves.

Can you see how, as we develop as children, we gradually lose our innocence and begin to become aware of do's and don'ts, of fears and shame, of guilts, yet at the same time feel raucous glee that we can stand, walk, and get into mischief all by ourselves. "Look Ma, no hands!" (Gemini).

Now the good news that Gemini has for us is that, thanks to the secret of the "switcheroo," whatever has been separated can also be reunited. And so we find that many outer world happenings in nature mirror processes that take place in the psyche. So, as it takes a mother and a father to create a baby physically, the very same process of *coniunctio* can take place within us. This is one of the profound meanings I tried to point out in *Jungian Symbolism* of the "Virgin" birth, the inner rebirth. Symbolically, we contain everything and are contained in everything, as the world is reflected in a drop of dew or a "now" holds eternity. Fortunately, since this truth is too great a one to bear, the function of the ego is to sort it out in terms of time and space, so that we can savor it here and there, now and then, sooner or later— the gift of Gemini!

Odin (Wotan), the Norse god of Wednesday (Mercury's Day), hung on the world tree of Yggdrasil for nine days and nights, after which he gave the gift of runes (the Norse alphabet) to humankind. So the counterparts of Hermes (Mercury), such as the Egyptian Thoth, are all connected to the idea of writing and communication. I hope you can see how astrology can help unravel the skein of symbolism everywhere in mythology and help us understand the profound meaning hidden within what often seems a succession of fanciful and impossible events. The greatest foe of mythology and religious symbolism is literalism, because it robs us of the immense hidden wisdom which is waiting there for all of us, for all time. Whenever we reject a myth for rational reasons, we ourselves are acting irrationally. But we need to know how to play Sophia's game of hide-and-seek; we need to learn the rules of how to play. Game is the object of hunting (Sagittarius), and in Gemini hunting is the game! "Seek and ye shall find. Knock and the door shall be opened." Well, 'tis getting late. I'll have more in my next letter!

Love,

ao

Indeed, I believe that we may claim with a very high degree of certainty that in this Halafian symbology of the bull and the goddess, the dove, and the double-ax, we have the earliest evidence yet discovered anywhere of the prodigiously influential mythology associated for us with the great names of Ishtar and Tammuz, Venus and Adonis, Isis and Osiris, Mary and Jesus. From the Taurus mountains, the mountains of the bull-god, who may have already been identified with the horned moon, which dies and is resurrected three days later, the cult was diffused, with the art of cattle-breeding itself, practically to the ends of the earth; and we celebrate the mystery of that mythological death and resurrection to this day, as a promise of our own identity. But what experience and understanding of eternity, and what of time, gave rise in that early period to this constellation of eloquent forms? And why in the image of the bull?

—JOSEPH CAMPBELL
The Masks of God:
Primitive Mythology

14

PROPERTY AND RESURRECTION

The Age of Taurus

(c. 4000–c. 1800 B.C. with interfaces)

Dear Friend,

A s you know, I used to teach children history in a private school on Long Island. I found the ninth-grade students quite enthusiastic about a course called "A Cultural History of Civilization." During the year we studied ancient history, taking time to read from prime sources, applying some of Jung's ideas about the collective unconscious, and detecting archetypal figures in the various mythologies. Through the year students would research and write about a subject of their own choice—art, alphabets, medicine, science, literature, etc.—as it appeared in each of the cultures we studied. Then we took a week to listen to and discuss the monographs. The students became mini-experts in their field, working with sources appropriate to their individual reading level.

I cannot tell you how much this amplified our textbook or how much I myself learned from my students. Where else would

I have learned, for instance, that the Egyptians invented the enema from studying the habits of the constipated ibis, which, thanks to its long arched bill, was able to siphon water into itself to relieve the situation? And where else would I have learned from an unprepared but imaginative student that "the collective unconscious is when a whole lot of people don't know nothing and don't know why they don't"? This same boy afforded another glimpse into the matter of the archetypal rival brothers. On a test which asked for a sample of four pairs, he came up with "Romulus and Remus, Balaam and Balak, Osiris and Set, and Abraham and Straus." I also learned from a fill-in test that the Assyrians drove hard bargains, which I hardly could deny, though I was looking for chariots, and that the Carthaginians fought the Pubic Wars. These are the serendipities of a teacher's life.

Anyway, I could give you over 250 examples of the Gemini motif in world mythology. In reviewing them I also noticed how many twosomes have balancing names, like Prometheus and Epimetheus or even those "Babes in the Woods," Hansel and Gretel, as well as Max and Moritz or Raggedy Ann and Raggedy Andy. The latter, like Hansel and Gretel, qualify for Gemini, though of opposite sex, because they are either siblings or children.

By somewhere around 3500 B.C., the Age of Gemini slowly gave way to the Age of Taurus, and true civilization could be said to have begun. (The word "civilization" embodies the Latin *civilis*, meaning "city.")

So let's review the characteristics of Taurus and its opposite sign Scorpio:

- Taurus the Bull, ♉, is a fixed earth sign, ruled by Venus, and it is the place of exaltation of the Moon. In the body it rules the throat, neck, and the quality of voice.

- In the world, Taurus is associated with agriculture, money, banking, real estate and property, and all matters dealing with permanence and security.

- It is a yin sign and by virtue of its rulers much associated with the feminine. Its process is involved with giving form. Its trap is rigidity and concretizing.

- Scorpio the Scorpion, ♏, is a fixed water sign, co-ruled today by Mars (according to the old system) and Pluto (according to the modern attribution). It rules the reproductive and eliminatory systems and is associated with all processes of recycling and transformation.

- In the world, Scorpio has to do with birth, sex, and death. This is found in *eros* and *thanatos*, Freud's concepts of sexual desire and death. (Freud, by the way, was a Taurus with Scorpio rising.) Scorpio also has to do with taxes, garbage disposal, fertilizers like manure, and on a higher spiritual level, resurrection. It is a sign of extremes. Three symbols are associated with it: the serpent, the eagle, and the dove.

While Gemini provides the conduit for kundalini up the spine, Scorpio provides the actual "serpent power" of libido, which travels up the *sushumna* as kundalini. Jung rightly defined this as psychic energy, which includes sexual desire in the lower chakras but which can be transformed as it ascends.

During the Age of Taurus, bull worship was prevalent virtually all over Eurasia. This is a fact, as we shall see from the numerous examples listed below. Even in China, the god of agriculture had a bull's head. I find it fascinating that astrology can give us a logical reason for this, one that escaped even Joseph Campbell when he wrote *The Masks of God* (as we can see from the epigraph to this chapter). Jung and Neumann offer psychological insight into what was happening in the unfolding of collective evolution. It is this, as well as history, to which astrology can connect.

You see, for civilizations to exist, agriculture has to be advanced sufficiently to provide a generous source of starch and protein for the diet of dwellers in a city. This means settling down (Taurus) and planting fields (Taurus), as well as raising cattle (Taurus) and fertilizing the fields (Scorpio). Within the cities, division of labor develops, and people live in more permanent brick or stone houses.

Now if you were a farmer in those days, what would you do after you planted your fields? Chances are, you would pray to the gods for water, good weather, no locusts, and, please, no pillaging wars! Whenever there is drought in our own times, many such prayers are still recited. Whenever we pray over something, we are expending psychic energy, and whatever we spend (Taurus) psychic energy (Scorpio) on, *we begin to feel that we own.* Anything we cherish, pray over, or treasure, because of emotional projections, acquires psychological value and results in attachment. We begin to say *my* land, *my* house, *my* children. If this is carried too far, we become possessed by our possessions, which is an enantiodromia (running into the opposite) peculiar to Taurus.

The motto of Taurus is "I have." You know how toddlers usually speak of themselves in the third person when they first begin to speak. "Jimmy wants milk," rather than "I want milk." The psychological beginnings of personal identity come with the first shrieks of ownership, "It's mine!" The claim to one's toys or blanket is a huge developmental step. For ancient farmers, it led to a sense of justified ownership of personal property, and when they banded together with other farmers, it gave rise to city-states and eventually a sense of collective nationalism (Taurus). Suddenly there was a new reason for waging wars to obtain more land and power—and the potential for dying to protect one's own property. This polarity is still a dreadful reality. Killing, as a process, alas, is ruled by Scorpio.

Next, the process of farming crops involves the planting or investing of seed in the ground with the confidence that it will yield a thousandfold: "God giveth the increase." Can you see that this is the identical process of savings (Taurus) and banking (Taurus), where money invested is expected to grow and yield interest? Nor does the connection end there. In the old days, wealth was counted in the heads (Latin *caput*) of cattle and livestock owned, as well as belongings (and that included wives), called "chattel," a cognate word. The same root is hidden in the word "capitalism," which oddly enough is carried on in the "stock markets" of the world. When things are going well, they are said to be "bullish." So when Merrill Lynch, the brokerage house, chose a bull as its logo and featured a bull on Wall Street in its television ads, one really has to laugh. I wondered if this was synchronicity or someone knew this mythology. Strangely enough, I met the man who did the filming for the ads; as far as he knew, it was synchronicity. Certainly it was apt. Nowadays, people even speak of making a "killing" (Scorpio) on the stock market.

Nor is that all. I have already mentioned the exchange of property (Taurus) for sex (Scorpio) in the custom of the dowry, when the wife brings her husband money, belongings, and, optimally, land. In the Old Testament, there are also many instances in which the custom was for the bridegroom to pay the father with livestock or service for his daughter. There was a custom in the time of the Mother Goddess under which every good woman in Babylonia was required to give herself sexually to a stranger once a year at the temple of the Goddess. Merlin Stone has pointed out the shift from this custom to a new regulation prohibiting adultery. That is when property ceased to be handed down matrilineally. A man needed to know his own children, so adultery became a sin (Scorpio) punishable by death (Scorpio). Inheritance (Scorpio) became patrilinear later in the Judaic Age of Aries, the Age after Taurus, though being Jewish still requires a Jewish mother. The oldest profession in the world also involves an exchange of money for sex, and many are the guilt-laden husbands who attempt to soothe angry wives with furs and jewels or gifts of money. As an analyst, you know that an excessive resentment about matters of property in marriages often masks deep sexual problems.

Needless to say, the exchange of property (Taurus) takes place again at death (Scorpio), and Scorpio also rules inheritance and taxes. (The Eighth House in a chart is the Second House to the Seventh of the partner.) After the tears for the departed, the next step is to consult the will and divide the estate. Thus money and property (Taurus) are recycled (Scorpio).

I have already written about the connections in the body between the voice and sexuality at puberty and in cases of hysteria. By now, the Taurus/Scorpio polarity should be fairly well established in your mind and we can move back into history.

Another curious synchronicity, historically speaking, is that the first myths of resurrection appear in the Age of Taurus. For the Sumerians, the word for plowing and sexual intercourse was the same, as was the word for the horizontal furrow in the field and the vulva of a woman. It was clear by then that the seed of grain (Latin *semen*) and the seed of a man served the same function in bringing forth new life. This idea lived on for centuries in the fertility rites of many agricultural areas in the world, rites carried out for the prospering of the fields.

In the words of Isaiah, "All flesh is grass"—it withers away, and yet it returns. These people perceived that human life had its seasons, too. So the farmer must have noticed that year after year his crops came up, ripened, were cut down, only to come up again at the appointed time. For the Egyptians, resurrection happened every day and night. The sun was swallowed by the goddess Nut, whose lovely body is the star-spangled night, and it is reborn every day. I have an illustration of Nut with cow's ears (Taurus), and she is arched over the phallic god Geb (Scorpio). So during this age people saw the motif of dying (which had already appeared in the myth of the hapless Gilgamesh) as a descent into the darkness of the earth and winter, but with hope of rebirth and renewal. Myths of resurrection are of a cyclical nature (Scorpio), and we find them in the stories of Isis and Osiris and Ishtar and Tammuz. The quest of Isis was for the re-membering of her dismembered brother and spouse. She found all her husband's parts but the one ruled by Scorpio, and Ra, the sun god, gave Osiris a golden phallus upon which Horus was conceived—another "virgin birth." Campbell has pointed out that all over the world, including the Americas, the great agricultural religions are tied to the astronomical calendar, to the stately dance of the sun, moon, and earth. Today this includes most of the major religions of the world: Buddhism, Christianity, Hinduism, and Judaism. The latter changed from being nomadic when the Hebrews settled down at the time the Temple in Jerusalem was built.

When I went to school, the prevailing attitude towards ancient mythologies was one of slight ridicule and rejection of people who could be so ignorant as to dance around a white bull, lifting their skirts to show their private parts, or pour bull's blood over a new king for his anointing. Even sillier were all those bare-breasted women waving snakes. I think it helps so much to understand that behind these symbolic gestures lie the hidden processes of psychological evolution. I doubt very much that people 5000 years ago knew they lived in the Age of Taurus. Not knowing makes the synchronicities at such a collective level even more extraordinary. It is imperative, I feel, as the world grows smaller and people and cultures intermingle more rapidly, that we learn the etiquette of tolerance and *take the time to perceive that symbols are always pointing to powerful intangibles common to all humankind.* They are the shorthand of wisdom. I beg of you to share this idea with others! The literalism resurfacing in well-intentioned but ignorant ways is a form of idolatry far more dangerous than bowing down to a bull was back in those days. It, too, mistakes the form for the content.

Up to now, the most perilous stages in history have come at the interface of Ages. During these transitional centuries an enormous tension of opposites builds up. The outgoing Age appears to bloom, in defiance of its own demise, in what the author William Irwin Thompson has called "the sunset effect." Thereafter it slowly goes to seed as the upshoots of the Age-to-be burst through the fresh new message so dreaded by the old. This is happening today. Regrettably, in the past too often the solution was outright genocide and persecution of the bearers of the older tradition, instead of gratitude for the positive values they offered. The other solution was theocide, killing the gods, turning them into the demons of the next Age, or reducing them to faint echoes in the characters of folk and fairy tales. Age by Age, this pattern has repeated itself. In the Age of Aries, the account of the genocide of the Canaanites and their old goddess religion is recorded in Joshua. In the Age of Pisces, the "pagan" gods of the Greeks and the Celts, and later the Hindus, were thrown down, destroyed, and denigrated by the Christians, who took over the mythos of those who gave us the Old Testament. Christianity glorified it, to be sure, in art and music, and in a whole civilization that spread over Europe and reached across the oceans to other continents. At the same time the Jews, the bearers of Judaism, were persecuted and reviled. This kind of collective destruction must and can stop in the Age of Aquarius if enough people understand what is going on and why. *We cannot kill archetypes*; all we can do is build new images and give them new names. Their divine processes and energies are far stronger than we know. Only symbols will unlock what they all have in common. If I have one prayer above all others, it is that this insight can be shared and learned before it is too late. We need to honor as one and the same the flame that burns through the varied lamps of all religions.

Well, forgive the outcry, but the news of the world lately has been so discouraging. Yet healing lies all about us, if we could only reach out and grasp it. I hope you understand why I feel so urgently about all this.

In my next letter, I plan to bring you "A Celestial Roundup." That's a lot of bull!

Love,

ao

Nut, Egyptian Sky Goddess
From a coffin in the Rijks Museum, Leiden

15

THE CELESTIAL ROUNDUP

Dear Friend,

I do not wish to overwhelm you with the contents of this letter, but it is important for the record to point out the indisputable evidence of synchronicity in history with the symbolism of an Age. So many are the "Bulls of Heaven" or "Bulls of Light" and their consort goddesses, the sacred cows, during the Age of Taurus that it's hard to keep track of them all. The important thing to remember is what they have in common.

The most persuasive symbol seems to have been that of the disk resting in the horns of the crescent.

Sometimes the disk is solar, in which case it would be lying in the horns of the crescent moon; sometimes it is lunar, the full moon resting in the horns of the solar bull.

From both an astrological and psychological viewpoint — especially since the Age of Taurus was to be followed by the birth of the collective ego in the Age of Aries—this would seem to suggest that the ego and the Self were not yet really separated. Consciousness and the collective Self were still one here, and the individual remained swallowed up in the collective, as Campbell and others have pointed out. This is the period when those remarkable mass burials took place—kings and queens buried with all their retinue, chariots, horses, and musical instruments. As many as forty attendants are found asleep in a row, with no indication of violence or suffering having taken place. In the famous grave of Queen Shubad, discovered by Sir Leonard Woolley in what was once Sumeria, not only was the bull prominently displayed on the famous harp, but bull's legs were also incised on each soldier's spear.

During this Age in Egypt, the greatest reward in the afterlife was the privilege of becoming an individual. The idea was at least forming, but not until after 1800 B.C. did the heroic wrenching out of the ego really take place. Then the myths shifted, and all the new heroes become bull-slayers. But in the Age of Taurus, it was mostly kings and queens who were recognized as individuals, and semidivine at that. The only horoscopes cast were for heads of state, since *L'etat, c'est moi* ("I am the state") was the rule. In Egypt, the title "Pharaoh" meant "House of God."

EGYPT. The most numerous examples of the Taurus-Scorpio polarity come from Egypt. Ancient Egypt was already in place by the Age of Gemini. In fact, it is said to be ruled by Gemini, and the uniting of the "Double Kingdom," Upper and Lower Egypt, is reflected in the "dual crown" worn by the Pharaohs. Though there were other theriomorphic gods and animals worshipped in Egypt, the chief among them at this time was the bull. Here are just some of the Egyptian bull (and cow) deities:

Apis, bull god of Memphis
Ra, Bull of Heaven
Osiris, Bull of Earth

Nut, sky goddess with cow's ears
Mnevis
Hathor, cow goddess, crowned with horns
Mentu, name of a bull appearing in Pharaohs' names
Bulchis, the bull god of Thebes

During this Age, bull horns adorned temples, tombs, and artifacts. When the demotic alphabet emerged, the first letter, still present in the letter *A*, which you are now reading, was called "aleph" for "ox." At first, it was written sideways, and by the time the Phoenicians spread the later "aleph-beth" across the Mediterranean, it had tipped upright. The Phoenicians, by the way, wrote from left to right on one line and right to left on the next, so as writing evolved some languages ended up with reversed letters. The Greeks called this *boustrophedon*, from their word for "ox-goading," because it proceeded in the same way that a farmer went plowing his fields. Today some computer printers type the same way!

The earliest bull cult is said to have been that of Apis, with a later one in Mnevis. A live white bull with special markings was installed with great pomp in a temple at Memphis, where it was worshipped and possibly eventually ritually sacrificed and eaten. Sometimes these bulls were mummified and buried with full regalia. Sacrifice may have replaced an earlier regicide. When such a bull was installed, at first only women were allowed to see him and to please him by exposing themselves (Scorpio). At death, the bull was said to be united with Osiris and was called Serapis. Archaeologists have found mummies of queens interred holding parts of a bull in their hands. Apis was sacred to the moon, since he was conceived by a moonbeam. The Moon is exalted in the sign of Taurus.

Since the great vegetation myth of Osiris was central to Egyptians, it was no wonder that the Scorpio side came out in all the extraordinary preparations for the afterlife, from pyramids to ornamented and well-stocked tombs and elaborate mummification.

From the concept of judgment after death—the soul being weighed on a scale against the feather of Ma'at—to the *Egyptian Book of the Dead*, we can deduce that this life was only a preparation for the next one.

Sex, as exemplified by the sacred aspect of the phallus of Osiris, was obviously given a prominent place and worshipped as an aspect of divine life force. This was enhanced by love as depicted in the beautiful myth of the quest of Isis, whose love and determination eventually rescued her consort after he had been cruelly hacked into fourteen pieces by his wicked brother Set. Curiously, there is a part in the story where Isis is guided on her way by scorpions. Both Inanna of the Sumerians and Isis are beautiful examples of feminine courage, love, and wisdom. In this Age of Taurus the goddesses had evolved from being the chthonic, brooding mysteries of the Age of Cancer to a new level of clarity and power. Taurus is ruled by Venus (Astarte, Aphrodite), so here the feminine takes on an aspect of consort as well as mother (Moon). We should also remember that this goddess of love is also the goddess of war. Her process is that of relationship and involvement with others.

MESOPOTAMIA (Today's Iraq!). Situated between the Tigris and Euphrates Rivers, the area yielded Enlil, bull god of Sumeria, and his consort, the cow goddess Ninlil.

A hymn of the times, recorded in cuneiform on a clay tablet, goes:

> *O lord of lands,*
> *lord of the word of life,*
> *O Enlil, Father of Sumer,*
> *thou who hast vision of thyself,*
> *overpowering ox, overpowering ox,*
> *overpowering ox, overpowering ox . . .*

The god was described as "crouching in the lands, like a sturdy mountain bull, whose horns shine like the brilliance of the sun full of splendor." The union of the divine bull and cow (Scorpio) was given as the origin of the lush fertile soil, so good for crops in the area (Taurus).

Near Ur stood a temple built in honor of the cow goddess, decorated with bulls and cows. Enlil eventually became a god of gods, so that lesser bull deities became known as the sons of Enlil. Statues of human-headed bulls and bull-headed or horned kings and priests have been unearthed there. Many of the seals and steles have horned figures placed under symbols of the sun and moon. One seal depicts a ritual marriage on an altar bed; under the bed is a scorpion! Later in Akkad, kings were given the title "Wild Bull," and you find huge statues of bulls with human heads and beards to signify their virility and power. It was in Sumer that the fantastic common grave of Queen Shubad was discovered. Another interesting note is that in this Age the earliest records of business transactions and of trade appear, all carefully noted on a tablet or papyrus.

THE NEAR EAST. Here we find:

Teshub, bull god of the Hittites
Asshur, gigantic winged bull of the Assyrians

Haddad, Ramman, and **Baal,** all fertility gods associated with storms and thunderbolts. Haddad's throne, at Heliopolis (Sun City), rested on statues of bulls; Ramman was addressed as "great and glorious bull, child of heaven, Lord of plenty."

El (Lord), bull god of the Canaanites, father of Baal (Son of the Lord)

That was a lot of bull!
The drawings of these particular bull gods endeared them to

me as a child. They appeared at the end of my mother's Bible, which often was the only picture book available to me in all those hotels in different countries. I would lie on Mother's bed and read the "Bible funny papers" and marvel at the different ancient alphabets depicted there as well.

Some believe that the name of the Semitic god Baal is derived from *Ba-el*, "son of El." The word for "God" just might also be the source of the words "ball," "bellow," and "bull." Baal became the god of those traveling Phoenicians who definitely connected with the people who eventually settled in Ireland and brought several bovine myths along with them. The Irish, in fact, are said to be ruled by Taurus. The Western Celts still celebrate Beltane, a spring festival now called May Day, falling in the sign of Taurus. And we still dance around the Maypole, celebrating the life force of spring. May Day is the midpoint, by the way, between the spring equinox and summer solstice.

Biblical scholars generally agree that the earliest god of the Hebrews was also a bull god: bull shrines existed at Bethel, Shechem, Shiloh, and Gilgal. At the latter stood a ring of stones or pillars which were anointed, not unlike the *lingam* in India. The last vestige of bull worship was finally overthrown at the time of Moses, who denounced the people sliding back to worshipping the Golden Calf. Certainly many clay and ivory images of bulls, cows, and man-bulls have been discovered in Palestine. I find all these connections absolutely mind-boggling!

GREECE AND CRETE. Here we find:

Poseidon, Bull of the Sea

Zeus, his brother, bull-ravisher of Europa, who fled over the Taurus mountains

The Minotaur, offspring of a white bull and Pasiphae, wife of King Minos on Crete. It was the task of Daedalus to engineer a scaffold to make this union possible.

In the Mediterranean area, the bull was also known as the "Earthshaker," and for good reasons. Theseus, who later killed the Minotaur, was himself the son of Poseidon. And it was at Knossos on Crete where the beautiful bull dancers leapt over the backs of the bulls and onto the walls and pottery of the period, while at the same time the bare-breasted goddesses were holding aloft their snakes (Scorpio). Knossos was largely destroyed by a powerful earthquake.

Finally, there was the great bull cult of Dionysus, the dating of which may be uncertain. Dionysus, a wild god of vegetation and wine, was often depicted with bull horns. Primitive orgies were celebrated in his honor by women, whose prime objective was mystical union with the bull god himself. At the climax of these screaming horror shows, a bull or goat or even some hapless male was torn apart alive, the prize being the phallus (Scorpio). Ritual processions called *phallophoria* were celebrated in Athens, in which several people would carry a huge member through the streets. This is less obscene than the May Day parades today in parts of the world where the huge phallic engines of death—tanks, cannons, and missiles—are the objects of attention. Both are the same Scorpio process, though one celebrates life and the other death. We still see the archetypal frenzy in teenage girls screaming at rock stars and trying to rip off pieces of the clothing of their idols. Mourners with genuine tears running down their faces still gather around the grave of Elvis Presley at Graceland, holding candles aloft, not realizing that they mourn the same archetype of Dionysus or Adonis, the fair young god of intoxicating music, dance, and sexual innuendo. In fact, today's religion finds expression in both the calm, Apollonian repetitive ritual of prayers and sermons and a fervent ritual involving more intoxicating music, chanting, dance, and even glossolalia. People today seem to have a great hunger for more direct and personal religious experience, hence probably the rise in interest in shamanism.

At the *tauroboleum*, a rite described powerfully by Mary Renault in *The King Must Die*, after a ritual marriage (Scorpio), the newly chosen king went through a barbaric baptism of the hot blood of a sacrificed bull. (Just after the Civil War in Spain, I attended a bullfight in Madrid. Eight bulls were killed. As we left the stadium, the poor and hungry were lined up to drink the blood.) Further east, the goddess Anahita was worshipped with a monthly sacrifice of a heifer. This was eventually incorporated in the worship of Ahura Mazda in Persia.

For us today so much of the Age of Taurus seems gross, obscene, and disgusting, but we have to realize that consciousness then was not what it purports to be at present. In a century which could witness a holocaust, we need to be mindful of how close beneath our civilized surface lies our own capacity for obscenity and barbarism. This is something Jung continually warned us about. Now we have Abu Graibh and Darfur and thousands of images of violence and sex abuse, daily on our televisions and worse yet, on game videos!

NORTHERN EUROPE. The origins of the Norse and the Celtic religions are not as easy to date, since these people were wandering for centuries. But according to Brian Branston in his *Gods of the North*, "the northwest Europeans were established in their 'old home' in Denmark and southern Scandinavia before 1800 B.C." According to Snorri's *Edda*, the first man, Buri, was licked out of rocks of ice by a cow whose name was Audumla, surely the first account of frozen food!

> She licked the rocks of ice, which she found salty. When she licked the rocks on the first day there appeared out of them by evening the hair of a man; the second day, a man's head; the third day, a man complete. He is called Buri, beautiful to look upon, great and mighty.

One wonders if that was the origin of the "cowlick."

The importance of bulls and cows in Irish myths is well known and reaches back into antiquity, we don't know how far. There was the Great Bull of Ulster, who was so big fifty men could stand on his back, and there was a bull feast at Tara followed by a ritual incubation. However, scholars have assumed that the "snakes" Christian Patrick expelled from Ireland were a euphemism for snake worshippers because, zoologically speaking, there never were any snakes there. The connection between Ireland and North Africa has been established as going far, far back, and one of the "settlings" of Ireland was said to be from Iberia (Spain), where the bullfights continue. In the *Tain*, a great bullfight between Finn and Dubh (white and black) takes place on a heroic scale, and there is the myth of the "Dun Cow." And, of course, there are bulls in Scotland too.

One of the most enchanting mythical creatures peculiar to both Ireland and Scotland is the "water bull," who comes out at night and fathers special cattle born with nicks in their ears. Sometimes the water bull takes the shape of a handsome lover and ravishes maidens by moonlight. Once when I was up on Conor Pass on the way to Dingle, I admired a small lake sitting in the lap of the mountain. Every year, no matter how dark the weather, I noticed it was always brilliantly shining. I was told, with a wink to be sure, and later I read that it shone because a water bull covered with jewels sleeps in its depths. You won't be surprised if I tell you that the kids I was traveling with at the time derived huge fun from identifying the local water bulls' progeny as we drove around the Hebrides, those Western Isles of Scotland. Practically all the cows had nicked ears!

INDIA. The list goes on:

Parjanya, bull god in the Vedas
Dyaus-piter (origin of Zeus and Jupiter)
Indra, Bull of Bulls, the thunder god

The first and most ancient civilizations all seem to have developed close to great rivers. In India the pre-Aryan cities were Harappa and Mohenjo-daro along the Indus River. Here the bricks were kiln-fired and more durable than those of Sumeria. There were highly sophisticated bathing arrangements and sanitary facilities, even sewers. Here, too, the cult of the bull flourished as is seen in terra-cotta statuettes and seals. These cities vanished suddenly; it is assumed that they were overwhelmed by the invading Aryans who brought with them their own bull gods. Parjanya, god of thunder and rain, was addressed in hymns in the Vedas as "The Bull of all and their impregnator, he wants the life of all things fixed and moving."

Dyaus, who etymologically prefigures Zeus and Jupiter (*Dyaus-piter* means "day father"), is called the red bull, rich-seed, who shines through the clouds and bellows downward. He is said to have fathered Indra, "the Bull of Bulls," and Agni, the god of fire. In India you find images of bull-serpents (Taurus/Scorpio). The serpent was sacred to Agni, as the ram was later.

Agni lives on in our word "ignition" and in "*agnoli*," the Italian for "little lamb." Agni reaches into the next Age of Aries.

In the Vedas, thunder is the bull's bellow, lightning his horns, and rain his seed sent to fertilize the earth, as in the myth of Jupiter Pluvius. And according to Jack Randolph Conrad, the author of *The Horn and the Sword* (a fascinating work on the history of the bull), the Sanskrit words for "bull" and "rain" come from the same root. Bulls were sacrificed to Indra in lots of one hundred (hecatombs), prefiguring similar sacrifices by the Greeks, as mentioned by Homer. Today, both bull and cow still remain sacred in India, and taurocide is strictly forbidden. All the products of their bodies are precious and vital in ritual and in the economy. I myself have seen the lovely "cow-dust hour," which comes as the cows head home to be milked in the evening and the late afternoon sun turns all gold. And I have watched boys making lovely patterns on the wall with dung balls slapped there to dry for later use as fuel. Butter is still poured over the stone *lingam*, and in the temples of Shiva, his bull Nandi watches over all. The peaceful pace and acceptance of all things natural are so lovely in this land. Cows are leisurely creatures that slow down traffic, bulls take mud baths, and sex is worshipped for its life-giving powers. People there still look upon nature, without prurience, as natural. Even today in Indian temples the sculpted *lingam* is united with the *yoni,* and they are worshipped together as a cosmic principle of *coniunctio* and creativity.

Just as a postscript, let me share something amusing. I began my research on all these bulls while we were still in California, startling the librarian by requesting all the books on bulls. I even got one, by mistake, on bull breeding. At the time a psychic in Los Angeles, said to be quite remarkable, had been recommended to us. When we went to see her, the second thing she said, shaking her head in disbelief, was, "I really can't account for it, but you seem to be surrounded on all sides by bulls." I guess, in a way, as you can judge by this letter, I was!

Summing up, can you see how mystifying all this bull worship remains to historians and archaeologists without the insight that astrology affords? It all occurred during the period when the constellation of Taurus hosted the point of the vernal equinox. Even in China, the god of agriculture had bull horns. Viewed symbolically and psychologically, the animal points to all those matters pertaining to Taurus: agriculture, fertility, physical power and endurance, cyclical resurrection, a respect for sex, birth and death, an awareness of a cosmic ecology based on astronomical rhythms. For us today, it points psychologically to our attitude towards "owning" material goods and property, to the exchange of money and values, to our ability to deal wholesomely or not with our sexuality and our attitudes toward death and dying. If any of us gets stuck in Taurus in our development, the trap will be identifying our personal worth with our wealth or possessions, or lack of them, a kind of "I am what I have" materialism, or in a rigid intransigence of opinion and fear of change. The cure, of course, is Scorpio's gift of contemplating the certainty of death and the impermanence of material possessions. As Christ put it, "What shall it profit a man, if he shall gain the world, and lose his own soul?" (Mark 8:36).

Personally speaking, I do not believe that renunciation of the material (Age of Pisces) is the challenge of today's Age. I see our task as learning the art of stewardship of money and goods, gratitude and respect for the world of form which is nature, and perceiving the inner light and consciousness within all of nature. The next step? A cosmic ecology and a personal and affectionate relationship to simple things. Noticing.

Well, I notice 'tis getting late, and time for the cow to jump over the moon!

Much love,

ao

So they gave their bodies to the commonwealth and received, each for his own memory, praise that will never die, and with it the grandest of all sepulchers, not that in which their mortal bones are laid, but a home in the minds of men, where their glory remains fresh to stir to speech or action as the occasion comes by. For the whole earth is the sepulcher of famous men; and their story is not graven only on stone over their native earth, but lives on far away, without visible symbol, woven into the stuff of other men's lives. For you now it remains to rival what they have done and, knowing the secret of happiness to be freedom and the secret of freedom a brave heart, not idly to stand aside from the enemy's onset.
                    —THUCYDIDES (c. 460–400 B.C.)
                         The Peloponnesian War

The hero is symbolical of that divine creative and redemptive image which is hidden within us all, only waiting to be known and rendered into life.
                    —JOSEPH CAMPBELL
                    The Hero with a Thousand Faces

—16—

EGO AND JUSTICE
The Age of Aries
(c. 1800–c. 7 B.C.)

Dear Friend,

I 'm sorry if I shot the bull too much, but it really isn't all bull (Taurus/Scorpio)! I guess I was trying to make my point by taking the bull by the horns! The more you look for evidence, the more there is. It is so exciting when you begin to see there is a menu, a cosmically ordered unfolding of meaning, and that humanity is an integral part. Humankind has been around for several millions of years, according to the latest count, but the last ten thousand show evidence of some incredible leaps in evolution in which we as human beings seem to play an increasingly important role. I do not happen to agree with the prognosis that our ultimate function is to generate computers which will render human life superannuated, though I have heard such prophecies made in all seriousness.

I confess there are times when I am appalled at the Aquarian scientific, mathematical frenzy that is driving some astrologers, placing them in a position of trying to subordinate astrology to rational control and ego dominance. This seems to me every bit as dangerous as the rejection of astrology by science. One should not, in my humble opinion, ever divorce astrology from its spiritual purpose and reduce it to statistics. Once the proof for astrology is there, hopefully, such statistically inclined astrologers can move on in another direction. Astrology is personal, every bit as much as it is transpersonal. Enough said.

I have one outstanding memory connected to rams, the symbol of Aries. I came upon two of them enclosed in a large field on the Isle of Iona in the Scottish Hebrides. With all that space to browse in, they were nevertheless engaged in a head-on pushing match. They even used their legs to try to unbalance each other, as wrestlers do. What was unforgettable was the depth and sonority of grunts, deep as those of a chorus of Tibetan monks. It struck me at the time that they epitomized their sign in their love of combat (Aries) and their choice to relate rather than either to share or to ignore each other (Libra). When I came back two hours later, they were still hard at it, ramming away and grunting. But by then they had a bigger audience of ewes lined up in the adjoining field. The rams' virility and strength helped me understand why they were to become sacred for so many people in ancient times.

As we come to the Age of Aries, bulls are out and rams are in. The heroes now are no longer of necessity gods or even semi-gods; more and more of them are human. And they become bull-slayers.

But first, to review:

- Aries the Ram, ♈, is a cardinal fire sign, ruled by Mars, and is the exaltation of the Sun. It is also the first sign in the zodiac, and its motto is "I am." Yahweh, the God of gods, translates into "I am that I am." In this Age, the number of names containing the sound of ram is astonishing: Ra, Ram, Rama, Brahman, Abram, Abraham, Amon Ra, Rameses, etc. You can even find the syllable "Mar(s)" in them backwards. Each carries the root idea of masculine solar fire and mortal hero. Keep that in mind as we continue.

- In the body, Aries rules the head and the muscular system, and by extension, all things that come first, including "me first!" It rules courage and initiative, war and adventure.

- Its archetype is that of the mortal hero. And this is a heroic age.

- Libra the Scales, ♎, is the opposite sign. Ruled by Venus and the exaltation of Saturn, its archetype is that of the feminine aspect of beauty, love, and, above all justice and proportion in all relationships, physical and personal.

Historically and psychologically speaking, several great events occurred during this Age: the concept of monotheism arose (a single god associated prominently with the Sun); with this came the birth of the collective ego; and a shift from a matriarchal to a patriarchal viewpoint took place. These changes came as the result of the gradual replacement of a theocentric society by an anthropocentric one. People became increasingly aware of their own strength and capacity to use their own reason; by the end of the Age, which was its flowering, they were already being advised by sages in India, China, and Greece of the wisdom of following "a middle way" (Libra). This was the great teaching of Socrates, Buddha, Lao Tzu, and Confucius, all born strangely within a hundred years of each other and living at the time of a great and most rare conjunction of Uranus, Neptune, and Pluto. These planets, of course, were unknown at the time. If you think about it, there is a logical sequence to these developments. As we grow stronger within ourselves, we tend to separate ourselves from our gods, our archetypal mother and father who seem the ultimate authority, and begin to identify increasingly with our own individuality. When this happened collectively, the natural consequence was to project Father God up with the sun, as sole source and giver of life, and to separate ourselves also from nature or Mother Earth, feeling that we—as it states in Genesis— were to have dominion over the earth. With the Hebrews, the separation was made complete and a covenant was established between God and man. Man identified now with himself (ego) and stood in danger of hubristic pride, one of the main motifs of Greek tragedy, as well as of the poignant story of David in the Old Testament. David was a hero, but also a vulnerable individual. His very humanity makes him both complex and lovable. He is the psalmist who prays to be kept from the "great offense" (Psalm 19:13), the sin of pride.

The realm of myth and the realm of history begin to overlap in earnest during the Age of Aries. Always remembering that a so-called myth is true of both the collective and the individual psyche, we find the mythic motifs recorded in the Pentateuch showing how vitally connected Judaism was to the Age of Aries and to its symbol, the Ram. In a way, Judaism begins with Abraham, who, obeying the voice of God, was willing to sacrifice his beloved son Isaac. Abraham and his father and his wife Sarah left Ur of the Chaldees and traveled to Canaan. Because Sarah was childless, Abraham fathered a son by Hagar, his bondswoman. This child, Ishmael, was cast out with his mother after the miraculous birth of Isaac to Abraham (whose name had been changed to mean "father of nations"). He was a hundred years old and Sarah ninety. Hagar and Ishmael became eponymic ancestors of the Semitic Arabs, while Isaac, through his son Jacob, became the ancestor of the twelve (sic) tribes of Israel. Everyone should remember the touching story of Abraham leading his beloved child up the mountain carrying firewood to make a burnt offering. Isaac asks innocently, "But where is the offering?"—not realizing that it is he himself until he is bound onto the altar and his father raises the knife to kill him.

> And the angel of the Lord called unto him out of heaven and said, Abraham, Abraham: and he said, Here am I.
>
> And he said, lay not thine hand upon the lad, neither do thou anything unto him: for now I know that thou fearest God, seeing thou hast not withheld thy son, thine only son from me.

> And Abraham lifted up his eyes, and looked, and behold behind him a ram caught in a thicket by his horns; and Abraham went and took the ram and offered him up for a burnt offering in the stead of his son. (Gen. 22:11–13).

Later in the history of the Hebrews, at the time when they were in bondage in Egypt, they were saved by the Lord speaking through Moses. They were protected from the slaughter of their firstborn by smearing the blood of sacrificed lambs (Aries) upon the doors of their dwellings, which were "passed over." Passover is celebrated to this day with the blowing of the *shofar,* a ram's horn.

Edward F. Edinger, in his book *The Bible and the Psyche,* has shown that the story of the Old Testament itself is a collective paradigm for the evolution of humanity. Two hundred years previously (in 1758) the German philosopher Johann Georg Hamann wrote: "Each biblical history is accomplishing itself in the life of each single man. All the miracles of Holy Scriptures take place in our souls." Perhaps the addition of astrology is only an extension of this idea. In this light, one can see that Moses is a great hero highly symbolic of the ego, in that like the ego within the psyche, he could lead his people (contents of the psyche) to the Promised Land (i.e., individuation) but could not enter it himself. Therein lie both the glory and the tragedy of every ego ever since.

After Moses had finally completed his own wanderings in the wilderness, he went up to Mount Sinai. He had a vision of a burning bush, a vision, we might say today, revealing that all life is holy. (The same idea occurs in the Welsh *Mabinogion* when Peredur has a vision of a tree half in green leaf and half in flame.) The Lord God gave Moses the Ten Commandments, and these are an instance of Libra balancing the Age. The Ten Commandments, the Code of Hammurabi, the Twelve Tablets of Roman Law, the Edicts of Solon, the Analects of Confucius, and the Noble Eightfold Path of Buddha were all first attempts at collective laws and precepts under which relationships (Libra) could be equably lived out, now that there were so many conscious individuals running around. We must understand ego in the Jungian sense, as the vehicle, the center of human consciousness. So psychologically, the story of Moses is one of highest significance. He is a great example of a mortal hero of courage, determination, loyalty, vision and obedience to his unseen Lord (Self). He was a true leader of his people. Strangely enough, to this day you find statues and pictures of him with ram's horns on his head: the statue by Michelangelo is a good example. One theory is that since the Hebrew word for "radiance" is the same as the one for "horns" except for the vowel, there might have been a mistranslation. But it is curious, nevertheless, that the horns on Moses are those of a ram.

The mythic element of Moses' story lies in his beginnings rather than in his end. He follows the pattern of so many other saviors: he is born of an unknown father and is set adrift in a basket in the bulrushes, rescued by the Pharaoh's daughter, and brought up by her. So he combines in his own experience the old and the new dispensations, just as in the following Age of Pisces, Jesus, born a Jew, was to bridge the old and the new Age to come.

Moses, besides being a hero (Aries), was above all a lawgiver (Libra). Among the many, many instructions for the building of the Ark of the Covenant are some of astrological import. One is the breastplate of twelve stones honoring the twelve tribes of Israel, each associated with a zodiacal sign, as still evidenced in a mosaic from a sixth-century synagogue. The covering for the tabernacle was to be a ram's skin. In the rules for setting up the new altar, which had four horns at its corners, the consecration called for sacrificing one bullock and two rams. The bullock's remains (Taurus) were to be burnt outside the camp—"it *is a sin offering*"—and elaborate rules follow for using every part of the sacrificed rams, ending with the following:

> And thou shalt take the ram of the consecration, and seethe his flesh in the holy place.

And Aaron and his sons shall eat the flesh of the ram, and the bread that is in the basket, by the door of the tabernacle of the congregation.

And they shall eat those things wherewith the atonement was made, to consecrate and to sanctify them: but a stranger shall not eat thereof, because they are holy. (Exod. 29:31–33).

Certainly this was a strong reminder to the backsliders Moses had chastened for continuing to worship the Golden Calf (Taurus).

EGYPT. Here, during the Age of Aries, Akhenaton also attempted a form of monotheism. He proclaimed the great god Aton, but as you know, that was not to last beyond his reign. However, those in Thebes worshipped the god Amon Ra (one of those anagrams for "ram"). At his temple at Karnak still stands a colonnade of forty ram-headed sphinxes. The temple is so constructed that on March 21 the sun, making its ingress into the sign of Aries, shines through the length of the temple and falls on the statue of the god. There are pieces of jewelry containing rams' horns rising out of bulls' horns. One such object is in the Boston Museum of Fine Arts. Amon Ra's symbol was the ram, and according to Frazer's *Golden Bough*, there was a yearly ram sacrifice, after which the ram's skin was placed upon the statue of the god, signifying a ritual sacrifice of the god. Besides Amon Ra, there were other ram gods in Egypt, and these seem to have been preeminent among the other animal-headed gods since they were associated with the sun.

As in Jerusalem in Judea and in Greece, Crete, India, and China, one of the new glories of the Age was its architecture. The greatest expenditure seems to have been on temples; from Solomon's Temple to the Parthenon, from the Valley of the Kings to the temples of Vishnu, everything was to the glory of the Creator. Some esoteric studies show that the mathematical proportions of some of these temples are the same as the proportions of the human body; every piece of the Parthenon is built according to the laws of the Golden Rectangle.

PERSIA. Another bull-slayer is Mithra. Statuary depicts him plunging a dagger into a bull while a scorpion bites the bull's genitals (Taurus/Scorpio). Mithra's exploits are recounted in the *Zend-Avesta*, and indeed Mithraism lasted well into the Piscean Age, rivaling Christianity. Mithra was part of a solar and fire religion, and all its initiates were men. The Age of Aries also was the time of Zoroastrianism and Mazdaism, again religions associated with Arian fire, masculine energy, and light.

Without wishing to burden you with more and more facts, I cannot resist pointing out that this Age, besides all the arts (Libra), saw a pouring forth of religious and philosophical writings, to say nothing of national epics, all containing heroic achievements. Here you find the Vedas, the Upanishads, the Mahabharata in India; the Zend-Avesta in Persia; the books that now form the Old Testament; the literature of Egypt; the drama, history, science, and philosophy of Greece; and the formation of the mythology of the Eddas and great sagas of the Norse that the Teutons and Celts would later set down. What science and technology have contributed to the twentieth century A.D. is certainly no greater than what the human soul poured forth collectively in the 500 years before the birth of Christ.

GREECE. Three myths and a trilogy of plays, Aeschylus' *Oresteia*, could be singled out as pointing specifically to the shift of viewpoint in that new age. One myth is the account of Apollo slaying the Python (Scorpio) near Delphi. This solar god symbolized the Apollonian triumph of intellect and reason and the beginnings of a masculine and rational rejection of the nonrational feminine, the Dionysian approach. In the *Oresteia* trilogy, the people of Athens are instructed in the horrors of the old feminine furies, the Erinyes, and their bloodlust and laws of revenge (Scorpio), and taught that the best solution to crime is to judge matters with a jury (Libra) and to determine punishment by a rational consensus. It was an idea whose time had come.

Theseus, of course, is the Greek bull-slayer, liberating the unfortunate youths and maidens who were the annual tribute to the Minotaur, the dark bull-man monster living in the labyrinth on Crete. With the help of Ariadne and her golden thread of wisdom, he succeeded.

The stories of Jason and the Argonauts and Odysseus in Homer's *Odyssey* are two grand myths of Aries. Jason's goal was to rescue the "golden fleece" of a solar ram which hung on a sacred oak at the temple of Ares (Mars). He and Odysseus are mortal heroes whose tales are of leadership and roistering manly adventure, but in which women are conquered (Circe), used (Medea), or extolled for their domestic fidelity (Penelope). This is also the period of Homer's *Iliad*, the glory of Greek drama, to say nothing of that artistic explosion never equaled again, the Golden Age of Athens (Libra). And these were confronted, at the same time, by the heroic austerities of Sparta (Aries), later fought out in the Peloponnesian War. It should come as no surprise that the goddess Athena appears on coins wearing a helmet adorned with ram's horns.

Perhaps one of the greatest contributions of the Age is the dawning of philosophy in both the West and the East. As people became self-conscious and separated from the Self, they needed to make a relationship with the visible and invisible worlds around them. Gone was the awesome fear of the unpredictable nature goddess, now supplanted with scientific observations and experiments. Man was taking charge of his own destiny, asking the questions of Socrates, whose answers were handed down by Plato to the great Aristotle and, in turn, to his student Alexander the Great. One can almost sense an intellectual euphoria the world over. It has its psychological counterpart today in individuals in late adolescence and early adulthood, when hard work, studies, and sports are balanced with long "bull sessions," those earnest philosophical discussions about the meaning of life. This is a glorious period in life, when young people suddenly think they know everything and feel almost omnipotent. From generation to generation their parents know better, and so it goes. Thirty-seven hundred years ago, a Sumerian father wrote in cuneiform on a tablet:

> You who wander around the public square, would you achieve success? Then seek out the first generations. Go to school, it will benefit you. My son, seek out the first generations, it will be of benefit to you. . . . I, night and day, am tortured because of you. Night and day you waste in pleasures.

A schoolboy's composition goes: "Where did you go?" "I did not go anywhere." "If you did not go anywhere, why do you idle about?" Somehow this brings the past very near to us.

ROME. This city-state was founded during this Age. It, too, had its epic in Virgil's *Aeneid*. Its laws were established, and its history of Etruscan kings unfolded, followed by the Republic and in turn by the emperors and the Roman Empire. Roman mythology was clearly an adaptation of the Greek, so the same gods prevailed, mostly with only some name changes. Here, too, the dialectic between the developing and heroic ego was matched with legal restraints. The name "Rome" came from the Etruscan *Ruma*, and one of their tribes was called Ramnes. Makes you wonder a bit. Another version, of course, is the story of the archetypal twins, Romulus and Remus, also cast out upon the waters as babies, this time saved and nursed by a wolf.

INDIA. Agni, the god of fire, rode on a ram. His name survives in the word "ignite" and in *Agnus Dei*, the lamb of God, slain in the Age of Pisces. Stories of innumerable heroes appear in the epic Mahabharata and the Ramayana. As in the West, architecture of the most stunning complexity arose, and there was a proliferation of advances in the arts and sciences.

CHINA. This was the age of the first great dynasties, the Hsia and Shang along the Huang Ho River. And as in the West, laws were being made uniform, and many public works, including the Great Wall, were constructed. At the end of the Age of Aries, the first great and tyrannical emperor, Shih Huang Ti, emerged, and since he wished history to begin with him (ego!), he had all the literature and historical records of his predecessors destroyed, including the works of Confucius, which were saved only because someone immured them in some houses among the bricks.

NORTHWEST EUROPE. Under the feet of the horned god (assumed to be Cernunnos) on the Gundestrop cauldron is a barely visible long serpent with a ram's head. Rams' heads appear on weapons and at the feet of statues of gods, but so far I do not have much information on the ram in northern mythology. However, the concept of the importance of the hero caught fire during this Age, and we have a plethora of them, all over Northern Europe and, in fact, the world over. The hero in Joseph Campbell's *Hero with a Thousand Faces* was born in this age.

It is frustrating for me, as you can imagine, to have to condense so much into so few words. The real purpose of this letter is to alert you to the psychological achievements of the period: those shifts involving ego development, the rise of the masculine principle, and the development of individual achievements which stand out to this very day. No longer do we have to rely only on the accomplishments of kings and leaders of tribes; we now have scientists, writers, artists, architects, astronomers, historians, senators, and lawyers, all individuals with unique contributions to make. With this staggering awareness of creative power and will emerges the necessity for just and peaceful relations among individuals, cities, and nations through the establishment of collective laws. We are still struggling with this; it is interesting to think of the United Nations, NATO, and the EU in this context. But can you see how the spirit and process of Mars pervaded this Age of Aries, both in its best and its worst aspects?

The Shadow of the Age, of course, was the loss of power and prestige of the feminine. In fact, this was the period when infant daughters were abandoned on mountain slopes to die, and when women were taken as hostages, sold into slavery, and often mis-used and abused. Their outcry, voiced in such plays as *Medea* and *Lysistrata*, mirrors the problem but does not solve it. Christianity, in the Age of Pisces to come, was to ameliorate matters in the beginning, but not for long. Jesus related well and kindly to women, but St. Paul was to lay the groundwork for "putting women in their place" as subservient to men, and much worse was in store. I suspect that men, having discovered their egos, were quite unready to surrender them as Jesus proposed. As I noted ear-lier, Tertullian, an early Church Father, was to question, "*Habet mulier animam?*" ("Does a woman have a soul?"). From Hypatia in Alexandria to Anna Bonus Kingsford and H. P. Blavatsky lie almost 1500 years, during which no woman in the West, outside of the Church, was to teach or write of esoteric matters with impun-ity. The great mystic Rabia was a Muslim and a daughter of the Near East. Some independent Christian women writers among the Beguines were martyred at the stake and their works destroyed.

Other aspects of the shadow of this Age were surely the inven-tion of gunpowder(!), which started out as fireworks in China, as well as wars with sophisticated weaponry; I think of Archemides' use of a solar mirror which focused the sun's rays and burned the sails of the enemy ships. The fate of the Carthaginians at the hands of the Romans is but one example. Babies were dashed to the ground, the hands of their mothers cut off, and the entire region was plowed under with salt so that crops would fail to grow.

One can ask, are we any better in this century? So much of the Age of Aries has still not been worked through the collective in the lives of individuals. Whenever and wherever you see mass hysteria, pandemonium, and the psychology of the mob at work, you see a regression to the task of Aries: the challenge of the individual ego to withstand being overwhelmed by the collective unconscious. The manipulation of the collective psyche was and is the forte of dictators; Hitler, for one, was a master of it.

One of the challenges of our own new Age is to see if we can be members of a collective psyche without losing our own conscious individuality. The stubborn and resistant nature of the U.S. citizen seems to be furthering this task. It may well be one of our most important contributions to the evolution of humankind. Lincoln, the Aquarian, put it succinctly: "You can fool all of the people some of the time ... but you cannot fool all of the people all of the time." Today, we shall have to wait and see.

To conclude, this great unfolding of human evolution has its counterpart in the individual. We, too, leave the uroboric phase of infancy and gradually acquire the glimmerings of consciousness. Then we separate ourselves from our outer environment and inner unconscious, to a point of identifying ourselves as individuals. By the end of the Age of Aries, the heroic ego was in place and idealized in men as bravado and what I think of sometimes as "mucho macho." Nowadays, this attitude is being challenged by a reemerging feminine. But sometimes you find that feminine equipped with every bit as much "mucho macho" in a Martian animus (or inner man), and the battle for supremacy is joined. It is so important to remember that "Mars" in the Age of Aries was a necessary archetypal process to pull humanity up out of the maternal unconscious. When a man steps forward bravely to serve his king (Self), as a knight would, his courage is used in the service of others, not just for himself, nor for the putting down of women or enemies. Rather, if the day will ever come, it may be used for the protection of the good, for the unity of nations, equality, justice, and love among men and women.

Getting late, must put down my pen!

Yet all for love,

ao

Myth is the poetry of religion.

THE FOUR NOBLE TRUTHS

There is suffering in the world.
Suffering is caused by desire and attachment.
Suffering can be removed.
Suffering can be removed through detachment and
by following the Noble Eightfold Path.

THE NOBLE EIGHTFOLD PATH

RIGHT VIEWS
Free from superstition and delusion
RIGHT ASPIRATIONS
High, worthy of the intelligent; worthy of man
RIGHT SPEECH
Kindly, open, and truthful
RIGHT CONDUCT
Peaceful, honest, and pure
RIGHT LIVELIHOOD
Bringing hurt or danger to no living thing
RIGHT EFFORT
In self-training and self-control
RIGHT MINDFULNESS
The active, watchful mind
RIGHT RAPTURE
In deep meditation on the realities of life.
                                        —THE BUDDHA

The masculine provides skillful means;
the feminine provides wisdom.
Both come together in
the enlightened being.
                        —LAMA TENZIN RIMPOCHE

—17—

FAITH AND REASON
The Age of Pisces
(c. 7 B.C.–c. 1800 A.D. and interface to 2012)

Dear Friend,

At the end of each Age a challenge appears that sets the stage for the incoming Age. To fully appreciate this, we have to put ourselves into the mindset of those earlier times. Imagine at the very end of Aries, having spent over 2500 years, give or take a few hundred, developing the concept of the brave masculine hero, the idea of one God, and of the sense of the importance of the individual and one's own self-conscious vehicle, the ego. You have all that in place, and then the emphasis shifts. Now the one God of a proud nation is to be shared with other nations. Furthermore, the truly brave heroes are to be the ones who can willingly sacrifice *themselves*, rather than some specified animal, as a martyred offering for the sake of God, risking every outer appearance of vulnerability and defeat in the process. The ego, so valiantly won, is to be surrendered to some unseen and unknown power rumored to exist within one's soul, though not defined nor really understood. That truly is a tall order. And for many, many people the world over, it still is. It was hard for Christians, as well as for Jews, but the message had already been prefigured in the East—for the Hindus in the Upanishads, by the beautiful and poetic figure of Krishna in the Bhagavad Gita, "The Song of God," and in the wise and gentle teachings of Buddha.

I have recently had a new insight into the spiritual and psychological impact of Christ on the Cross: now at the end of this Age could it not be that the message of this divine drama is that we can become *conscious* of the existence of an indwelling Christ, a Divine Guest (Jung's Self) or Atman? "Christ Consciousness" could now be seen as a term for an awareness open to all humankind, not just the prerogative of only one religion. Remember, that is what the mystics of them all have expressed for centuries. This is a huge step: each individual ego being a unique expression of the same Spirit; our ego having our name and representing who we *think* we are, but discovering that who we *really* are is the ONE common source for all of us.

The concept of transpersonal love (Neptune, ruler of Pisces, is the higher octave of Venus, whose process is more that of *eros*) is another thing that evolved in consciousness during the Age of Pisces. This means love even for your enemies—a love to be called *agape* in the West, a love expressed as *ahimsa* (nonviolence) in the East, a love which would set self-martyrdom above killing one's persecutors. This seems ironic given the situation today. Negative Neptune yields fanaticism and obsession.

In the Age of Pisces the dichotomy shifted to that of faith and reason, ultimately in the West to become the struggle between religion and science, or Pisces and its opposite sign, Virgo. It must have been as difficult and startling a concept as one can imagine. A good illustration lies in the story of a little boy in Sunday school hearing the story of the crucifixion of Christ. He listens intently, getting redder and redder in the face, until finally exploding with, "Hell, where were the Marines?" Confronting Aries with Pisces is not unlike confronting the Terminator with Jesus limp on the Cross.

There is no denying that the icon for Western civilization in the Age of Pisces has been that of the Cross, symbolic of the process and the difficult challenge that image implies. At another level, the cube represents matter, the manifestation of the 4 symbolic elements:

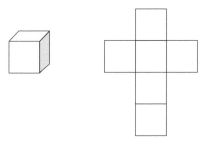

No matter what one's religion today, there can be no doubt about the cultural impact of Christianity: the majestic sweep of art, architecture, music on the one hand but also the horrifying religious wars and violent efforts at conversion. On the Virgo side came the rich gifts of the rediscovery of Greek philosophy, the building of universities, medicine and science, all of which we owe to the Moors and Islam coming into Spain. This has been wonderfully captured by Richard E. Rubenstein in *Aristotle's Children*. There was a brief Golden Age (900–1100 A.D.) in Spain when Jews, Christians, and Muslims worked together translating the ancient texts and living together peacefully. Maybe we have forgotten to be grateful for this reprieve from the Dark Ages! Much later, the swing between the Age of Reason (Virgo) and the Romanticism (Pisces) of the nineteenth century that followed provides yet another example.

We have seen God revered by cattlemen in Taurus the Bull, by shepherds in Aries the Ram; now we were asked to become fishermen in Pisces the Fish. Christianity is the religion that, consciously or unconsciously, chose to align itself specifically with that symbol. But Buddhism, Islam, Sikhism, and Bahá'í are also among the great religions of the Piscean Age, just as Judaism began during the Age of Aries but continued into the Age of Pisces. Jesus, a Jew, is said to have been born circa 7 B.C., at the time of a conjunction of Jupiter and Saturn in Pisces. This conjunction was so close that the two planets appeared as one gigantic, brilliant star when seen with the naked eye. So there might have been good reason for the astrologers (magi) of the time to be impressed and to make some predictions that would have disturbed the reigning King Herod. There is much dispute all these millennia later about the literal accuracy of many biblical accounts. This much we know: The fact remains that the *image* of Jesus served as a bridge between the Ages. Viewed symbolically, which we desperately need to do, a luminous message comes through, handed down mythically and symbolically from earlier sources and rediscovered in subsequently discovered Gnostic texts. The current split between fundamentalists of all stripes, which seems so painful to the rest of us, could so easily be healed by looking at the Bible and the Koran in a symbolic way. Literalism can become a form of idolatry. This is why the avatars spoke in parables, so the stories could be understood on many levels, each revealing a more profound understanding. And astrology offers us a golden key to that symbolic insight.

Though Buddhism began five hundred years earlier, its precepts of peace, compassion, nonviolence, and the pursuit of inner wisdom and detachment make it a description of the "One Way" to self-realization that still complements the teachings of Jesus. Buddhism came as a reform and extension of Hinduism, in much the same way that the teachings of the New Testament are for Christians an extension of the Old Testament, and the Koran, rather than denying either of these bodies of wisdom, according to Islam, is a crowning of both. Of them all, Buddhism (and Taoism in China, and Zen in Japan) is by nature the most Piscean and nondenominational. One can be both a Christian or a Jew and a Buddhist, since Buddhism offers a methodology for enlightenment in which there is no need or desire for conversion.

I have placed the heart of Buddha's teachings at the head of this letter, so you can see its wisdom for yourself. Here there is no insistence on creed. In that regard, it is akin to the practices of Sufism, the mystical essence of Islam. All the great religions seem to have an inner tradition of mysticism at their heart. Perhaps these are waiting to flower in our Age of Aquarius. It almost seems that way. We shall hope and pray and see.

To understand the deeper meaning and connections to this Age, let's look at Pisces again:

- Pisces the Fish, ♓, is co-ruled by Jupiter and Neptune. It is a mutable water sign, yin, and is the exaltation of Venus. The sign is usually drawn with the two fishes swimming in opposite directions. Already we know this to be significant, as the Ages are moving backward through the constellations while we move forward in the inner wheel of the tropical zodiac of the signs.

- In the body Pisces rules the feet. (Jesus washed the feet of his disciples as a ritual act, which the Pope reenacts on Maundy Thursday.) In the world, Pisces rules oceans and large bodies of water. Above all, it rules peace and compassion, *agape*. It also rules music, poetry, and devotion. In the psyche, it carries the unconscious, which is the source of the conscious. Its positive archetype is the mystic, that great hero in the invisible world of soul. Thus it rules meditation. Neptune, you remember, rules all mind-altering substances. The negative traits are self-pity, lack of self-esteem, and being wishy-washy.

- Now contrast Pisces with Virgo the Virgin, ♍, which is the opposite sign. This is a mutable earth sign, also yin, ruled by Mercury, whose processes in this sign become grounded in logical, precise discrimination and rational common sense. Above all, Virgo loves truth and understanding. She is the epitome of reason and definition. It is probable that the feminine asteroids—Pallas ⚶, Ceres ⚳, Juno ⚵, and Vesta ⚶, et al.—will be said to rule Virgo. They have the right so to do, since they belong to an orbit between Mars and Jupiter. Do you remember the astronomer Bode's law?

He found that the proportion of the distances of the planets from Mercury through Saturn is the same as the proportion of the frequencies of the notes on a guitar string! Shades of Pythagoras' "harmony of the spheres."

- In the body, Virgo rules the intestines, which discriminate between the useful and the useless in the nourishment passing through them. Here the good is extracted from the mixture and put in order.

- In the world, Virgo rules the traditional sciences, rationalism, and all kinds of classifications and details. It is associated with granulation and the miniaturizing of things. Seeds and all they symbolize belong to Virgo. Negative traits would be fussiness, criticism, and hyper-perfectionism.

- Psychology itself involves analysis (Virgo) and synthesis (Pisces).

A great Piscean message came into the world with Jesus Christ, but with it the terrible Shadow of Virgonian dispute. Within three centuries, Christians were killing Christians over rules and regulations, hair-splitting theological definitions, arguments about right and wrong, and countless new opportunities for sins, mortal and venial. For me this Shadow is symbolized by the pointing finger of a scold. Here came the Four C's—complaining, comparing, criticizing, and condemning—and the trail of their ensuing woes. Never before in history have so many been condemned by the personal judgment of so many others, nor was there ever before such idolatry of rules and regulations per se, despite Jesus' reminder that we were not made for the Sabbath, but the Sabbath for us.

The entire concept of measuring time began with clocks devised to order the periods for prayer in monasteries. Since then, all of us are being driven by the seeming lack of time in which to fulfill our responsibilities. Schedules and measurements are all the gift of Virgo. The struggle between the outgoing Age and the incoming one was fierce and cruel on both sides. The Romans persecuted and killed Christians for sport in the Coliseum, while trying everything possible to stamp out the new religion. Piscean men and women were burnt (Nero is said to have used them for living torches), mauled by lions, tortured, and reviled. Yet the new Age prevailed (something we ourselves must remember). Then it was the Christians' turn to destroy as much as possible of the glorious heritage of the former Age. Libraries were sacked and burned, "pagan" religious ideals were mocked, ridiculed, and put down, centers of learning closed or destroyed, and the one pagan woman teacher and philosopher in Alexandria, Hypatia, ripped from her podium and flayed alive with oyster shells. All this was in the name of Jesus Christ. Nor did it end there, as you know. The religious wars, big and small, have never really ceased. As Joseph Campbell warned, we *must* learn to understand each other's mythologies. For many in the world, alas, they *still* are worth killing and dying for.

Islam, the second great religion in the West, also has its beauty of faith and devotion, accompanied by a great many duties and requirements. Both Christianity and Islam depend on dogma, largely fashioned after the departure of their founders. And each of the religions has its holy book—the Bible and the Koran. Judaism is also a religion of the book, the Torah and the Talmud. Unfortunately, all three have several sects that too often came or still come to blows!

The Sikhs, too, are connected to one great book, the Adi Grantha, that is read aloud twenty-four hours a day, every day, in enclosed glass booths situated on the four sides of the huge rectangular pool at the Golden Temple in Amritsar, India. When we were at the temple one evening, we witnessed the moving ritual portage and uncovering of the actual great book, wrapped in seven cloths and covered with marigolds. It was raced at high speed across a narrow bridge to the temple, carried by porters on a golden palanquin to the nerve-shattering blare of gigantic trumpets. Once in the temple, it was uncovered ceremonially by several turbaned and bearded men, who read from it the wisdom of forty avatars from all religions. Then it was rewrapped and returned equally dramatically to where it was housed for the night. The Golden Temple is set around this huge pool surrounded by white marble walks and buildings. Music and song quaver over the rippling waters day and night, hauntingly beautiful. A sacred tree has been touched by so many hands, its trunk is like a smooth varnished piece of furniture!

All such holy books containing wisdom, guidance, and regulations are ruled by Virgo. Though the alphabets are the gift of Gemini, the contents of any how-to book are Virgo; the Virgin is the goddess of prose, just as Venus exalted in Pisces is goddess of poetry and music. So these holy books blend both signs. Today you could say that Virgo is left-brain and Pisces right-brain, in terms of linear versus imaginal thinking.

The shadow side of Virgo manifests itself.

The impact of these tensions of opposites in the last 2000 years has filled libraries with volumes of theologies, historical events, commentaries thereon, and disputes about them. Complicated dogmas, rules, rituals, taboos are all Virgo, as is the ideal of perfectionism and the sin of scrupulosity. All I can do in this letter is point out the basic underlying tension and polarity. Another Piscean step came with the discovery of Neptune in the mid-nineteenth century. Neptune rules the process of dissolving. As soon as it was discovered, art lost its borders in impressionism, music lost its obedience to set rhythms with Debussy and others; ether and radium dissolved other borders. Spiritualism came under scientific scrutiny and the psyche was suggested as a reality.

Christian associations with the fish are many. The disciples were to be "fishers of men"; baptism takes place in a *piscina*, literally a fish pond; even today, the bishop's mitre or triangular hat is a fish head. Even the word "episcopal" has a fish (*piscis*) hidden it. The Virgin is usually symbolically depicted in the *vesica piscis*, obtained by intersecting two circles:

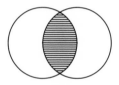

Reversed, the *vesica piscis* forms)(, the symbol for Pisces. Even in pre-Christian times this symbol was associated with the yoni, and fish were eaten in honor of the love goddess. Freya, the Norse one, gave us Friday. *Vendredi* (French for "Friday") is the day of Venus; until recently it was a day to eat fish for Roman Catholics. We still call a person who has difficulty relating (Venus) a "cold fish." A Christian church is built like a ship, its long body called the "nave." The logo of Christ is the two curves of the fish, found to this day in the catacombs. Being Christian was dangerous in the early days of persecution in Rome. A Christian, not knowing if a stranger shared his faith, would draw one arc of the fish and the other person, if Christian, would complete it. A non-Christian would think the Christian was just doodling. In those days, the Greek word for "fish," *ichthys*, was an anagram for the phrase in Greek for "Jesus Christ, Son of God, Savior." In the New Testament, besides the Virgin Birth, we find the miracle of the loaves (Virgo) and fishes (Pisces), and Jesus told John and Peter, both fishermen, to cast their nets (Virgo) on the other side.

Jung has written extensively on the symbolism of the aeon of Pisces, and it is fascinating reading. The images of Jesus as the slain lamb (Aries-ego), the Paschal lamb, not only refer to the fading of the previous Age of Aries the Ram, but hint at the great psychological task awaiting us at the collective level. That task involves a willingness to make of ourselves "a full and willing sacrifice." We are to take the ego we worked so hard to acquire and offer it up with devotion to a higher power within us, to the Divine Guest, the Christ Within, the Atman, or whatever name the mystical traditions of each religion give to that center and totality of our individual psyches. It is a divine drama, and as this Age of Pisces gradually gives way to our already dawning new Age, you can see how far we are from completing it. The curse of the pointing finger is still among us, internationally, nationally, politically, within all institutions and families, right down to the accusations with which we flagellate ourselves in the privacy of our own consciences.

Pisces, in turn, which rules all mind-altering substances, can also be the shadow side of Virgo. Given the rate of people seeking escape from "reality" in drugs and alcohol, you really begin to wonder how the simple message of Jesus' "new commandment" got lost—the commandment "to love one another even as I have loved you." So the complete and loving gifts that Pisces and Virgo have to exchange within our psyches are far from having been accepted. Virgo's positive gift is loving and practical service and genuine humility. Think Red Cross, or *Medecins sans Frontières*. For me, it is epitomized in the way the Swiss, a Virgo people, run their country and its affairs. At the personal level, one can think of Mother Teresa, born a Virgo and dedicated to loving service. Her message, however, is also prophetically Aquarian when she says, "I believe in person to person and that God is in everyone."

After the period of the terrible persecutions and martyrdoms of the early Christians, one of the trends of the Age of Pisces was the withdrawal of men and women from the world into hermitages and, later, monasteries, in order to meditate, pray, and pursue a mystical and introverted direction. (In the natural zodiac, Pisces is the twelfth sign, and the Twelfth House in any chart rules one's attitude toward seclusion and introspection.) This introversion is very Piscean. Such monastic orders also flourished in the East and still do. For East and West the basic vows of chastity, obedience, and poverty were deemed essential. This implied renouncing nature and placing the highest value upon the intangibles of the world (introverted Pisces). Later the monastic orders of the extraverted West became more involved with education, caring for the sick, and providing for the poor, all of which is Virgo. The Celtic Christians and St. Francis of Assisi were exceptional examples in that their renunciation did not exclude nature. Francis celebrated it in his love for birds, animals, and flowers, Brother Sun and Sister Moon. Just read his famous prayer in the light of the union of Pisces and Virgo, so entwined are they in terms of ego-sacrifice, love, compassion, and service.

A PRAYER OF ST. FRANCIS

Lord, make me a channel of Thy peace
That where there is hatred, I may bring love,
That where there is wrong, I may bring forgiveness,
That where there is discord, I may bring harmony,
That where there is error, I may bring truth,
That where there is doubt, I may bring faith,
That where there is despair, I may bring hope,
That where there are shadows, I may bring Thy light,
That where there is sadness, I may bring joy.

Lord, grant that I may seek to comfort
Rather than to be comforted;
To understand, rather than to be understood;

To love, rather than to be loved.
For it is by giving that one receives;
It is by self-forgetting that one finds;
It is by forgiving that one is forgiven;
It is by dying that one awakens to eternal life.

It is hard to imagine, short of the words of Jesus himself, an example that better illustrates the union of these two signs. Again, Mother Teresa's "We can do no great things, only little things with great love," would be another combination of Virgo's care for practical detail and loving Pisces.

Psychologically speaking, it is not easy to surrender one's ego. First you must develop one, to be aware that you have one. Secondly, you have to be really convinced that there is something within you greater than what you ordinarily think you are. Sacrificing ego can be downright dangerous. There is the story of the great Sufi mystic al-Hallaj, who in a great moment of illumination completely surrendered his ego. Joyfully he ran out to share his great discovery: "I am Allah!" he shouted, "I am Allah!" People accused him of blasphemy and killed him. But they say that as his blood trickled out onto the dusty ground it formed the word "Allah." In order to accomplish this surrender today, Jung maintains, we need to learn to think with our hearts and be willing to take up our own cross rather than projecting all our burdens onto Christ. This is what he wrote in a letter to Dr. Dorothee Hoch on July 3, 1952:

> Educated people . . . would be much more readily convinced of the meaning of the gospel if it were shown them that the myth was always there to a greater or lesser degree, and moreover is actually present in archetypal form in every individual . . .
>
> Instead of bearing ourselves, i.e., our own cross, ourselves, we load Christ with our unresolved conflicts. We "place ourselves under his cross," but by golly not under our own . . .

Have your congregation understood that they must close their ears to the traditional teachings and go through the darknesses of their own souls and set aside everything in order to become that which every individual bears in himself as his individual task, and that no one can take this burden from him? We continually pray that "this cup may pass from us" and not harm us. Even Christ did so, but without success.

Yet we use Christ to secure this success for ourself. For all these reasons theology wants to know nothing of psychology, because through it we could discover our own cross. But we only want to talk of Christ's cross, and how splendidly his crucifixion has smoothed the way for us and solved our conflicts. We might also discover, among other things, that in every feature Christ's life is a prototype of individuation and hence cannot be imitated: *One can only live one's own life totally in the same way with all the consequences this entails...*

But Christ accepted a cross that cost him his life. It is fairly easy to live a praiseworthy truth, but difficult to hold one's own as an individual against a collective and be found unpraiseworthy. Is it clear to your congregation that Christ may possibly mean just this?

For me, this is the best summation of the challenge and task for individuals before they can move on to understanding what comes next in the Age of Aquarius. The ego, as I have pointed out before, does not have to die; it only has to surrender, to turn its face to the inner Self or Christ Within and relate to it in a spirit of devotion. Only then can one understand the blessing, "May the peace of God be with you, and the glory of his countenance shine upon you." The willing service and humility of the ego are the gift of Virgo, and the "peace which passeth understanding" is then the gift of Pisces. It is there waiting, lovingly and patiently, for us to come.

Love and peace, wherever you are,

ao

*M*an possesses a dual nature, a phenomenal ego and
an eternal Self, which is the inner man, the spirit, the
spark of divinity within the soul. It is possible for a man,
if he so desires, to identify himself with the spirit and
therefore with the Divine Ground, which is of the same
or like nature with the spirit. . . . Man's life on earth
has only one end and purpose: to identify himself with
his eternal Self and so to come to unitive knowledge
of the Divine Ground.

— ALDOUS HUXLEY

*M*en float sticks upon the water and
think that they have divided it.

— RAMAKRISHNA

*S*plit a piece of wood, and I am there.
Lift up the stone, and you will find Me there.

— THE GOSPEL OF THOMAS

*P*RAYER FOR *M*YSTERY
A Celtic Prayer

*Y*ou are above me, O God
You are within.
You are in all things
yet contained by no thing.
Teach me to seek you in all that has life
that I may see you as the Light of light.
Teach me to search for you in my own depths
that I may find you in every living soul.

— J. PHILIP NEWELL

18

INDIVIDUAL AND COSMOS
The Age of Aquarius
(c. 1800 A.D.– c. 4000 A.D.)

*In the words and deeds of the past there lies hidden a
treasure that men may use to strengthen and elevate their
own characters. The way to study the past is not to confine
oneself to mere knowledge of history but through application
of this knowledge to give actuality to the past.*

—I CHING

Dear Friend,

You ask, *What about the Age to come?* Well, that is the big
question and one that astrology can certainly help answer.
If you are convinced, as I am, that the past has shown a
pattern strangely and wonderfully connected to the unfolding of
the Ages, then it is worth looking at what the tasks and the traps
might be in the Age we are entering. Psychologically speaking,
those of us who have come through our own inner Age of Pisces
are ready for Aquarius. From studying the meanings of the sign,
I have come to believe that the new dialectic will involve the true
discovery of the inner Self, the Divine Guest within us, and with
it the need to recognize this in *all* people and in nature as well:
it will be the dialectic of the individual and the cosmos. More

simply stated, it could mean the discovery of the sacred in the commonplace, a reconciliation of the transcendence and immanence of spirit—a cosmic ecology, if you will—a deep understanding of the interdependence of all life.

The great Native American Chief Seattle wrote of this concept to President Franklin Pierce in 1855. Here are a few memorable lines he wrote:

> How can one buy or sell the air, the warmth of the land? That is difficult for us to imagine. We do not own the sweet air or the sparkle on the water. . . . Each pine tree shining in the sun, each sandy beach, the mist hanging in the dark woods, every space, each humming bee; every part of the Earth is sacred to my people, holy in their memory and experience.
>
> We are part of the Earth and the Earth is part of us. The flagrant flowers are our sisters. The reindeer, the horse, the great eagle are our brothers. The rocky heights, the foamy crests of waves in the river, the sap of meadow flowers, the body heat of the pony—and of human beings—all belong to the same family. . .
>
> Teach your children what we have taught our children, that the Earth is our mother. . . . One thing we know, which the white man may one day discover, our God is the same God. You may think now that you own God as you wish to own our land; but you cannot. God is the God of ALL people and God's compassion is equal for all. This earth is precious to God, and to harm the earth is to heap contempt upon its Creator. So love it as we have loved it. Care for it as we have cared for it. . . .
>
> Humankind has not woven the web of life. We are but one thread within it. Whatever we do to the web, we do to ourselves. All things are bound together. All things connect. Whatever befalls the Earth befalls also the children of the Earth.

Here nuclear physics, laser beams, and holograms, all ruled by Aquarius (as is astrology itself), will lead the way to a scientific confirmation, perhaps, of what Chief Seattle is writing about. We materialists have fallen into the trap of what the Hindus term *maya* or the illusory appearance of the universe, and we fail to perceive the *unus mundus*, the "one world" of the mystics and the alchemists. We, because of our physical vehicles, are forced to perceive in terms of time and of the three dimensions of space and miss finding it because we are not shown how! It is when we see it *only* in this habitual way that the Earth becomes mere matter to be bought and sold, wasted, and defiled. We lose the perception that St. Francis and Chief Seattle share— the holiness *within* the wholeness of this world. "There is another world and it is hidden in *this* one."

The hologram, which is produced by laser beams, provides a three-dimensional reality suspended in space that you can put your hand through! Furthermore, every single fraction of a hologram can produce the whole image. This *process* is similar to that of our own bodies, in which each cell carries the signature of our identity in the DNA/RNA of the genetic code. If you can still hold the image of that process, can you see how it could help us understand the words in Genesis "and God created man in his own image" as meaning that every part of the universe, down to the smallest atom, contains the imprint of its Creator? We human beings, men and women, also carry the creative principle within our psyches, within our inner suns—our Divine Guest—which at one level are united as sparks with the "Sun behind the sun," the mystery of God. Gradually the privilege and poetry and "imprisoned splendor" of what it could mean to be a human being, in tune with our true nature, might not only be accepted scientifically and religiously but lived out. In the coming Age, there is opportunity for science and religion finally to exchange proof and sacrament.

Should this be true, then we already recently have had prophets among us in Jung, Einstein, Teilhard de Chardin, Joseph Campbell, Matthew Fox, and among the many men and women who are heralding the reemergence of Hagia Sophia, the feminine wisdom hidden in nature and within each of us, without which we cannot give inner birth to our true selves in the process of individuation.

It has long been known that this process has a methodology, a science or gnosis, but it has been kept dark because of potential misuse. One of the features of the new Age is that more and more of these techniques are being revealed to those willing to be responsible for them. Much of this will depend on our understanding the intrinsic nature of synchronicity. In a letter to Karl Schmid, Jung wrote:

> Synchronistic phenomena are very often connected to archetypal constellations. This much can be determined by experience...
>
> Synchronicity is not a name that characterizes an "organizing principle," but like the word "archetype" it characterizes a modality. . . . It is legitimate to ask yourself what it is that carries the qualities of the archetypal and the synchronistic, and to pose the question, for instance, of the intrinsic nature of the psyche or of matter.

It is 150 years now since Emerson, Thoreau, and the Transcendentalists wrote of Indian philosophy in America. Not everyone realizes that the body of wisdom of the Vedas, the Upanishads, and the Bhagavad Gita only reached Europe for the first time in the late 1700s. These works were translated into Italian and German, and because of the American Revolution, most young Americans chose German universities rather than Oxford and Cambridge to further their education. It was they who brought the news of these translations to Boston. They offered the first radical change in philosophical views in centuries. Thoreau gave part of this wisdom a pragmatic Yankee twist when he interpreted *ahimsa* (nonviolence) as civil disobedience. Later this idea inspired a young Indian lawyer in South Africa called Mohandas Gandhi, who used it to free India from British rule. This in turn inspired Martin Luther King, Jr., and the civil rights movement in the United States. There was a compelling picture in the newspaper of a student holding some flowers up to a bayonet held by a soldier in front of the Pentagon. In the small space between blade and petals, East and West were finally meeting. That's Aquarius! When ideas begin to affect the entire globe, which happens today whenever we turn on TV for the news, we are furthering the Aquarian process. But the timing of Eastern wisdom coming West in the late eighteenth century is important because not only did it coincide with three great revolutions, it coincided with Herschel's discovery of a new planet, Uranus, the ruler of Aquarius, in 1781. This planet had been hitherto unknown, and its discovery was followed by those of two more planets, Neptune and Pluto, in subsequent years. A possible third one is Chiron, quite recently discovered. But its small size has raised the question whether it is a true planet or a comet. Astronomers are leaning toward the latter opinion. In any case, astrologers are excited about it. In general, it looks as if a new planet is discovered when humanity is ready to evolve to the process it represents.

Today the biggest discovery of all is that of our own planet Earth; we are seeing it in a totally new way. I believe the icon of this Age is the photograph of Earth taken from the moon by the astronauts. With this picture, for the first time we can look at our lovely, fragile home objectively. This view from the moon is as great a shift in viewpoint as the one now required within us.

Mary Baker Eddy, Anna Bonus Kingsford, and Helena Petrovna Blavatsky in the latter half of the nineteenth century were, as far as I can make out, among the first women to seriously address themselves with impunity to metaphysical matters outside of the Church. Despite the number of brilliant women in the West who lived from the fourth century on, few had freedom of expression, and most were put to death on charges of heresy. As I wrote in *The Dove in the Stone*, we are only just beginning to appreciate the terrible suffering of these women, among them the Beguines in the late Middle Ages. So the slow emergence of women who are allowed intellect and permitted to express their thoughts and share them equally with men is another sign of the Age. I realize, with profound gratitude to this country and this Age that I can write these letters to you without fear of being put to death. Four hundred years ago, give or take a few, one poor Englishwoman was burned to death for having a copy of a Psalm in her apron pocket. Despite the tides of current fundamentalism in *all* the great religions, which serve to sum up the Age of Pisces, the eon rolling in will surely bring with it a new tolerance, respect, and understanding of all faiths. A holistic attitude will prevail (and not just in medicine).

Years ago, one of my friends gave me a lovely gift, which she had made herself. It was a crystal box, cube-shaped, with a lid. One day when I was teaching a course on the cultural history of civilization, I brought the box to class. I put a candle in it, lit the candle, and then held in front of it the symbols of the various religions we had studied, which I had drawn on tissue paper. The children could see that the same light shone through each. It seemed to make quite an impression. Then suddenly one of the students jumped up in delight. "Wow!" she cried. "You could put any one of us in front of that, and the same light would be shining through each of us." "Yes," spoke up another, "that's what the Atman's supposed to do. Right?" Right. Then another one came up to the box. He had cut a square of black paper and punched a few holes in it. When he held it in front of the cube, only a few little pricks of light shone through. "I think that's the way most of us are," he commented glumly.

Well, the discussion got very animated, believe me. I heard things like, "Then you need to get enlightened, dummy!" "Is that what they mean by being illuminated?" "Is that why saints have halos and all that light drawn around them?" "Is that what the Transfiguration of Christ was about?" The class was so filled with ideas, with everybody talking at once, that I asked them then and there to write down their thoughts. Everyone grabbed paper, and the pencils flew. I wish I could have made an anthology of the comments those students made, as young as they were. One even suggested that to work on yourself, in this light, was not to be narcissistic, and if you were accused of self-absorption, you could just say you were washing windows. Another used the image of stained glass windows in a church, which look like nothing until lit up from within. Wisest of all were the words of one shy girl, "If I know my own light exists inside me, then I just have to know it is in everyone else, even if it is hidden or obscured." For me as a teacher, it was the proof perfect that education (Latin *ex ducere*, "leading forth") is just that: the "drawing out" of the wisdom that is latent in us all. "In-struction" is simply building in or explaining the system, the trellis, of a particular discipline, made to hold up the creative and living growth upon or within it. After forty-odd years of teaching, in one way or another, I realize I have never taught a thing. At best, I could only fan the flame within my students and maybe create a situation for an attack of insight.

It is my conviction, from the Jungian perspective, that when teachers can relate Self-to-Self with their students, the students feel loved and respected. Then they cease to fear and put up barriers, so more learning can flow in and out. In retrospect, I know this from the few wonderful teachers I myself was privileged to have. Alas, much of education proceeds on an ego-to-ego basis, but then so does most of life.

Since astrology can point to universal processes functioning in anything in the phenomenal world, it is a good guide in helping us see what the great religions of the world have in common esoterically rather than focusing on the many exoteric things that make them different. This will be one of the tasks in the new Age. Aquarius is by nature tolerant and freedom-loving. Maybe, for once, we won't have to put down the previous Age and demean it. Maybe for once we can be grateful rather than scornful of the past; maybe we can say "thank you" to the Grandfathers and Grandmothers as the Native Americans do.

Ramakrishna, the Hindu saint, was an Aquarian and a great believer in interfaith dialogue, and he also had a fine sense of humor. At one time in his life, he decided to practice what it would be like to be a Christian, a Jew, a Muslim, a Buddhist, until he truly understood them all. In each instance, he practiced the religion in question with utter devotion until he had a full realization ending in a vision of Christ, of Moses, of Muhammad, and so forth. He even tried living as a woman for a brief period, so that he could have a deeper understanding of women. He also married. Needless to say, not everybody understood his extraordinary actions, and some serious questions came up as to whether or not he was fit for his work as guardian of a Hindu temple. So a convocation of experts and sages was called from all over India. Ramakrishna was examined and questioned thoroughly and at length for several days. Then he was told to await the decision. Finally he was summoned. When he entered the room, all the sages and experts bowed down to him and pronounced him an avatar, a great teacher for his time. Ramakrishna stood before them solemnly, and then his face broke out in a wide grin. "Phew!" he exclaimed, "I thought you were going to tell me I was nuts!"

Muhammad said that any philosopher who taught a metaphysics he had not himself realized was just a donkey carrying about a big load of books. Ramakrishna realized all the religions. He became illuminated, and when people would come and ask him to speak of God, he would ask, "With or without form?" as simply as we would ask how you take your tea, with or without milk.

I am sharing this because Ramakrishna had the Aquarian view of honor and respect for all faiths, finding through his own experience that they were equally valid and that they all served the same purpose: reuniting individuals with their truest and deepest natures, the part in them that is a spark of God. All the rest is social embroidery, adaptation to regional and social requirements. You would not and should not expect an Eskimo and a tropical islander to have the same rituals. But we should recognize that all those human beings who instinctively seek to find meaning and peace within themselves discover it when they connect to whatever for *them* is the Divine Ground, as Huxley and Tillich called it. Each of the avatars said "There is only One Way!" If we think in terms of *verbs* (processes), then they were describing the *same* "only way"—the way from the ego to the Self within. Each of them experienced the bliss and "peace that passeth understanding," and in their time and culture sought to share it with humanity. But because we think literally, if my guy is right, yours must be wrong! People all over the world are killing each other for this reason, even as I am writing. In this sense, Jung has given us an immense gift for the future. By using psychological terms, which carry no specific religious semantics, he has made sense of how to approach this inner age-old process within each individual psyche. This opens the way for us all. So today we seem to use the word *spiritual* in preference to *religious*.

Now, in the light of psychological evolution, let's take a closer look at Aquarius and its complementary sign Leo.

- Aquarius the Water bearer, ♒, is a fixed air sign, yang, and it has been called the sign of the Common Man. Its ruler is Uranus (Saturn, according to the old system). The squiggles of the glyph become symbolic of vibrations.

- The opposite constellation is Leo, ♌, the Lion King, ruled by the Sun.

- Therefore, Aquarius is the *detriment* of the Sun, meaning that here the concept of monarchy is modified by the idea that we can all be kings and queens in our own right, another way of defining democracy. The ruler (Leo) becomes now the minister of the people (Aquarius). Note that the water symbol does not signify a liquid but rather living waters and vibrations of invisible energy: *prana* and kundalini in the body, and electricity, radio waves, X-rays, computers, cell phones and the like, as well as aviation, space travel, or cosmic rays.

- In the world, Aquarius rules governments by and for people, society in general, the collective community, friends, transpersonal love, as well as communications dependent on invisible energy such as radio and television. (We display its ruler, Uranus, ♅, on our rooftops!). It has much to do with space travel and exploration, technology as well as globalization, international aid and cross-cultural finances. The sign can be extremely detached and impersonal, which is one of its traps. This is the dichotomy of the collective (Aquarius) and the individual (Leo).

- In the psyche, this sign has to do with higher intellect (Uranus is the higher octave of Mercury) and intuition; it governs idealism, abstract concepts, and our perceptions of space and interest in space exploration and the cosmos. *Star Wars* and *Star Trek* have paved the way—and I even remember the prophetic comic character *Buck Rogers*!

Leo, a sign that is highly individual, personal, and caring, rules processes that can balance the detachment of Aquarius with true warmth and feeling. As the centuries roll by, this will become crucial. You see this reflected even in architecture. Today's skyscrapers and collective business centers are abstract, implacable, windowless cubes of glass and steel (Aquarius), while palaces and castles built at the height of the monarchies are flamboyant and richly ornamented, surrounded by elaborate parks, plaisances, and fountains. There is nothing cozy about Aquarius! Today nature is not invited, but I believe it will be. In the beginning, this is one of the traps. We are in danger of becoming not so much anthropocentric as technocentric. We have no windows to open, so we breathe polluted air. We watch nature films from our living rooms. We do not work in the outdoors, so we have to exercise on machines. Sometimes it's downright funny, but sad. This is what Jung meant by enantiodromia, the running into the opposites.

As I have mentioned before, few astronomers or astrologers agree about the dating of the dawn of this new Age, but its symptoms certainly coincided politically with the end of the eighteenth century and the discovery of its ruler Uranus by a "common man," William Herschel, who was an amateur astronomer and a German musician living in Bath in England. This was the time of those three great revolutions on behalf of the common man: the American, the French, and the Industrial Revolutions. And from then on, with the discovery of how to cast iron, the whole world of manufacturing began with a vengeance. Monarchies were toppled, and the cry was out for three famous Aquarian principles: *Liberty, Brotherhood,* and *Equality.* These are the cornerstones of the sign. And in the last two hundred years, the collective has struggled through many different political experiments intended somehow to benefit the common man (though so often they fall into the old trap of Leo elitism anyway): communism, socialism, democracy. I don't think fascism is a viable option, since it has elitism built in from the very beginning. But collectively, all over the world, we are still trying to find the best solution for representative government, without dictatorship, and a fair distribution of wealth and property, plus a guarantee of personal freedoms. The famous Four Freedoms (freedom of speech and worship, freedom from fear and want), are certainly Aquarian. We obviously are still working on them. But even the concept of a United Nations (Franklin D. Roosevelt was an Aquarian) or a European Union have been huge steps in the right direction. One of the striking things about the student uprising in China in 1989 was its spontaneous collective nature. It did not seem to have its focus in one particular leader. The poignant statue of "the goddess of democracy" was an Aquarian icon. Since then a number of countries have freed themselves from despotic governments.

Today we have the European Union, a stunning organization, which nations beg to join, reversing centuries of wars and conquests. A common currency and passport—who would have dreamed this but Aquarius?

Another of the clearest indications of Aquarius is the spontaneous arising all over the world of "centers," "*kibbutzim*," "groups," and "communities" based on widely diverging philosophies and practices, yet capable of friendly interchange. Our mail is filled with notices of one international conference after another. I spoke twice at International Transpersonal Association conferences, one in Bombay and one in Davos, Switzerland. (Each word in the title of this organization is Aquarian.) Members of thirty-seven countries attended. This is an age of workshops and seminars to which people flock with genuine and voluntary commitment. Nobody forces them with bribes to heaven or threats of hell, yet people attend, because they wish to. Can you imagine a hundred years ago such events taking place as "Holding Hands across America" or the "Harmonic Convergence" or the hymn "We are the World"? That's Aquarius!

To some, perhaps, much of this seems downright silly, but there is humility in being willing to risk being a fool (Uranus) for God. Certainly our beginnings in this Age are accompanied by eccentric "weirdos" and "kooks." But then, I suppose, St. Simeon Stylites and his imitators sitting on top of a sixty-foot pillar for over twenty-five years might have been deemed a mite odd, even in his time. We need to be tolerant and keep a sense of humor while all this sorts itself out. We have to remember the anonymous Englishman who invented the use of the umbrella. He took his wife's parasol to keep himself dry while walking down a village street in the rain. He was hooted at and ridiculed, if not stoned by village urchins. But when people saw that he kept dry, they soon became converted. England has been a land of "bumbershoots" ever since.

Naturally, the Shadow of the Age stares us straight in the eye, and astrology can help point it out. The dark side is too great a detachment, too much emphasis on the collective, overlooking the individual. Politically, this has already proven to be a disaster, as recent history in this century has shown us. But now we are killing transpersonally as well. From nuclear warfare to terrorism and random crime in the streets, the idea is "Don't take this personally, bang, you're dead!" Random groups in planes or on boats or just passing by are shot, burned, and killed. And the awesome event of 9/11 has turned into a global nightmare. More and more innocent bystanders, who have nothing personally to do with the matter at hand, are losing their lives. Alas, that too is Aquarius. According to Jung, the only way that we can help the collective Shadow is to work assiduously on our own. This means observing ourselves, catching ourselves as we put the blame on others for things we cannot admit repressing within our own psyches. In that light, our shame becomes our blessing angel, the redemption of Saturn himself. Shame is a small price to pay in the long run for consciousness—ask Adam and Eve!

I think psychologically two of the worst phrases we use are "It's your fault!" and "If only..." I had a client once with Saturn conjunct the Moon. She was in her seventies. I asked her about her mother and a heated torrent of blame ensued. Her mother had ruined her life! This, I had to point out, offered two possibilities: either her mother was receiving her inner projection of the archetypal Mother or she was indeed a monster. The client chose monster. In that case, shouldn't she thank God that she was not a monster too, and how could she not have compassion with such a woman who had to live with herself 24/7! I pointed out the reason for my question in the chart which accurately described the way unconsciously she had processed the archetypal Mother. It was as if she could drop a heavy load of blame as we sat together. Her eyes filled with tears.

Social security and government welfare are also Aquarian, but they, too, are transpersonal. There is no love (Leo) tucked into the envelopes with the checks, only tax money offered up, probably grudgingly. Toll-booth green lights say "Thank you!" More and more we are being reduced to ciphers and numbers. That, too, is Aquarius. The depersonalization of HMOs is reducing many doctors to filling out papers rather than healing patients. I know this. My son is a psychiatrist.

The highest suicide rates are in those countries where the government controls the security and welfare of all its citizens. Perhaps it is just because life is so institutionalized and transpersonal that the recipients of public aid are starved for personal love and care. The same is true for hospitalization and the care of the aged. Once the personal touch, the kindness, and the love are left out, the bodies of the sick and the old become cases or packages, materials simply to be manipulated with great efficiency but little or no personal compassion. All these examples are what can happen when there is too much Aquarius without its balance of Leo.

At the end of my classes, meetings, or workshops, I have tried to illustrate this needed balance by an instant communion called a "yum-yum." In a yum-yum (an old Tibetan custom, of course!) we stand in a circle and put our arms over the shoulders of the ones next to us, then we throw back our heads in a great Y-U-M! Then we bend into the circle, sounding as rapidly as possible "yum-yum-yum-yum!" as if life itself were a delicious meal (which it certainly can be). This is chanted in unison three times, followed by "hugs to the left and hugs to the right!" The yum-yum itself is very Aquarian, but the hugs left and right are the reminder that transpersonal good is dependent at the same time on personal touch and affection towards your immediate neighbor. This may all sound a bit silly, but believe me, it not only works, it's fun.

When we were in northern India, we went with a group to Dharamsala to meet His Holiness, the Dalai Lama. After that marvelous privilege and experience, we were invited to visit the huge Tibetan orphanage which is supported by a number of different countries. It is an enchanting place and full of lovely Tibetan children. At the end of our visit, about a hundred of them came to see us off as we got on our bus. I suggested a yum-yum. In seconds, all the kids were in a huge circle and, despite the language barrier, knew instinctively how to proceed. We had a humongous yum-yum, filled with joy and merriment. So it is now truly "an old Tibetan custom." We still see their radiant faces and hear the laughter as the hugs went on and on while they jumped around each other. The biggest yum-yum I know of so far was at the Davos Conference and had some twelve hundred people in it. It is my hope that the custom will be carried on, since it is by nature so Aquarian/Leo. It requires no previous preparation, costs nothing, can be done with two or with any number, knows no language or age barriers, and ends the most serious of colloquia in high affection and good humor.

Teaching in the round is symbolically wise. When teacher and class or preacher and congregation confront each other, so often true learning and spiritual exchange are lost. I think Christ hinted at this. In the apocryphal Acts of John you find a description of the Round Dance and the words, "He who does not join the dance mistakes the occasion." So, whenever and wherever it is possible or appropriate, have the courage to dance, to hold hands, to unite wisdom with joy and joy with wisdom. Truly, they belong together in the Age to come.

Not long ago, I learned that a theoretical physicist named Dr. William Tiller, a professor at Stanford University, had discovered through biofeedback that when two people hold hands the energy is squared. So when ten people hold hands, the energy is that of a hundred. Since we define entropy as a winding down of energy, could we not call this *syntropy*, the revving up of energy? This can only be done by human beings and might explain the meaning of Christ's saying, "When two or three are gathered together, there am I also."

In 1998 I traveled to a Peace Conference on the Isle of Iona in the Scottish Hebrides. It was very Aquarian: seventy-two leaders of various spiritual groups from places as far apart as Norway, Japan, Israel, Holland, and the Americas were all gathered together to prepare for the upcoming Centennial Peace Conference in The Hague. I quoted my teacher M, who, fifty-four years previously, had predicted that the coming spirituality would consist of small groups of people gathering together to discuss and meditate voluntarily. Then he cocked his head and said there was one problem: we would not know how many of us there were! So here was a first step. We might be making history. I pointed out that perhaps St. Paul did not know he was making history; maybe he was just giving "workshops" in Ephesus, Corinth, and Rome. Things are changed by what comes after, as Anne Tyler wisely wrote.

Anyway, as we gathered daily in a circle, holding hands, I suddenly realized that we had solved the insoluble problem of "squaring the circle"! You have to think outside the box. Incidentally, one week after the Peace Conference in The Hague, the war in Kosovo ceased. Could there have been a connection?

So YUM-yum-yum-yum-yum-yum and hugs to the left and hugs to the right, to you, dearest of friends.

And love, always, transpersonal and personal!

ao

*With our eyes open, we share the same world.
With our eyes shut, each of us enters his own world.*
—HERACLITUS

Divine forces are diffused in things.
—CORNELIUS AGRIPPA VON NETTESHEIM

There are two orders in this art [of the Philosopher's Stone],
*that is beholding by the eye and understanding by the heart,
and this is the secret stone which is rightly called a gift of
God . . .* [it] *is the heart and the tincture of the gold,
which is sought by the philosophers.*
—PETRUS BONUS, alchemist, 1564

The believer [of Allah] *. . . will be told: "Since you
have made such exertions to get this close to Me, I am
not going to let these strenuous efforts of yours come to
nothing. I am showing you My Beauty, for which you
have felt such longing." In all the things of this world,
that person now sees, feels, and senses the presence of God.*
—SHEIKH MUZAFFER OZAK AL-JERRAHI
Irshad: Wisdom of a Sufi Master

Heaven is spread upon the earth, and men do not see it.
—THE GOSPEL ACCORDING TO THOMAS

19

THE GIFT OF
A STREETLAMP

Dear Friend,

Not so long ago there was an item in the newspaper stating that two mathematicians, with the help of a computer, had worked on the numerical challenge of pi. They carried it out to 480,000,000 places. Had the number been printed, the paper would have stretched six hundred miles, yet no apparent pattern of repetition was discovered! I found this fascinating because it reinforces further the psychological truth hidden within what Jung called the archetypal mandala, the circle as a symbol for wholeness, rather than completion, as an eternal symbol both for God and for the individual psyche.

You would swear that just by looking at the circle above you could know its totality, its area. But since the formula is πr^2, we know that it is undefinable and limitless. The symbol of the circle itself provides a mysterious paradox of order, containment, and unity filled with a potentially limitless diversity.

I remember looking out the window at the snow falling thickly onto the street one winter's night when I was a homesick child living in a Swiss boarding school. As it fell, I noticed that wherever there was a streetlight there was a perfect circle, a nimbus of light in motion. Despite the continuous changing of crystalline flakes, the circle of light remained constant. I think I was about nine years old at the time, and I remember the sense of comfort this gave me, though I could not have put it into words. It hinted somehow at a hidden potential for permanence and order underlying chaos and randomness. Since that time, I have seen this circle of light repeated in rain, in fog, in the reflection of a single moon in hundreds of puddles. We all have—it is obvious. But much later I learned something very important: there is an extra step that we can take when we make such observations.

- Step one is to look.
- Step two is to notice.
- Step three is to draw any logical conclusions from what we observe, which is what science and technology do. But there is a further step awaiting us in this Age to come.
- Step four is to *connect what we have noticed to its possible spiritual implication!*

This means taking the outer matter into one's own psyche and reading the physical manifestation as a possible metaphor for meaning. Read this way, the whole manifest world can become one's guide and teacher. It is like the cube that my teacher M once showed me; we see only half of it, three sides at a time, yet unconsciously we supply the other three. Thus, in principle, it is possible to find an inner meaning in whatever we notice and experience.

This is a conscious application of synchronicity. Paracelsus hinted at it in the expression *das Zuwerfen der Natur* (nature's capacity to reveal its hidden light, the *lumen naturae*). Whatever your eye lights upon will yield up its secrets if you know how to perceive the process it is embodying. We need only to set up an inner dialogue with it. Most synchronicities occur when we are in a heightened state, that state of syntropy, or when we are revved up for one reason or another. It is then that we constellate the archetypes that dwell in what can best be described as the *unus mundus*, that place where time and space as the ego experiences them do not exist. (Lest this seem dismaying, it is something we all experience in dreams. There we find space that takes up no space and time out of time.) But just as we so often see the images arising out of a chart as synchronistic, through active contemplation we might see synchronistically through the veil of "matter" to the hidden wisdom it conceals. As the poet George Herbert (1593–1633) so beautifully expressed it:

> *A man that looks on glasse*
> *On it may stay his eye*
> *Or if he pleaseth, through it passe*
> *And then the heav'n espie.*
>
> *This is the famous stone*
> *That turneth all to gold;*
> *For that which God doth touch and own*
> *Cannot for less be sold.*

Science has made its name through steps one, two, and three, but it stops short of step four. Its province, it maintains quite rightly, is not metaphysics. But I think, dear friend, we could coin a new "scientific" term for what I am suggesting and what astrology and Jung's alchemists point to—a word that would be the very antonym of metaphysics: *endophysics!*

This would direct us to a very simple truth: that the wisdom and proof we seek are also *within* the physical, not only *beyond* it (*meta-*). This suggests that we do not have to rely only on outer sources, whether books or teachers or discarnate and supernatural gurus, to find what we are looking for. A daisy will do any day, or a windowpane, or a piece of Christmas wrapping paper *perceived in the right way*. Among many other things, a daisy can teach us about centering; a windowpane about divisions and transparency;

the wrapping paper about the gift of spirit concealed in the wrapping of the material and manifest world or in our own bodies.

By taking the way of endophysics, step four, we can call upon our inner potential, the feminine process of the Holy Spirit, Hagia Sophia or Holy Wisdom, to connect the "outer and visible sign" with the "inner and spiritual grace [*meaning!*]" which is its truth, thereby making them one. This is the definition of a sacrament, and it may someday be possible for us to live sacramentally in the commonplace of our everyday lives with the help and guidance of Sophia. It will be her Age, as Joachim of Fiore predicted. Her motto is *omnia coniungo* ("I unite all"). This would indeed be a conscious application of synchronicity, which Jung defined as a meaningful coincidence of outer event and inner significance. Then instead of waiting for synchronicities to happen spontaneously as a kind of random revelation (perhaps with the help of astrology's gift of identifying those "divine processes" concealed in events or things or "matter"), we can choose to move and have our being more often in the deeper and greater reality of the *unus mundus*, symbolized by the mandala, the circle underlying the seeming randomness that the ego calls life.

It is the Self, the Atman, the Divine Guest, who dwells as centerpoint and totality in that invisible circle of our individuality and in the cosmos at one and the same time. Yet we can only become conscious of this Self with the help of our ego, which orbits it at the circumference. The radius of Hagia Sophia, the Holy Spirit, unites the two and represents "the Only Way."

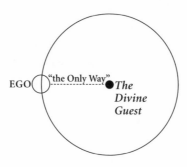

Step four could be a conscious step, once the Piscean sacrifice of ego-identification has been made. Then ego would reach out, in love and trust, for the gift-bestowing inner hand of our Divine Guest, our direct inner connection to Spirit. The gift itself is insight, the "aha!" of inner revelation that in the past was the grace of usually only mystics, poets, and children. But we *all* have the capacity for step four. When we make the effort to take it, ordinary life becomes extraordinary and "intro-ordinary," or touched by a secret joy, a kind of magic and wonder. It reminds me of Elizabeth Barrett Browning's words: "Earth's crammed with heaven and every common bush afire with God." As I tried to share in *The Dove in the Stone*, it really only takes "a loving eye" to see the connections and thus find heaven on earth.

You can see by extension that if "things" in nature and all around us can teach us through synchronicity, the outer experiences of our lives can also be perceived as metaphors of what our individual psyches hunger for and require on our way to individuation. By applying the fourth step to the events in our lives, the same kind of noticing can be fruitful, and the same search for spiritual implications can give us amazing understanding and insight.

Just as random snowflakes reveal the circle of light, so the seemingly random encounters, pains, and joys in our lives can yield a meaningfulness when perceived in that light. We always see through the lens of who we happen to be at any given moment because, as astrology teaches us, we process any shared experiences through our own individual perception, thus making them our own. The astrological chart describes how the characters appearing in the outer drama of our lives, the traumatic events of our childhood, etc., "synchronize" with our perceptions of them. In this fashion we serve one another, appearing in each other's plays as parents or villains or witches, friends, teachers, lovers. More often than not, we come across as actors playing these archetypal parts for one another, often releasing painful insights and wisdom as we go. So if you follow that thought, you will see that to love your enemy would be to recognize the mask that he or she is forced to wear in your drama, a mask that does not necessarily coincide with who the person really is. Our projections fashion the masks with which we cover others' faces. And they cover ours with masks of their own needs. To forgive an enemy, then, would be to lift off the mask we ourselves have placed there. Beneath it, we might find a hurt, frightened, bewildered, and above all unloved person like ourselves. "It takes one to know one."

Fear, pride, lust as overweening desire of any kind, anger, hatred, greed all exist. So do sickness and death. My impression of what Jung was trying to impart is that if we acknowledge rather than deny or disapprove their reality, we can redeem and transform them through a psychological and alchemical process within each individual psyche. This is a labor of blood, sweat, and tears—and a labor of love.

It was a monk known as Evagrius Ponticus who, in the fourth century A.D., identified the seven deadly sins. He also had a remedy for them: *apatheia*, meaning dispassionate detachment (not apathy in today's sense). Only through detachment can consciousness have integrity. All too often, the emotions of guilt, defiance, and shame clutter up the process of redemption through conscious awareness. Pain, suffering, and self-loathing are common to us all as we travel the Path, but as the *I Ching* points out, to fight one's faults is to strengthen them; better to use the energy in the forceful pursuit of the good. In the meantime we can console ourselves with the adage, "Every saint was once a sinner."

Astrology teaches that every vice is some planet's virtue misapplied. So the potential redemption comes from detached observation of oneself with compassion, rather than self-loathing, followed by an effort to redirect the process in a wiser direction. This can be done only with conscious intent.

I recall when I first met my teacher M at the age of twenty-one, every one of my sins and shortcomings rose up to confront me. I was appalled and wallowed almost two weeks in genuine remorse, until he finally grinned at me and said, "Dearie, if you would spend as much energy on changing as you do on all those waterworks, we'd get along a lot faster." Later he pointed out to me that to sacrifice the daily fruits of one's actions to God, as in karma yoga, means *all* one's actions, failures included. Learning to sacrifice one's failures is a hard lesson. I also remember a story he told of a disciple and his Master which brought on more waterworks. It went something like this: There was once a young student on the Path who fervently vowed to his Master not to indulge in certain wrongdoing. No sooner promised than he fell back into temptation with his old cronies. He was so ashamed of himself that he avoided his teacher and even crossed the street to hide from him.

One day, however, he literally collided with him rounding a corner. The Master looked at his student and shook his head. "My son," he said, "don't hang around with your enemies. When you are being good, they will taunt you, and when you are doing wrong they will encourage you. If you insist on going on the wrong path, come to us who will bear your burden until you are strong enough."

In conclusion, astrology and psychotherapy can come together in revealing some of the "hidden agenda" of any given psyche. Each ego will have unconsciously set up its own unique needs, often as a defense mechanism to protect itself in one way or another. At the same time there is a greater hidden agenda, that of the Self, which partakes of the unity of Spirit. This agenda, were it to be comprehended, might answer the great why of existence itself. It is indeed well hidden in the obvious!

So I myself can only go back to the painful windowsill of my childhood and be grateful to the streetlamp for its blessing image of the circle of light behind the brightly falling snowflakes. That circle remains as mysterious as the nature of pi, but as lasting a promise as ever-encircling love.

And so, dearest friend, as I end this cycle of letters, I can but encircle you with my love.

Pass it on!

ao

GLOSSARY

Astrological Terms

Astrological Age. A period of approximately 2300 years, with several centuries of interface before and after, during which the point of the vernal equinox (0 degrees of Aries in the tropical zodiac) traverses a constellation in the sidereal (visible) zodiac. That is, when the sun rises on the day of the vernal equinox (around March 21), it will have this constellation in the background. For example, the Age of Taurus is the period when the constellation of Taurus hosted this point. The point of the vernal equinox moves at the rate of 1 degree every seventy-two years.

Ascendant. The line formed by the eastern horizon. The cusp of the First House. The sign of the zodiac crossing this cusp at the time of birth is called the *rising sign*. It describes what Jung called the *persona*, the "mask" or personality that we normally use in dealing with the external world.

Aspects. The geometrical angles formed in the 360 degree circle by two or more planets. The main aspects are:

> Conjunction: 0–8 degrees
> Sextile: 60 degrees
> Square: 90 degrees
> Trine: 120 degrees
> Quincunx: 150 degrees
> Opposition: 180 degrees

For further information see chapter 6.

Cusp. The line dividing one house from another, or the separation of one sign from another.

Degrees. A degree is one 360th part of a circle. Each sign has 30 degrees. A planet will occupy a position in degrees of a sign. For example, on November 13, the Sun is in 20 degrees of Scorpio.

Detriment. The designation of the sign opposite to the sign "ruled" by a given planet. Example: the Moon rules Cancer but is in its *detriment* in Capricorn, i.e., it functions with less ease.

Ecliptic. The apparent path delineated by the sun as it shifts position throughout the year in its apparent orbit around the earth.

Elements. Fire, air, water, earth: the four ways energy manifests, according to ancient beliefs. Psychologically, our capacities to act, to think, to feel, and to be practical. See diagrams in Table E for four triplicities of signs.

Equinox. Occurs when the sun reaches 0 degrees of Aries (the vernal equinox) or 0 degrees of Libra (the autumnal equinox) in the tropical zodiac. The first moments of spring and fall; the days in the year when there are equal hours of day and night.

Exaltation. Designates the sign which, by nature of its element and quality, is most harmonious with the process of a given planet. Example: The Sun is *exalted* in Aries but *falls* in Libra.

Fall. A planet in a sign which, by the nature of its element and quality, is least in harmony with the process of a planet is said to be in fall there. Example: Mars *falls* in Cancer but is *exalted* in Capricorn.

Glyph. The pictograph or symbol for a sign, planet, or aspect.

Horoscope. The chart of the heavens drawn up for the birth time, date, and place of an individual or an event.

Houses. The twelve arcs or divisions of space surrounding the Earth. See diagram in chapter 10 for the Placidus system used by the author. The houses remain fixed while the signs move clockwise through them every twenty-four hours. There are various house systems. The main coordinates are the east-west horizon and the vertical zenith-nadir (noon-midnight points).

Natal astrology. The branch of astrology dealing with the charts of individuals. There are other branches, such as mundane (which concerns cultural events), horary (which studies the moment when questions are posed), etc.

Platonic Year. A period of approximately 26,000 years; a complete cycle of the Precession of the Equinoxes through all twelve constellations.

Precession of the Equinoxes. The westward march of the intersections of the celestial equator and the ecliptic through the sidereal zodiac (the visible constellations). A complete cycle takes approximately 26,000 years. See chapter 11.

Ruler. Term used for a planet whose process coincides naturally with the sign it occupies. Example: Jupiter is ruler of Sagittarius; its detriment is in the opposite sign of Gemini. See diagram of the natural zodiac, Table A.

Zodiac (or natural zodiac: see Table A). A depiction of the signs and their planetary rulers in natural sequence, for convenience and symbolic understanding, but not a factual zodiac. Its divisions are named Aries, Taurus, etc.

Sidereal zodiac. The belt of twelve visible constellations of stars circling the solar system. They are of unequal width. Used especially by Eastern astrologers. Divisions are also named Aries, Taurus, etc.

Tropical zodiac. The twelvefold division of the ecliptic or apparent path of the Sun. These are the twelve signs used primarily by Western astrologers. They are "invisible" and conceptual divisions of 30 degrees each, related to the four key points in the division of the seasons: the first days of spring, summer, fall, and winter.

Jungian Terms

Anima, animus. "Personification of the feminine nature of a man's unconscious and the masculine nature of a woman's" respectively (Jung).

Archetype. A primordial image appearing universally in myths and fairy tales, corresponding to "irrepresentable, unconscious, preexistent forms" that are part of the inherited structure of the human psyche.

Collective unconscious. The level of the unconscious beneath the personal unconscious, shared universally by humanity through time and space. The instincts and archetypes form the collective unconscious. As dreams emerge from the individual, so myths and fairy tales arise from the collective unconscious, and they share universal motifs.

Coniunctio. The union of opposites, often resulting in a third. Example: the *coniunctio* of outer and inner experience can give birth to meaning. The *hieros gamos* (Greek, "sacred marriage") is an example of a *coniunctio*.

Ego. The center of consciousness in the psyche. The sense of the temporal personality, "I." It mediates between outer and inner experience and also deals with the unconscious contents of the psyche as they arise.

Individuation. The process and purpose of individual self-realization and fulfillment. The ongoing quest for the inner Self.

Psyche. The totality, conscious and unconscious, of an individual's inner life.

Self. The center and totality of the psyche; in religious terms, the Atman or the Christ Within (the Divine Guest). Not to be confused with the ordinary "self" usually referred to as "I," which Jung calls the *ego*.

Shadow. The personification of those parts of ourselves we deny or disapprove of, which we unconsciously project onto others. The collective Shadow is projected by groups onto other groups or nations upon other nations, hence the importance of integrating the Shadow on an individual basis.

Synchronicity. An acausal view of time in which relevant coincidences occur—a coincidence of an outer event with an inner psychic meaning. (The astrological chart mediates through synchronicity.)

Temenos. From the Greek, meaning "sacred precinct." Everybody's psyche can be seen as a *temenos*, as sacred.

Unus mundus (Latin, "one world"). The unity sometimes experienced as underlying the apparent dualities in the time-space continuum.

BIBLIOGRAPHY

Aldington, Richard, and Delano Ames, trans. *New Larousse Encyclopedia of Mythology*. London: Hamlyn, 1982.

Aquinas, Thomas (attributed to). *Aurora consurgens*. Edited by Marie-Louise von Franz. Translated by R. F. C. Hull and A. S. B. Glover. New York: Pantheon, 1966.

Blair, Lawrence. *Rhythms of Vision*. New York: Schocken, 1976.

Bly, Robert, ed. *News of the Universe: Poems of Twofold Consciousness*. San Francisco: Sierra Club, 1980.

The Book of Common Prayer. Greenwich, Conn.: Seabury, 1953.

Branston, Brian. *Gods of the North*. London: Thames & Hudson, 1980.

Bynner, Witter. *The Way of Life according to Lao Tzu*. New York: Capricorn, 1962.

Campbell, Joseph. *The Masks of God: Primitive Mythology*. New York: Viking, 1960.

———. *Historical Atlas of World Mythology*. Two volumes. New York: Harper & Row, 1988.

———. *An Open Life: In Conversation with Michael Toms*. Burdett, N.Y.: Larson, 1988.

Charpentier, Louis. *The Mysteries of Chartres Cathedral*. Translated by Ronald Fraser. London: Thorsons, 1972.

Chevalier, Jean, and Alain Gheerbrant, eds. *Dictionnaire des symboles*. Paris: Seghers, 1973.

Conrad, Jack Randolph. *The Horn and the Sword: A History of the Bull as Symbol of Power and Fertility*. Westport, Conn.: Greenwood Press, 1957.

Davidson, H. R. Ellis. *Gods and Myths of Northern Europe*. Baltimore, Md.: Penguin/Pelican, 1969.

De Santillana, Giorgio, and Hertha von Dechend. *Hamlet's Mill: An Essay on Myth and the Frame of Time.* Boston: Gambit, 1969.

De Vries, Ad. *Dictionary of Symbols and Imagery.* Amsterdam: North Holland Publishing Co, 1981.

Durant, Will. *The Life of Greece.* New York: Simon & Schuster, 1939.

———. *Caesar and Christ.* New York: Simon & Schuster, 1944.

Edinger, Edward F. *Ego and Archetype: Individuation and the Religious Function of the Psyche.* New York: Putnam, 1972.

———. *The Bible and the Psyche.* Toronto: Inner City Books, 1986.

Eliade, Mircea. *A History of Religious Ideas, Vol. I: From the Stone Age to the Eleusinian Mysteries.* Translated by Willard R. Trask. Chicago: University of Chicago Press, 1978.

Eliot, T. S. *The Complete Poems and Plays, 1909–1950.* New York: Harcourt, Brace & World, 1971.

Emerson, Ralph Waldo. *Essays.* New York: Thomas A. Crowell, 1926.

Encyclopaedia Britannica. Eleventh Edition. Cambridge, U.K.: Cambridge University Press, 1910.

Flower, Robin. *The Irish Tradition.* Oxford: Oxford at the Clarendon Press, 1970.

Fox, Matthew. *The Coming of the Cosmic Christ.* New York: Harper & Row, 1988.

Frankfort, Henri, et al. *Before Philosophy.* Baltimore, Md.: Penguin/Pelican, 1972.

Frazier, James George. *The Golden Bough.* New York: Macmillan, 1979.

Freke, Timothy, and Peter Gandy. *The Jesus Mysteries: Was the "Original Jesus" a Pagan God?* New York: Three Rivers Press, 1999.

Gimbutas, Marija. *The Goddesses and Gods of Old Europe.* Berkeley: University of California Press, 1982.

Grof, Stanislav. *Realms of the Human Unconscious.* New York: Viking, 1976.

Hartmann, Franz. *The Life and Doctrines of Paracelsus.* New York: Macoy, 1932.

Hitching, Francis. *Earth Magic.* New York: William Morrow, 1977.

The Holy Bible. King James Version. Oxford: Oxford University Press, 1928.

Homer. *The Iliad.* Translated by E.V. Rieu. Baltimore, Md.: Penguin Books, 1959.

Howell, Alice O. *The Dove in the Stone.* Wheaton, Ill.: Theosophical Publishing House, Quest Books, 1988.

———. *Jungian Symbolism in Astrology.* Tempe, Ariz.: American Federation of Astrologers, 1999.

———. *The Web in the Sea.* Wheaton, Ill.: Theosophical Publishing House, Quest Books, 1993.

Jobes, Gertrude. *Dictionary of Mythology, Folklore, and Symbols.* New York: Scarecrow Press, 1962.

Jung, C. G. *Collected Works.* Translated by R. F. C. Hull. Twenty vols. Princeton, N.J.: Princeton University Press. 1957–1979.

———. *Memories, Dreams, Reflections.* Edited by Aniela Jaffé. New York: Pantheon, 1963.

———. *Letters, 1906–1961.* Edited by Gerhard Adler and Aniela Jaffé. Translated by R. F. C. Hull. Two volumes. Princeton, N.J.: Princeton University Press, 1975.

———. 1996. *The Psychology of Kundalini Yoga.* Edited by Sonu Shamdasani. Princeton, N.J.: Princeton University Press, 1996.

Kaplan, Aryeh. *Waters of Eden.* New York: National Conference of Synagogue Youth/Union of Orthodox Jewish Congregations, 1982.

Kingsford, Anna Bonus. *The Perfect Way*. New York: Macoy, 1924.

Kramer, Samuel Noah. *History Begins at Sumer*. Garden City, N.Y.: Doubleday, 1959.

Lawrence, D. H. *The Complete Poems of D. H. Lawrence*. Edited by Vivian De Sola Pinto and Warren Roberts. New York: Viking, 1971.

Markale, Jean. *Women of the Celts*. Translated by A. Mygind, C. Hauch, and P. Henry. Rochester, Vt.: Inner Traditions, 1986.

MacCana, Proinsias. *Celtic Mythology*. London: Hamlyn, 1970.

MacGregor, Geddes. *So Help Me God*. New York: Morehouse-Barlow, 1970.

McNamara, William. *Earthy Mysticism*. New York: Crossroads, 1987.

Mascaro, Juan, trans. *The Upanishads*. Baltimore, Md.: Penguin, 1971.

Massey, Gerald. *The World's Great Year*. Edmonds, Wash.: Sure Fire Press, 1988.

Munro, Eleanor. *On Glory Roads*. New York: Thames & Hudson, 1987.

Muzzafer Ozak Al-Jerrahi, Sheikh. *Irshad: Wisdom of a Sufi Master*. Translated by Muhtar Holland. Amity, N.Y.: Amity House, 1988.

Neumann, Erich. *The Origins and History of Consciousness*. Translated by R. F. C. Hull. Princeton, N.J.: Princeton University Press, 1954.

———. 1974. *The Great Mother*. Translated by Ralph Manheim. Princeton, N.J.: Princeton University Press, 1974.

The Oxford Book of American Verse, 1902–1949. New York: Oxford University Press, 1950.

The Oxford Book of English Verse, 1250–1918. Oxford: Oxford at the Clarendon Press, 1949.

O'Driscoll, Robert. *Celtic Consciousness*. Edinburgh: Canongate, 1982.

Paracelsus. *Selected Writings*. Edited by Jolande Jacobi. Princeton, N.J.: Princeton University Press, 1969.

Patai, Raphael. *The Hebrew Goddess*. New York: Avon, 1978.

Rees, Alvyn and Brinley. *Celtic Heritage*. London: Thames & Hudson, 1961.

Reid, Vera. *Towards Aquarius*. New York: Arco, 1971.

Rostovtzeff, M. *A History of the Ancient World*. Translated by J. D. Duff. Two volumes. Oxford: Oxford University Press, 1926, 1938.

Rubenstein, Richard E. *Aristotle's Children: How Christians, Muslims, and Jews Rediscovered Ancient Wisdom and Illuminated the Dark Ages*. Orlando, Fla.: Harcourt, 2003.

Shakespeare, William. *The Complete Works*. London: Collins, 1939.

Sheldrake, Rupert. *A New Science of Life*. London: Blond & Briggs, 1981.

Stone, Merlin. *When God Was a Woman*. New York: Harvest/HBJ, 1978.

Swami Prabhavananda and Christopher Isherwood, trans. *Bhagavad-Gita: The Song of God*. New York: New American Library, 2004.

Teilhard de Chardin, Pierre. *The Phenomenon of Man*. New York: Harper & Row, 1955.

Thomas, P. *Epics, Myths and Legends of India*. Bombay: D. B. Taraporevala & Sons, 1980.

Toynbee, Arnold. *A Study of History*. New York: Weatherman, 1979.

Watts, Alan. *Myth and Ritual in Christianity*. Boston: Beacon, 1968.

Wilhelm, Richard, and Cary Baynes, trans. *I Ching: The Book of Changes*. Princeton, N.J.: Princeton University Press, 1961.

INDEX

Quest Books

encourages open-minded inquiry into
world religions, philosophy, science, and the arts
in order to understand the wisdom of the ages,
respect the unity of all life, and help people explore
individual spiritual self-transformation.

Its publications are generously supported by
The Kern Foundation,
a trust committed to Theosophical education.

Quest Books is the imprint of
the Theosophical Publishing House,
a division of the Theosophical Society in America.
For information about programs, literature,
on-line study, membership benefits, and international centers,
see www.theosophical.org
or call 800-669-1571 or (outside the U.S.) 630-668-1571.

Related Quest Titles

The Dove in the Stone, Alice O. Howell

The Guide to Horoscope Interpretation, Marc Edmund Jones

Jung: A Journey of Transformation, Vivianne Crowley

Stars, Cycles, and Psyche (DVD), Alice O. Howell

The Waking Dream, Ray Grasse

The Web in the Sea, Alice O. Howell

To order books or a complete Quest catalog,
call 800-669-9425 or (outside the U.S.) 630-665-0130.

Praise for Alice O. Howell's
THE
HEAVENS DECLARE

"Alice Howell's rich and thoroughly engaged life comes across to the reader's delight in this entertaining and innovative presentation of the twelve zodiacal signs and constellations. Through a series of letters to the lay reader, she explains both the limited number of astrological "facts" and its infinite number of possible permutations. Steeped in Jungian insight, her connections draw from alchemical, mythic, and spiritual understanding and assist anyone who wishes to transmute the inevitable sufferings of life into the wisdom of individuated serenity. Astrology, as Ms. Howell presents it for every man and woman, is a humble but rewarding lesson in wonder and awe."

—MICHAEL YORK, author of *Pagan Theology: Paganism as a World Religion* and Professor of Cultural Astronomy and Astrology, Bath Spa University, UK

"Using her extensive knowledge of symbolism and Jungian psychology combined with an intimate writing style, Alice Howell has the unique ability to convey the profundity, mystery and sacredness of astrology without falling into the traps either of literalism or of obsessive reliance on techniques. If I were limited to only one book to introduce others to this ancient art, this would be the one I would choose."

—JAMES FRAZIER, author of *C. G. Jung: Synchronicity, Astrology, and Mercurius*